THE LONG DEFEAT

To Margaret

[signature]

October 2017

THE LONG DEFEAT

*Cultural Trauma, Memory,
and Identity in Japan*

Akiko Hashimoto

2015

OXFORD
UNIVERSITY PRESS

OXFORD
UNIVERSITY PRESS

Oxford University Press is a department of the University of
Oxford. It furthers the University's objective of excellence in research,
scholarship, and education by publishing worldwide.

Oxford   New York
Auckland   Cape Town   Dar es Salaam   Hong Kong   Karachi
Kuala Lumpur   Madrid   Melbourne   Mexico City   Nairobi
New Delhi   Shanghai   Taipei   Toronto

With offices in
Argentina   Austria   Brazil   Chile   Czech Republic   France   Greece
Guatemala   Hungary   Italy   Japan   Poland   Portugal   Singapore
South Korea   Switzerland   Thailand   Turkey   Ukraine   Vietnam

Oxford is a registered trademark of Oxford University Press
in the UK and certain other countries.

Published in the United States of America by
Oxford University Press
198 Madison Avenue, New York, NY 10016

Library of Congress Cataloging-in-Publication Data
Hashimoto, Akiko, 1952–
The long defeat : cultural trauma, memory, and identity in Japan / Akiko Hashimoto.
pages cm
Includes bibliographical references and index.
ISBN 978–0–19–023915–2 (hardcover : alk. paper)—ISBN 978–0–19–023916–9 (pbk. : alk. paper)
1. World War, 1939–1945—Social aspects—Japan.   2. Collective memory—Japan.
3. Nationalism and collective memory—Japan.   4. Group identity—Japan.   5. National
characteristics, Japanese. I. Title.
D744.7.J3H37 2015
952.04—dc23
2014039666

FOR DAVID

Contents

Acknowledgments

This book is a result of my longtime interest in the defeated nations of World War II. As an adolescent moving with my family, I shuttled between the cultures of both the losers and the winners—Japan, England, and Germany—and could not help but notice how "the war" seemed to influence the way people carried themselves. Many questions stayed with me from that time, and this book is part of my attempt to answer them.

In the years of research leading to the publication of this book, I have accrued encouragement, information, advice, and criticism from many people. I am grateful to all of them for freely giving their time and knowledge. Special thanks are due to the many people who guided me and collaborated with me during fieldwork, especially the informants, respondents, and those who provided crucial introductions to people whose views have shaped my understanding of cultural trauma and war memory.

In the early phases of the study, when war memory became a central focus of my academic interest, I developed a method of shadow comparisons that underlies this book. Albrecht Funk was an early influence from whom I learned so much through our discussions comparing the German and Japanese cases. His enthusiasm for this project was invaluable from the beginning. Iris Landgraf also helped me learn about the younger generation in Germany, which she exemplified. My fieldwork in Hamburg would not have been possible without the help of Herbert Worm, Matthias Heyl, Yasuko Hashimoto Richter, Tommy Richter, and over a dozen local informants and interviewees who welcomed me and guided me with their knowledge.

In Japan, I learned much about the complexities of war memory from the wisdom, courage, and kindness of many people. Watanabe Shin generously provided crucial contacts for my fieldwork in Yokohama. I am indebted to Koshio Masayoshi and Kobayashi Katsunori of Kanagawa Prefecture for introductions, and over a dozen local informants and interviewees who generously took the time from their busy lives to guide me with their knowledge. I am especially thankful to Miwa Seiko for facilitating my work in Yokohama, and for her friendship and assistance over many years. Many others offered hospitality when I visited different sites, especially Kazashi Nobuo in Hiroshima, Yamabe Masahiko, and Watanabe Mina in Tokyo. Young Japanese participants in my focus group interviews were forthcoming with gusto while finishing all the pizza. Thank you for sharing your experiences with me. Iwata Eriko facilitated these focus groups with enthusiasm and tenacity. I also appreciated the discussions with Kohno Kensuke and Hara Yumiko at the NHK Broadcasting Culture Research Institute in the early phases of this research.

As the project evolved, I benefited greatly from the intellectual exchange at the Yale University Center for Cultural Sociology. I am grateful to Jeffrey Alexander for inviting me to join the Cultural Trauma Project. His generous advice and guidance has been invaluable. I am also grateful to Ron Eyerman for sharing his wealth of knowledge on cultural trauma. My chapter "Cultural Trauma of a Fallen Nation: Japan, 1945" appearing in the Cultural Trauma Project publication *Narrating Trauma: On the Impact of Collective Suffering,* edited by Ron Eyerman, Jeffrey C. Alexander, and Elizabeth Breese (Boulder, CO: Paradigm, 2011) comprises the kernel of ideas from which *The Long Defeat* developed; parts of that chapter have found their way into chapters 1 and 3 of this volume. The Center's workshops were important in crystallizing my approach to the study of cultural trauma and memory. I gained much also from the comments by Elizabeth Breese, Phil Smith, Bernhard Giesen, and other participants of the workshops.

I much appreciated the financial resources that made it possible for me to carry out the different phases of this project, especially a grant from the Abe Fellowship Program of the Social Science Research Council and the American Council of Learned Societies with funds provided by the Japan Foundation Center for Global Partnership. I am grateful to Frank Baldwin for his early support and to Takuya Toda-Ozaki for his ongoing counsel. Faculty research grants from the University of Pittsburgh, especially the Japan Council, the Asian Studies Center, the University Center for International Studies,

and the Dietrich School of Arts and Sciences were critical in carrying out the latter phases of this study. Publication of this book has been aided by grants from the Richard D. and Mary Jane Edwards Endowed Publication Fund and the Japan Iron and Steel Federation Endowment.

Hiroyuki Nagahashi Good, the Japanese studies librarian at the University of Pittsburgh's Hillman Library, has been a pillar of support and invaluable at all phases of this research. Kazuyo Good also aided me with various library requests. At the early phase of research, I received support from Sachie Noguchi, who is now at Columbia University's East Asian Library, and Maureen Donovan at Ohio State University's Cartoon Research Library. My work would not have been possible without the many research assistants who helped me with the painstaking work of data collection, analysis, organization and management: Patrick Altdorfer, Christiane Munder, Georg Menz, Masahiro Okamoto, Yasumi Moroishi, Yasumasa Komori, Sachiko Akiyama, Eriko Iwata, Shuso Itaoka, Yoichiro Ishikawa, and Yoshimi Miyamoto.

Many colleagues and friends have stimulated my thinking and conceptualization on cultural analysis during the years in which this project has been in the making. Many thanks are due to the successive chairs of my department who extended support to me during this long-term project: the late Norman Hummon, Patrick Doreian, John Markoff, Kathleen Blee, and Suzanne Staggenborg. I also appreciate the staff at the Department of Sociology at the University of Pittsburgh for their valuable support. My colleagues at the Japan Council of the University of Pittsburgh were generous with their support and warm encouragement, especially Keith Brown, Tom Rimer, Hiroshi Nara, Richard Smethurst, Mae Smethurst, Brenda Jordan, Gabriella Lukacs, David Mills, and the late Keiko McDonald. For their constructive comments on parts or all of the draft manuscript, I am especially grateful to Kathy Blee, John Markoff, Hiroshi Nara, and Dick Smethurst. Thank you, Dick, for letting me audit your HIST1000. I would also like to acknowledge the support and friendship of colleagues at the University of Pittsburgh, especially Hideo Watanabe, Janelle Greenberg, Martin Greenberg, Alberta Sbragia, Sabine von Dirke, Amy Remensnyder (now at Brown University), and Ellis Krauss (now at the University of California, San Diego).

This book has also greatly benefited from the discussions at lectures and seminars I have given at various institutions—among them Yale University, Harvard University, Cornell University, University of San Francisco, University of Georgia, University of Texas, Austin,

University of Virginia, George Washington University, Metropolitan State University, UCLA, the Hiroshima Peace Institute, the London School of Economics, as well as the University of Pittsburgh. I am grateful to the organizers of these events for their gracious invitations. The discussions greatly helped shape my arguments. I am especially indebted to insightful comments over the years from Alexis Dudden, Jeffrey Olick, Helmut Anheier, Yudhishthir Raj Isar, Mariko Tamanoi, Andrew Gordon, Ted Bestor, Len Schoppa, Barry Schwartz, Mikyoung Kim, Laura Hein, Mark Selden, Franziska Seraphim, and Peter Katzenstein. I have also been fortunate to receive warm encouragement from Bill Kelly, John Campbell, Sheldon Garon, Fred Notehelfer, Mary Brinton, Patricia Steinhoff, Norma Field, Robert Smith, and John Traphagan.

Many good people have shared my life throughout the time I have been working on this book. Keith Brown has been a wise and trusted friend throughout my career at Pittsburgh. Kathy Blee cajoled me to finish the book and believed that it could be done even when I faltered. Hiroshi Nara was always ready to cheer me on. I shared many good suppers and companionship with Esther Sales and Pat Doreian. Lucy Fischer and Mark Wicclair have been thoughtful and delightful companions, as have Linda Serody and Alan Meisel. JoAnn Brickley shared the gift of her friendship and counsel. My dear friends Tamara Horowitz and Keiko McDonald did not live to see this book completed but their special influences are embedded in it.

At Oxford University Press, I would like to thank my editor James Cook for his special interest in this work and his thoughtful guidance. I am also indebted to India Gray and David Joseph for intelligent copyediting and efficient production, and Peter Worger for assistance. I am grateful to the anonymous reviewers for Oxford University Press for their comments on the manuscript which greatly aided the revision of this book. I also want to thank Mitch Reyes and Jennifer Kapczynski for their critical feedback on chapter 1 at the Lewis and Clark College's Writing Retreat. Mary Susannah Robbins held me to a rigorous writing schedule, gave me valuable feedback, and encouraged me to carry on at a crucial time when writing the book.

Finally, I want to express my deepest appreciation to my husband David Barnard whose loving and abiding support made the journey of this project possible. I am so lucky to count him as my life partner, best friend, supporter-in-chief, and editor extraordinaire. He not only read and edited every word and comma in the manuscript, but he also lived and breathed them with me. This book is lovingly dedicated to him.

THE LONG DEFEAT

1

Cultural Memory in a Fallen Nation

Growing up [youth] in Tokyo in the 1960s, my daily trip home from grade school took me through a crowded walkway at Shinjuku station bustling with small shops and kiosks. It was a long, busy passageway that connected a new subway line and a suburban line at one of the largest commuter hubs of the city. Sometime in the early 1960s, this walkway came to be lined everyday with amputated middle-aged men wearing tattered cotton military uniforms that revealed conspicuously their missing arms, artificial legs, glass eyes, and other disfigurements. Some would sit still on the ground or keep their heads bowed—motionless as commuters hurried by. Others played melancholy, amateurish tunes on a harmonica or an accordion. It took some time for me as a child to realize these men were there to collect money from the passersby, and that their war misery was on display, in a sense, for that purpose. These traces of war were easy to find when we children looked around and paid attention. Sometimes we saw them in plain view, like the panhandling veterans. Other times we caught or overheard woeful stories in family conversations—air raids endured, properties destroyed, relatives lost. As children we did not know how the Asia-Pacific War came about, or what exactly to make of it, but we understood that it was the single most destructive ordeal that the adults had experienced. ✓ Something dreadful had happened. Early images and perceptions like these would ultimately color our understanding of the war as a national trauma.

How do memories of national trauma remain so relevant to culture and society long after the event? Why do the memories of difficult experiences endure, and even intensify, despite people's impulse to avoid remembering dreadful pasts and to move on? This book explores

G, Confede, J

these questions by examining Japan's culture of defeat up to the present day. I survey the stakes of war memory after the defeat in World War II and show how and why defeat has become an indelible part of Japan's national collective life, especially in recent decades. I probe into the heart of the war memories that lie at the root of the current disputes and escalating frictions in East Asia that have come to be known collectively as Japan's "history problem."

Memories of difficult experiences like war and defeat endure for many reasons: the nation's trajectory may change profoundly, as it did when Japan surrendered sovereignty in 1945; collective life must be regenerated from a catastrophic national fall; and losers face the predicament of living with a discredited, tainted past. In this process, the vanquished mobilize new and revised narratives to explain grievous national failures, mourn the dead, redirect blame, and recover from the burdens of stigma and guilt.[1] The task of making a coherent story for the vanquished is at the same time a project of repairing the moral backbone of a broken society. This precarious project lies at the heart of Japan's culture of defeat, a painful probe into the meaning of being Japanese. Understanding this project is crucial for assessing Japan's choices—*nationalism, pacifism,* or *reconciliationism*—to address the national and international tensions it faces today.

The influence of defeat on Japan's postwar culture has been immense, long-lasting, and complicated.[2] Japan lost sovereignty after surrendering in 1945, and it was occupied for seven years by the winners, who imposed radical reforms in nearly all aspects of society from governance and law, to economy and education. Japan's perpetrator guilt in the war was defined explicitly at the Tokyo War Crimes Trials (1946–1948), which indicted Japan's military leadership for committing crimes against peace and other violations of war conventions. At the same time, the tribunal and numerous other war crimes trials in Asia overlooked the possible guilt of many others in the military, bureaucracy, government, business, and—controversially—the Emperor. Since then, long-standing fissures have emerged within Japanese society over who was responsible for the war and who was guilty. These fissures continue today. Underlying the fissures are two fundamental questions: *Why did we fight an unwinnable war? Why did they kill and die for a lost cause?* In answering these questions, people bring different narratives to bear, debate different rational positions, and opt for different solutions; but ultimately, the answers are formed by personal and political reactions to the memories of massive failure, injustice, and suffering. At the heart of these debates are concerns not only about war responsibility but also about national belonging, the

Are there war massacres in J?

Vick Fr For.

relations between the individual and the state, and relations between the living and the dead.

Japan's war memory is one of the most crucial issues of the global memory culture on wars and atrocities that has surged since the 1990s. There are many volatile, unresolved issues: the territorial disputes with China, Korea, and Russia;[3] the treatment of war guilt and war criminals at commemorations ("the Yasukuni problem");[4] and the claims for compensation and apology by wartime forced laborers, forced sex workers ("comfort women"),[5] and prisoners of war (POWs). Conflicting memories of the troubled past that underlie them also fuel Japan's national controversies—called the "historical consciousness problem" (*rekishi ninshiki mondai*). Far from arriving at a national consensus after seventy years, the cleavage separating different war memories and historical claims deepened in the 1990s with many disputes: the mandate to use patriotic symbols (the national flag and anthem)[6] and inculcating patriotism in schools; the treatment of Japan's atrocities (e.g., the Nanjing massacre) in textbooks and popular culture;[7] and the claims for compensation and health care by the victims of air raids and atomic bombings.[8] These issues continue to test the core of Japan's postwar identity and culminate today in the critical question of remilitarization, altering the pacifist constitution that has anchored national life since 1947.

Poland

3

The difficulty of coming to terms with national trauma is known to many national cultures that have been transformed by memories of catastrophic military failure: examples include postwar Germany and Turkey, post–Algerian War France, and post–Civil War and post–Vietnam America.[9] Facing the challenges of culpability for death, violence, and loss, some nations have responded by mythologizing the lost cause as in the post–Civil War American South;[10] some by martyring the dead soldiers as in post–World War I Germany;[11] while others have chosen to focus on recovery through radical reform, as in post–Ottoman Turkey.[12] Research suggests that nations suffering the crisis of defeat or conquest respond with persistent attempts to overcome humiliation and disgrace, although they differ in approach. This book surveys Japan's case after World War II, building on German historian Wolfgang Schivelbusch's work *Culture of Defeat*.[13]

1-2-3

Comparative

By tracing the many ways in which the vanquished recount their war memories to postwar generations, I move beyond established methods that focus on formal policies and speeches and instead examine the textures of historical and moral understanding in the everyday life of the broader postwar culture. I survey the narratives of war that circulate in families, popular media, and schools to

assess how people have come to terms with the difficult national legacy of trauma, loss, guilt, and shame. I focus mainly on the decades between 1985 and 2015, when war memory took a transnational and global turn. My analysis finds that Japan's war memories are not only deeply encoded in the everyday culture but are also much more varied than the single, caricatured image of "amnesia" depicted by Western media. I suggest that there is no "collective" memory in Japan; rather, multiple memories of war and defeat with different moral frames coexist and vie for legitimacy. I make this case by identifying different trauma narratives that emerged for different social groups with diverse political interests. I then extend this inquiry to probe how negative memory influences and motivates postwar national identity.

Columbus Day

Cultural Trauma, Memory, and National Identity

Maurice Halbwachs suggested that collective memory is always selective according to different conditions of remembering the past.[14] Memories are not fixed or immutable but are representations of reality that are subjectively constructed to fit the present. The struggle for control over memory is rooted in the conflict and interplay between social, political, and cultural interests and values in particular present conditions. Memories of wars, massacres, atrocities, invasions, and other instances of mass violence and death become significant referents for subsequent collective life when people choose to make them especially relevant to who they are and what it means to be a member of that society. Some events become more significant than others because we manage to make them more consequential in later years to better understand ourselves and our society. Jeffrey Alexander has called this process "cultural trauma," which occurs "when members of a collective feel they have been subjected to a horrendous event that leaves indelible marks upon their group consciousness, marking their memories forever and changing their future identity in fundamental and irrevocable ways."[15] The horrendous event emerges as a significant referent in the collective consciousness, not because it is in some way naturally ineffaceable but because it generates a structure of discourse that normalizes it in collective life over time.[16] In the process, the memory of the event is made culturally relevant, remembered as an overwhelmingly damaging and problematic collective experience and incorporated, along with all of its attendant negative emotions, as part of collective identity.[17]

AIDs

My home state: Tanay Columbus Day

Those persistent negative emotions are the most powerful motivator of moral conduct and are critical for understanding how cultural trauma is regenerated over time.[18] Cultures remembering negative historical events are driven to *overcome* the emotions and sentiments that accompany them. Those sentiments have been continually reinscribed in memory and passed on to successive generations. They include the desire to repair a damaged reputation; the aspiration to recover respect in the eyes of the world; the wish to mourn losses and recover *Indo,* from censure; the longing to find meaning and dignity in the face of *Turk,* failure; the hope to shield family and relatives from recrimination; *US* and the urge to minimize the event or pretend it never happened. *Poland,* Satisfying these yearnings and hopes is a long, ongoing project not only to refashion memories but also to mend a broken society. In this recovery project, memories are realigned and reproduced—to *VS* heal, bring justice, and regain moral status in the world—with vary- *G,* ing degrees of success. Understanding this repair project is crucial *SAfr* to explaining the persistence of the cultural trauma, the culture of *Austral* defeat, and also Japan's "history problem." *US*

Today we live in an emerging "culture of memory" where remembering the national past has become vitally relevant for living in the present.[19] Oral history movements, new museum and memorial constructions, and political movements to right past wrongs have proliferated around the world especially since the 1980s. They are all examples of a trend in which remembering the past has become a crucial experience for forging collective identity.[20] The 1990s through the 2010s—the period covered in this book—has also been a crucial time for Japan to look anew into the national past to envision its future. This has reignited past political feuds and old controversies over how to narrate national history, and reawakened the public consciousness that continues unabated through today. The post–World War II gen *kec—* eration, now two-thirds of the population, has entered the fray as new *for* stakeholders to play their roles in framing the national script. The different positions of the generations have meant that people bring more diverse motivations to reframe the history of the lost war. At the same time, rapidly changing geopolitics has brought new uncertainties about unresolved war issues vis-à-vis Japan's Asian neighbors, such as the spiraling lawsuits filed against Japan for compensation claims, demands for apology,[21] and the contested descriptions of events in history textbooks. These issues and others refueled since the 1980s prefigured Japan's history problem, the ramifications of which underlie and aggravate many of Japan's most vexing challenges in its international relations today: the rising popular antagonism toward

Chinas

Japan in East Asia; the increasingly provocative territorial skirmishes with China, South Korea, and Russia; and the persistent belligerence from North Korea.

The culture of memory arises at a significant time of growing awareness that historical knowledge is neither fixed nor uniform. Universal claims for truth are increasingly suspect for many in late modernity, posing challenges to the act of framing a national metanarrative. There is increasing recognition that historical representations have become subjective, political projects in this search for usable pasts.[22] It seems no longer possible today to produce a single, definitive public history shared commonly and objectively within and among nations.[23] This poses a special challenge in East Asian societies like Japan where legitimate and valid knowledge of national history has heretofore been centralized by the state.[24] In a post–Cold War world that requires a broader reorganization of knowledge, the contradiction between the historical relativism that has emerged in the global arena on the one hand, and, on the other, the goal of official history which is to inculcate a particular truth has become increasingly acute.[25] In these times of flux, it is not surprising that Japan has seen a surge of acrimonious disputes and, indeed, a rise in neonationalism among those who perceive global change as threatening to their self-identity.

Contentions over war memory across the East Asia region strike at the core of Japan's project to recover its moral foothold in the long wake of its calamitous defeat. Several issues stand out as particularly inflammable: the redress for wartime sexual forced labor ("comfort women"); the culpability for brutal massacres (especially the Nanjing massacre); and the attempts to rehabilitate the perpetrators and war criminals as martyrs (the Yasukuni Shrine). Predictably, this type of project is fraught with deep fissures among stakeholders who embrace diverse perspectives and goals. The carriers of memory—Japanese intellectuals, educators, politicians, lawyers, commentators, media critics, activists, and others who retell the past—assign different meanings to the national fall, complicating the prospect of forging a unified national metanarrative.

My analysis of the deep fissures in Japan's postwar memory builds on German sociologist Bernhard Giesen's typologies that illuminate the different constructions of trauma narratives in civil society.[26] I propose that there are three categories of conflicting trauma narratives vying for moral superiority within the complex landscape of cultural memory in Japan. They are different in how much they emphasize human failures and how they depict the moral character of *heroes, victims,* and *perpetrators* of the war. They are also different in how they

perceive the relationship between winner and loser, and the stakes of memory. In short, they differ in the moral interpretations of defeat and in the courses they chart for national recovery.

A Tale of Three Moralities: The Divided Narratives of a Cultural Trauma

Moral understandings of war vary in time, place, historical context, and political-cultural traditions.[27] In the just war theory rooted in the Western Augustinian Christian tradition, war is theorized and justified by the idea that the use of mass political violence can be ethically appropriate.[28] World War II was an example of such a just war for the Allied powers that defeated the Axis powers who were deemed to be unjust aggressors. This perspective rooted in Western theology, however, is not a cultural universal across the wide spectrum of human history. More pragmatic and ubiquitous is the realist, crude recognition that a "good war" is a war that ends in victory, expands political power, and promotes national interests. In the long history of warfare in Japan, different standards have prevailed: the premedieval system of legitimating war by authorization of the imperial court; the feudal system of legitimating warfare by victory;[29] and, in modernity, fitfully adapting to the West-initiated system of regulating wars by international conventions and treaties. It is therefore not surprising that along the way, Japan has embraced degrees of realism and relativism in constructing notions of good and bad wars without subscribing to absolutist principles. Although the just war philosophy does not readily "fit" in a Japanese cultural context that evolved outside the Judeo-Christian civilizational orbit and grew from polytheistic traditions where moral relativism is a pragmatic way of life,[30] Japan nevertheless adopted the concept to justify its actions in World Wars I and II. In Japan's adaptation, the just war framework meant that the Asia-Pacific War was the "Sacred War" fought for the Emperor to protect the "Greater East Asia Co-Prosperity Sphere" from Euro-American, white, colonial aggression. After the national collapse of 1945, many reacted to the abrupt inversion of moral order that rendered their "right war" to be the "wrong war" by reverting back to a realist moral relativism (*kateba kangun, makereba zokugun*).

This abrupt inversion of the moral order, and widespread cynicism about war, all but ensured that conflicting trauma narratives would emerge in postwar Japanese society. Over the decades, three categories of trauma narratives have emerged, diverse but deeply etched in the national sentiment. They are different in how they assess the moral import of military and political actions, and in how they characterize the negative legacy of failures and losses in the war. Each points Japan in a different direction for shaping its future.

The first category of narratives emphasizes the stories of fallen national *heroes*. These narratives embrace a "fortunate fall" argument, which justifies the war and national sacrifices in hindsight by claiming that the peace and prosperity of today are built on those sacrifices of the past. These heroic narratives tend to promote a discourse of indebtedness that is heard often in official speeches at commemorations. It is an ameliorative narrative intended to cultivate pride in national belonging; at the same time it diverts attention from the culpability of the state in starting and losing the war.

A second narrative promotes empathy and identification with the tragic *victims* of defeat. Here a vision of "catastrophe" prevails—an unmitigated tragedy of epic proportions—accentuating the total carnage and destruction wrought by ferocious military violence. This discourse of suffering and antimilitarism is found often in family stories; popular culture stories; and the pacifist embrace of the victims in Hiroshima, Nagasaki, and scores of other cities crushed by atomic bombings and indiscriminate air raids. This narrative also tends to divert attention, in this case from the suffering of distant others that the Japanese victimized in Asia.

The third type of narrative contrasts with the first two by emphasizing Japan's *perpetrator* acts of imperialism, invasion, and exploitation in China, Korea, and Southeast Asia. This is a narrative of a "dark descent to hell," stressing the violence and harm that Japan inflicted, with varied attribution of malicious intent. The most difficult and controversial of the three narratives, this vision, and its discourse of regret, is often found in investigative journalism, the news media, documentaries, academic publications, and intellectual discussions as well as some veterans' memoirs and oral histories. Civic movements and friendship organizations dedicated to reconciliation in East Asia largely presuppose the acceptance of this perpetrator narrative.

This cacophony of memory narratives, far apart in moral sentiments and interests, accounts for the disarray in the nation's representation of its metahistory. This problem is evident even in the naming of the war: "the Pacific War" became a standard name for the war imposed by the US occupation and is still often used in the fortunate fall narrative. A countervailing name, used by Japanese progressive intellectuals and educators, also gained ground and is often used in the dark descent narrative; this name "the Fifteen-Year War" recognized the salience of Japanese imperial aggression in East Asia for a decade preceding the war in the Pacific. Subsequent designations used to sidestep such naming politics have been "the Asia-Pacific War," "the Shōwa War," "World War II," and, as people became weary of the political baggage that each name carried, the war ultimately came to be called "the last world war," "that war," and even "that unfortunate period of the past." This problem of representing "that war" arises at every turn, from commemorative speeches and history textbooks to museum exhibits. The hundreds of regional, specialized "peace" museums scattered across the nation must address this history problem by not presenting a comprehensive national history of the war; rather, they present partial stories of cultural trauma, selectively emphasizing perpetrators, victims, or heroes. Thus the common Western criticism that Japan leaves so much of war history unexamined points the finger in the wrong direction: it is not about national amnesia but about a stalemate in a fierce, multivocal struggle over national legacy and the meaning of being Japanese.

Narrating Fallen Heroes: The Fortunate Fall

From Robert E. Lee of the American Confederacy to German Field Marshall Erwin Rommel in World Wars I and II, to John Wayne in the film *Green Berets* (1968), there are many stories of well-known heroes of a lost war. Regardless of where and how the heroes fought, these popular narratives allow their actions and even their downfall to be framed as an act of courage and selfless sacrifice. Historian George Mosse explored this proclivity to celebrate fallen soldiers by examining how the war dead were martyred in Germany after World War I to dissipate the pain of failure and to relieve the guilt of the survivors.[31] Martyrdom allows the living to say that soldiers did not die in vain. In the Japanese version, the narratives of fallen heroes often also claim redemption for them in that their death ostensibly contributed to making Japan's future better and brighter—the "fortunate fall."

A well-known example of this genre in Japan is the story of the fallen heroes on the battleship *Yamato*, one of the most iconic narratives of sacrifice for a greater cause in Japan's World War II history. The largest battleship ever built, it sank north of Okinawa in April 1945 with a crew of 3,000 men as it was deployed for a tactically dubious suicide sortie only months before Japan's defeat. This patriotic tale recounts the last moments of the men in the battleship and the torment among the young officers as they desperately questioned the meaning of their impending death for a war that was certain to end in defeat.

Moments before the ship sank under an overwhelming bombardment by seven hundred American bombers, Captain Usubuchi makes the now-famous statement that his impending death is rendered worthwhile because his sacrifice can serve as an awakening, a rallying cry for a better national future:

> Japan has paid too little attention to progress. We have been too finicky, too wedded to selfish ethics; we have forgotten true progress. How else can Japan be saved except by losing and coming to its senses? If Japan does not come to its senses now, when will it be saved?
>
> We will lead the way. We will die as harbingers of Japan's new life. That's where our real satisfaction lies, isn't it?[32]

What this twenty-one-year-old officer meant by "progress" is vague enough that different meanings can be attributed to it, such as peace, justice, security, or prosperity. It is also easy to fault the logical contradiction of a young man claiming to contribute to a future that he will not experience. Yet this contradictory logic is at the core of the idea that links progress to sacrifice, which engendered the collective belief that Japan could rebound and recover. In this requiem for the dead, the courage and discipline of the men facing certain death are emphasized without directing blame or resentment toward the state leadership that ordered the mission with no fuel to return home. This story of *Yamato*, recounted in many films, documentaries, textbooks, and even political speeches,[33] inspires ideas that range from nationalism to anti-Americanism, supranationalism, and pacifism. Avoiding condemnation of the heroes as perpetrators of an aggressive war, narratives like those of *Yamato*'s fallen heroes are remade and updated regularly in the popular media.[34] Other examples of this genre include the bestsellers and films *Eternal Zero* (*Eien no zero* 2009, 2013) and *Moon Light Summer* (*Gekko no natsu* 1993), both about Zero fighter pilots who never returned; these successor narratives aim to mobilize indebtedness and praise for the war dead.

Narrating Victims: The Catastrophe

From the *Diary of Anne Frank*, now translated in sixty-seven languages, to the iconic photo of the "Napalm Girl" (1972) running naked on a road after being burned by a South Vietnamese air force attack, there are voluminous narratives of innocent victims of tragic wars

Jap. Victims —
Dresden Victims

and other catastrophes. Regardless of where and how the victims are persecuted, these narratives frame their suffering as the result of brutal, callous oppression, and inexcusable acts of torture and injustice. Historian Jay Winter, recounting the carnage of World War I in Europe, argued that it was important for people to make sense of the slaughter via a culture of remembrance and mourning in order to grieve and heal from the devastating experience of loss.[35] This "popular piety" is evident also in the Japanese narratives of victims, and it is a key ingredient for catharsis and atonement.[36] Significantly, the Japanese state and military are often the *shadow perpetrators* in these narratives, which explicitly or implicitly encode their culpability for the victimization.

Nakazawa Keiji's semiautobiographical comic *Barefoot Gen* (1973–1987) is arguably the most iconic antiwar literature of this genre in Japan. Written by a survivor of the Hiroshima blast, the story represents unmitigated "catastrophe," offering a tragic narrative of the obliteration of Hiroshima through an intimate family portrayal of day-to-day survival after the atomic bomb. Based on a true story, it is a powerful interweaving of personal history and world history, telling the horrific effects of the nuclear blast and radiation with rage, agony, and despair. The graphic details of the atomic blast are depicted to maximum effect.[37]

Gen unequivocally indicts the war as absolute evil. Moreover, the war was brought on recklessly and unnecessarily by the Japanese military and the imperial state that heartlessly and ineptly misled civilians to deathly destruction and suffering. All the suffering emanating from this atomic bomb could have been averted if only the war had been stopped earlier, if only the military state had the sense to accept the Potsdam Declaration sooner. *Gen*'s message is clear: authorities like the state, the military, the Emperor, the American military, and American doctors (who collected clinical data from the radiated victims) cannot ever be trusted again.[38] Thus, even as the story progresses from obliteration to rebuilding new life, it carries a bitter undertone, since nothing can really undo the permanent damage to people's lives and bodies, and the culprits are not brought to justice.

Gen's iconic status cannot be overstated. Used widely and easily accessible in schools in the past four decades, *Gen* has reached successive postwar generations and shaped popular consciousness about the violence of militarism. Many have attested to the psychological trauma of learning about Hiroshima in childhood first from *Gen*, whether in school libraries, in peace education classes, on commercial television, or in cinemas.[39] Equivalent to Anne Frank's story as a story of victimization used to educate, *Gen* mobilizes empathy and pity and sends the

each section has a key
cultural representation - film, a novel,

clear message that we must take control of our own lives and have the strength to say no to war and nuclear weapons, so as never to become such victims again. Little connection is made, however, between the bomb and the fifteen-year war that preceded the blast, even though Hiroshima was a military city. The audience gains no insight from *Gen* that much of invaded Asia welcomed the atomic bombs dropped on Japan at the time. (For example, *Gen* is largely rejected by Korean audiences.)[40] For the most part, *Gen* has become a tale of victims of a brutal war, extolling the theme of suffering.

The mobilization of victimhood in stories such as *Gen* succeeds in feeding into the larger cultural trauma of the fallen nation and emerges not as an anti-American sentiment but an antimilitary sentiment. Stories of this genre are created up to today, with similar themes of the meaningless destruction and breakdown of moral and material order. Other examples of this genre emphasizing the helplessness of orphans and civilians on the home front are *Graves of the Fireflies* (1988), *The Song of Sugarcane Fields* (2004), and *To All the Corners of the World* (2007).[41]

Narrating Perpetrators: The Dark Descent to Hell

From *Eichmann in Jerusalem* (1963) to the documentaries of the My Lai massacre (1968) and Francis Coppola's film *Apocalypse Now* (1979), there are many tales of infamous perpetrators of a lost war in the popular culture. Regardless of where and how the perpetrators carried out their actions, their narratives tend to frame them as disturbed, troubling men who have gone over the deep end or over to their sadistic and evil side. American historian Christopher Browning traced the history of German perpetrators in World War II who cold-bloodedly executed Polish civilians en masse as part of their regular daily jobs.[42] These perpetrators were brought to justice in trials at the hands of their own countrymen in the 1960s. Japanese perpetrators of World War II, by contrast, stood trial at the hands of the victors and their victims but not their own people—a development complicated by the exoneration of the Emperor by the American occupation, and the Cold War. Nevertheless, Japanese perpetrator narratives also expose malevolent acts committed by their own people, based on the belief that uncovering and facing your own people's dreadful past is intrinsically important for individuals and society alike. Moving forward, turning a new page, and making a clean break from the past call for self-examination of one's moral failures. When it comes to recovery and healing from military violence in particular, this approach presumes the necessity of facing squarely the darkest and least acceptable aspects of the self. *of one's national history*

One of the most influential figures to shape the public discourse on war guilt in postwar Japan is historian Ienaga Saburō, a prolific scholar of war history and war responsibility.[43] Ienaga is also the well-known plaintiff who waged the longest legal battle against the state over how to teach the national past. Motivated by remorse at having been a passive bystander during the war, Ienaga devoted himself to righting the wrong by publishing perpetrator history in school textbooks, claiming that the state was especially culpable and responsible for the war and how it was carried out.[44] His three lawsuits spanning 32 years *story* (1965–1997) helped keep alive the critical narrative of national history in the public arena, especially the dark chapters of the war: invasion, rapes, and plunder in China; the biological experiment Unit 731; the Nanjing massacre; the forced labor of colonial subjects and POWs; and the victimization of civilians in Okinawa.[45] Ienaga's narratives hold that the war was an illegal war of aggression in violation of international conventions, driven by Japan's economic and political ambitions to control northern China, which culminated in a 15-year conflict. He does not spare the state:

Brits in Burma on rr film

> The fifteen-year war was an unrighteous, reckless war begun with unjust and improper goals and means by the Japanese state, and . . . starting the war and refusing to end the war in a timely fashion were both illegal and improper acts of the state.[46]

fascism viewed from Italy; 1922 1920s, Ethiopian war

Ienaga's lawsuits raised public awareness of Japan as perpetrator and spurred citizens' movements and civic organizations to support his ongoing efforts. A favorable verdict for his second lawsuit emboldened other history textbook writers to increase their coverage of perpetrator history in the 1970s and 1980s.[47] Scores of popular history books, novels, documentaries, even manga cartoon history books for school libraries, and other cultural media followed with robust narratives of Japanese perpetration in Asia during the periods of colonization and war. As I show in chapters 3 and 4, teachers, activists, artists, cartoonists, and the media routinely recounted and disseminated these stories, exposing the children to Japanese acts of perpetration more than had been done in the past, thereby reproducing the cultural trauma of the war for the next generation. However, such public reckoning with perpetrator history has also been met by fierce rebuttals, such as the defamation suit filed against Ōe Kenzaburo, the Nobel laureate whose

"Okinawa Notes" in 1970 referred to the involvement of the Japanese military in the mass suicides of Okinawan civilians.[48] Updated perpetrator narratives today are reproduced nationally in the media by journalists and academics; in the international arena they have successfully engaged broader media through feminist and human rights activists.

[handwritten: Who unveils Trauma. — Mr. Roberts, survivors, feminists, investig journalists, etc]

Divided Memories in a Culture of Defeat

As these distinct narratives show, a nation's memory of war and especially of its defeat does not produce a monolithic, consensual picture but creates a conflictive and polyphonic public discourse. Heterogeneous memories such as these are in fact more common than people assume especially within a time span of a few generations from the event.[49] For example, Konrad Jarausch and Michael Geyer discuss the "fractured, multiple, intersecting" memory narratives of Hitler's war, the Nazi regime, and the Holocaust since the 1989 reunification, showing that individual accounts in the German case are also replete with contending recollections. The official German policy of contrition notwithstanding, stories of perpetrators, victims, bystanders, and collaborators coexist based on different perceptions, experiences, and self-interests. These are ultimately irreconcilable and incapable of engendering a coherent, unified account for the nation.[50] In the German case, divided memories have emerged from a specific set of social and political conditions: the different West-East political regimes during the Cold War, different generational influences, diverse battlefront and other wartime experiences, and different ideological assumptions that have become inescapable for unified Germany.[51]

French memories of war have also failed to produce a national consensus: the discourses of resistance heroes are interspersed with perpetrator narratives of Vichy crimes and victim narratives of Nazi-occupied France in their national self-understandings.[52] Similarly in Austria, victim narratives of Nazi annexation have ceded ground to righteous heroic narratives as well as perpetrator narratives of military collaboration. Each narrative offers a partial account of a "whole" that remains elusive and incongruent.[53]

Japan's divided memory culture also resonates with that of post-defeat nations of World War I like Turkey after the Ottoman Empire,[54] and postcommunist nations like Hungary and Poland after the Cold War.[55] This recent comparative scholarship is especially insightful in illuminating the predicament of *non-Western* nations, defeated by *Western*

Finland

nations, who are compelled to revise the meaning of their totalitarian pasts in a manner that conforms to the West's expectations of how they *should* "come to terms" with such a past. The pervading sense that there is an "acceptable" and "civilized" way for liberal democracies to confront their totalitarian past by "seeking the truth" is a common thread that ties together the cultures of defeat in these disparate cases. As this book will also show, what is "appropriate" to remember, based on a universalized West European model, derived from the Holocaust experience and rooted in Western anti-Semitism, constrains and sets complicated hurdles on non-Western memory cultures in their efforts to address past wrongs.

In the case of Japan, the tarnished memory and ambivalent sentiments about heroes, victims, and perpetrators of the militarist totalitarian past have erupted to the surface in many proxy political disputes, such as the question of remilitarization in the new global geopolitics. From the first time Japan sent the Self-Defense Force (SDF)—as Japan's de facto standing military is known—to join UN Peacekeeping operations overseas (in 1992, after the Gulf War) the question of whether any Japanese soldier could again harm or be harmed by another foreign national has been insistently present. As Japan developed new security legislation (2004) precipitated by 9/11 and to address North Korea's missile threats (1998, 2006, 2009, 2013, and 2014), the contentions have been intertwined with fears of giving too much power to the SDF and trusting military leaders again. When the neonationalist faction of the parliament succeeded in revising the Basic Law of Education (2006) and brought patriotism back to public school curricula, it raised fears for some, and hope for others, that Japanese children may be induced to believe again that dying for the country was a worthy goal. These were not merely disputes between political hawks and doves, but evidence of fissures at the core of the antiwar national identity that had been fostered over the course of the long defeat.[56] Today, as the geopolitical tensions in East Asia escalate and Japan's military capabilities grow, the trepidation over possible involvement in another military conflict has also heightened. Whether people are for or against the new interpretation of the constitution that would now allow a limited level of collective self-defense (2014), the anxieties underlying this new shake-up of what "peace" means in a pacifist nation have reignited, fed by memories of the disastrous last war run by uncontrolled military power.[57]

In Japan's postwar history, the chronology of the narratives of war heroes, victims, and perpetrators starts with the Tokyo War Crimes Trials (1946–1948). As one of the instigators of a world war with the largest casualty in modern history, Japan could hardly escape culpability. The total death toll of World War II is estimated at 60 million, of which one-third occurred in Asia.[58] During Japan's incursions in East and Southeast Asia and the South Pacific, an estimated 20 million Asians were killed, not only from warfare but also from civilian raids, plunder, rape, starvation, and torture.[59] The civilian death toll of the Asia-Pacific War was overwhelming: around one million in Japan from the atomic bombings of Hiroshima and Nagasaki and the air raids in hundreds of cities; over 16 million in China; and under 2,000 from the United States. The deaths rates among soldiers were high especially toward the end of the war: about 2.3 million Japanese soldiers died at a death rate of 38%, which was higher than that of German soldiers (33%), and 19 times that of American soldiers (2%).[60] Because the Japanese military fought across the vast expanse of the Asia-Pacific region where supplies of food, medicine, and ammunition were broken off, approximately 60–70% of the soldiers died not from combat but from starvation, disease, and abandonment. Half of their remains have been repatriated but the rest are, to date, scattered across the vast region. Only a small percentage was taken prisoner given the official prohibition on surrender, and the last of them returned in 1956. It took decades to complete the repatriation of several million civilians and ex-soldiers.[61]

At the tribunal, Japan's perpetrator guilt was defined explicitly by the Allies in a "victors' justice" that blamed Japan's military leadership for committing crimes against peace and other violations of war conventions. The indictments of perpetrators also included culpability for atrocities such as the Nanjing massacre and the Manila massacre.[62] In addition to the Class A war criminals indicted at the Tokyo Trials and then executed, thousands of perpetrators in the lower ranks were tried and indicted as Class B and C war criminals for carrying out war crimes throughout East and Southeast Asia (1946–1951).[63] However, national reckoning with a larger scope of guilt by untold, often lesser known perpetrators remained elusive. The Emperor—who had by then renounced his "divine" status—was not held culpable for crimes against peace and escaped prosecution. The Japanese people at large were also held unaccountable as they were said to have been misled by a deceptive militarist state. Tens of thousands of civilians were purged as collaborators of the wartime regime, but many were depurged even before the end of the occupation as the Cold War intensified in East Asia.[64]

The chronology after Japan regained sovereignty in 1952 is relatively straightforward. After the conservative Liberal Democratic Party

(LDP) came to dominate the Japanese government in the mid-1950s, the economic imperatives of material growth and stability took priority over punishment for past deeds, while the political imperatives of security and alliance with the United States took priority over reconciliation with communist China and the Soviet Union. When these conservatives stabilized their foothold as the stewards of unprecedented economic growth in a nation determined to make up for the astronomical losses of the war, they gained institutional control over the official metanarrative of the war, which they sought to characterize as a tragic conflict fought reluctantly but bravely for national survival. In this heroic narrative, the present growth and prosperity were the hard-won rewards built on past national tragedy.

The opposition, however, skeptical and distrustful of the conservative account of unmitigated progress, forcefully dissented and joined forces with myriad countervailing social groups and movements, such as the teachers' union and pacifist movements that were in the 1960s and 1970s opposing the US-Japan Security Treaty, nuclear tests, and the Vietnam War. These groups, led by educators, intellectuals, journalists, unionists, and activists, claimed that the war had been waged by ambitious leaders of an aggressive state who carried out reckless military invasions and colonization, resulting in great pain and suffering in Asia. Centrists, in turn, staked a narrower claim, emphasizing the domestic toll that total war had inflicted on Japan, such as the victims of the atomic bombing of Hiroshima and Nagasaki and of the thousands of air raids carried out by American forces. For the centrists, the war was a tragic conflict fought foolishly by a dysfunctional military state, only to end in a monumental defeat.

The contentious politics of memory in the 1960s and 1970s reached a point where different stakeholders came to share a measure of agreement in remembering the Japanese side of the suffering. Even if they disagreed on whom to designate as heroes, victims, and perpetrators, or how to remember Asian suffering inflicted by Japan during the war, they shared a memory of their own losses and could not deny the visible hardship that was around them. As such, the cultural trauma could be normalized as veterans and civilians, rich and poor, elite and downtrodden could at least forge a common ground in their antipathy for war. Ultimately this developed into powerful antimilitary and antinuclear sentiments that became integral to the culture of defeat.[65]

In the 1980s and 1990s, a global memory culture began to coalesce around emerging human rights and transitional justice movements that focused on redressing past wrongs. Pressured by neighboring East Asian nations and the international media, Japan's long-standing

War monuments

problem of reckoning with the past became an international concern on many fronts: disagreements over self-justifying history textbooks, struggles over official apologies, compensation suits filed by former colonial subjects and victims, controversial commemorations of the war dead and war criminals, disputes over museum exhibits, and others. A most significant example was the redress for former "comfort women" who were forced as sex workers to service Japanese soldiers during wartime, and who began to break their silence and claim redress from the Japanese government. Emerging as a transnational feminist movement against sexual violence, the "comfort women" case succeeded in bringing the world's attention to victimization of women in war, while also tarnishing the carefully crafted image of "innocent" Japanese soldiers.[66] Such developments were catapulted not only by global trends but also domestic events that transformed the conditions of memory making such as the death of Emperor Hirohito, the end of the monopolistic rule of the LDP, and the collapse of the bubble economy; and regional events such as the rising political, economic, and cultural importance of East Asia, especially China. The contentious disputes of these decades resulted in the growing recognition for the perpetrator past in popular culture, as well as efforts for reconciliation by broad international coalitions of citizen's movements.

from the Balkans + China + Korea

By the early 2000s, there emerged a neonationalist backlash to the efforts to bring about reconciliation to East Asia.[67] It was a response to the globalization of "the history problem" that accompanied the shifting balance of political power in East Asia with China's spectacular economic rise.[68] As Japan's anxieties grew in the face of an economic downturn, recession, unemployment and rising inequalities, its problems in the post–Cold War international order also mounted: the continuing dependence for security on the victor, the United States; the failure to be part of the victorious coalition in the Gulf War (1990); and the failure to gain permanent membership in the UN Security Council reserved for the winners of World War II (2005). Recognizing the ghost of the traumatic defeat in the deepening morass, some Japanese critics have called it "the Second Defeat" or "the Third Defeat."[69] The international and national disputes have worsened in the 2010s, most visibly in the irreconcilable claims on the border islands, the nationalists' hate movements on both sides of the sea, and the demands for more apologies and compensations.

These deep fissures in Japan's war memories that I have described are also reflected in scores of national public opinion surveys. For the most part, these reveal a three-way split in the national reckoning with the war legacy, divided in their evaluation of the character and conduct of the war and its consequences.[70] They are divided among three answers: (1) the war was bad and should have been avoided; (2) the war was bad but could not have been avoided; and (3) the war was inevitable given the threatening circumstances of the era. This diversity in presuming Japan's culpability corresponds to the varied memory narratives that will be shown throughout this book. National surveys confirm this trend: a 2006 survey published by the largest Japanese national newspaper *Yomiuri* for example revealed that one-third (34%) believed the Asia-Pacific War was a war of aggression, while another third (34%) agreed that only the Japan-China War, and not the Pacific War, qualified as a war of aggression. About 10% believed that neither conflict was a war of aggression, while 21% were undecided.[71] The fissure is also evident in a 2006 survey by the *Asahi* newspaper with the second-largest national circulation: a third (31%) of the respondents thought that Japan waged a war of aggression in China, while less than half (45%) believe it was both a war of aggression and a war of self-defense.[72] This diversity of views in the defeat culture is shown time and again in opinion polls and national surveys, and tends to hold a steady pattern across generations; they cannot be explained monocausally by generation, gender, or political party affiliation.[73]

Such divisiveness has its consequences, especially in a culture of defeat: asked whether they trust their political leadership, Japanese public opinion is endemically negative: only 23% of Japanese trusted their political leadership, leaving Japan ranked 127th out of 135 nations in the world.[74] At the same time, asked in a comparative survey about whether they "take a positive attitude" toward themselves, the Japanese ranked lowest in self-esteem scores among 53 countries.[75] It is not hard to imagine that these overall trends derive in some measure from the negative national memories of a difficult past internalized by those who long to repair and recover from that legacy.

About This Book

Collective memory studies teach us that our social act of remembering is always selective according to different conditions of remembering the past. This book assesses war memories not as fixed recall but as representations of reality that are subjectively constructed in particular present conditions. To assess such conditions of memory making as cultural constructs, it is important to take account of the sentiments, values, and motivations of ordinary people, not only decision-makers and intellectual elites. Accordingly, my analysis explores both producers and consumers of war memory and uses a wide range of sources—from personal testimonies and interviews to popular cultural media material—to explore the variety of ways that Japanese identity is shaped in families, schools, and communities.

Such everyday sentiments are on display in many settings: family kitchens and living rooms, school classrooms, in newspapers, on television, and on the Internet. Examining the popular narratives in these disparate places offers an insight into a wide range of moral values and motivations for remembering. To this end, I analyze the contents of popular narratives that reference the war, defeat, and colonial legacy: newspaper editorials, letters to the editor, best-selling books, high school textbooks, educational cartoons, films, animated films, television documentaries and debates, children's stories, cram school crib notes, formal and informal speeches, biographical memoirs, Internet sites and blogs, and public and private museum exhibits. I also delve into direct and published interviews, as well as ethnographical fieldwork and focus groups interviews to elicit and decipher the cultural assumptions and values that inform the meaning of the war and the legacy of the defeat. Taking this triangulation approach allows me to consider diverse snapshots of memory communicated in everyday life in the mass media, in school classrooms and at home.[76] This analysis focuses on the period 1985 to 2015 and presents a sociological account of how people refashioned and reinscribed the cultural trauma from different perspectives, while negotiating the tension between moral frameworks and emotions in these recent decades. Through this exploration, the study asks whether healing from the scars and escaping from the prison of history can ever be complete, especially if the trauma itself, in the end, is incomprehensible and irreparable.

As a book that assesses Japan's case in the context of the global "culture of memory," my analysis also uses a method of *shadow comparisons,*[77] critically applying concepts and ideas generated from works on difficult memory and cultural trauma in other societies. Because the critical work on German memory is wide, varied, and thorough, I draw on it often to illuminate patterns in Japan and to derive insights into meanings by implicit or explicit comparison. In particular, I draw on the works of sociologists, psychologists, and historians of Germany: Aleida Assmann, Bernhard Giesen, Jeffrey Olick, Gabrielle Rosenthal, Dan Bar-On, Robert Moeller, Omar Bartov, Dirk Moses, Konrad Jarausch, and Michael Geyer. Other comparisons that shed light on the Japanese case are studies of post–World War I Turkey, post–Vietnam War America, and postcommunist Central Europe.

This comparative approach allows me to observe the commonalities in the meaning of cultural trauma in different cultures of defeat.[78]

My sociological approach builds on the work of many others. Among them are the work of American historians of contemporary Japan such as John Dower, Carol Gluck, Alexis Dudden, Laura Hein, Mark Selden, Yoshikuni Igarashi, and Franziska Seraphim, and anthropologists Mariko Tamanoi and Lisa Yoneyama. They have blazed the trail with their close observations of memory making in disparate cultural settings of Japanese society. My work is also informed by the work of Japanese sociologists such as Oguma Eiji, Yoshida Yutaka, Fukuma Yoshiaki, Sato Takumi, Ueno Chizuko, and Shirai Satoshi, and critical scholars of war memory such as Kato Naohiro, Takahashi Tetsuya, and Narita Ryūichi all of whom have illuminated many aspects of Japanese society that are inflected by the negative legacy of war and defeat.

This book is grounded in the epistemological position that the distinction between history and memory is at best blurred,[79] and that memory narratives do not render definitive truths about historical events and facts.[80] Rather, I see memory narratives as vehicles of communication that reveal the attachments and anxieties of the narrators in negotiating their self-identity. Interpretations of contentious difficult "facts" diverge because people want to make the past more bearable and the present more palatable. This perspective, however, raises the question of how the research can set the parameters for choosing the trauma narratives to examine from a diverse range. In this study, I have selected samples of trauma narratives by assessing their salience, relying on circulation figures, sales figures, popularity rankings, and wide distribution. Another selection criterion was the staying power of the cultural products diffusing the narratives, measured in the number of remakes and types of medium in circulation, reviews, advertising, blogs, and other audience responses. Wherever possible, I have pursued universal sampling as my sampling strategy especially for the newspaper editorials of five national newspapers (*Asahi, Yomiuri, Nikkei, Mainichi,* and *Sankei*), series of public testimonies and memoirs, as well as commemoration literatures.

After this introductory chapter, the next chapters describe how the memories of war and defeat are discussed in three areas of everyday life: the family, the popular media, and school. I illustrate a wide range of memory narratives and their narrators in those settings and consider their different national visions. Chapter 2 introduces the reader to the former soldiers and describes how they tell their stories of their war experience. The cultural trauma has left indelible scars on many of them, and it has impacted how they told their war stories to their children and grandchildren. Surveying 430 cases, I find that many chose to present themselves as powerless victims and used that narrative to repair their biographies. Smaller contingents acknowledged their war responsibility, and fewer still talked of their war exploits. The postwar children and grandchildren, in turn, sought out stories to construct "family albums," piecing together selected war memories to make coherent family narratives.[81] This intergenerational repair project effectively transmitted the cultural trauma of war as something "close to home" rather than a worldwide event.

Chapter 3 describes how Japan remembers the war and the war dead at the annual commemorations on August 15. I show how the political performances and the popular media discourses divide rather than unite the nation over the questions of war guilt and national sacrifice. Surveying the political performances on August 15 from 1985 to 2014, as well as the media discourse surrounding those commemorations in newspaper editorials, television, and film, I find that many of Japan's memory makers responded positively to the international pressures to right past wrongs in the 1990s, yet faced a severe backlash in the 2000s.[82] Thus the impact of the global politics of regret on Japan has been mixed.[83]

Chapter 4 illustrates how the war is taught to Japan's school children in the classroom and during school trips. I argue that despite being stereotypically branded by the Western media as attempting to whitewash the past, teaching of war, peace, and national history to Japan's next generation actually succeeds in raising pacifists. The chapter covers a wide range of teaching material and memorial sites from peace museums across the country to forty-six social studies textbooks, and well-known children's history comics (manga) series. I argue that that negative emotional memory, especially the fear of repeating violent conflicts, has been used effectively to motivate peace education. A surprising proportion of perpetrator accounts are found in the material on the war that children learn, along with accounts of heroes and victims. Such cultural trauma stories are often transformed into morality tales aimed at preventing a repetition of the national failure.

Chapter 5 considers Japan at the crossroads of becoming a "normal country"—a nation possessing the full military capability to wage war. The post–World War II generation, now two-thirds of the population, must come to many decisions in the increasingly tense and uncertain geopolitics of East Asia. I consider these questions in the international setting where the global movements for redress have intensified scrutiny on Japan's violent past. I conclude with three strategies of overcoming Japan's "history problem" at play today that correspond to the three trauma narratives illustrated throughout the book: nationalism, pacifism, and reconciliationism. I focus this discussion on the current dispute about revising the postwar peace constitution that has never been altered and show how the ripples of the past war directly reach decision-making today. Finally, I compare Japan's case to Germany's and consider the lessons that may apply transnationally.[84]

2

Repairing Biographies and Aligning Family Memories

A war story told in my family when I was growing up was about the Tokyo air raids in May 1945 when my grandfather's home in Komazawa was scorched by one of the hundreds of thousands of incendiary bombs dropped by American air squads. As narrated to the children—usually by my mother—it was not a story about a lucky family that escaped death from night raids that killed hundreds of thousands, but a story about an unlucky family that was devastated by the twist of fate that left them financially and emotionally distressed for a long time. It was always added that the house had been the crowning achievement of my grandfather's career, built from his lifelong savings, and therefore its loss, together with all other possessions, left him a distraught man. Told from the viewpoint of the family, the story elicited awe, sadness, and pity, but because it also lacked any sense of historical and political context and proportion, to me as a child it sounded as if the hundreds of American B-29s had flown all the way to Tokyo that night specifically to destroy my grandfather's house. War memories like these recounted in Japanese families tend to focus on personal anguish that overshadowed everything else at the time. Only decades later did I learn of the heavy Japanese air raids on Chinese cities like Chongqing that equally obliterated civilian homes and killed tens of thousands.

War stories recounted in this way to many postwar children as a "dreadful experience" (*imawashii taiken*) in family memory tend to concentrate on events occurring in the last years of the war when Japan's losses had mounted exponentially and defeat was imminent. Partly for this reason, many personal stories told about the war from both the battlefront and the home front tend to focus on the experiences of extreme deprivation, danger, and near-death around 1945. Therefore, many survivors recall helplessness—from incinerating air raids, pounding defeats, debilitating diseases and malnutrition, to slayings, evacuations, and rapes—when any sense of security had completely eroded for almost everyone. This sense of trauma and despair left indelible scars on those who experienced it and impacted how they would tell their war stories to their children and grandchildren. The large accumulation of these trauma narratives in postwar society would open the way to much criticism toward Japan's propensity to take the victim's view of the war, more often than the perpetrator's or the hero's.[1]

Marianne Hirsch calls this type of knowledge *postmemory*, an imagined understanding of trauma by those who did not experience the event itself but grew up deeply influenced by it. In practical terms, it is the experience of inheriting cultural trauma from parents and grandparents that then becomes the backdrop against which family relationships and social identity are formed. The trauma itself may be often too difficult to represent or communicate fully, and it may not even be understood fully. Nevertheless, the taboos, preoccupations, and anguish of the trauma are transmitted through close relationships and emotional ties, and become the shared cultural and cognitive frames to interpret the events across generations.[2] This notion of postmemory is relevant for understanding war memory because war discourses today are reproduced mostly by postwar generations who inherited such frameworks of interpretation. It also shows how personal and intimate connections shape the moral evaluation of war for postwar generations in ways that are more real and intimate than school textbooks and cultural representations.[3] Personal memories passed on in the family have shaped the sentiments of public intellectuals and artists, politicians, and bureaucrats more profoundly than is usually recognized. Family memories are visceral and cut to the bone; they carry the deep emotional content of what is at stake when living in a war, however poorly articulated. This notion is echoed by many: for example Ōtsuka Eiji, a well-known commentator of contemporary culture, recognizes that even as he turned his back to the tedious war stories of his parents when he was growing up, "I can feel what my father wanted to convey to me without being able to articulate it, and I am certain it is the basis of what I write about today."[4] Others of the same generation reinforce this point, like Kawaguchi Kaiji, the author of the best-selling *Zipang* (a story about altering the course of World War II with time travel), who acknowledges that his work is really a "quest to understand what kind of people our parents really were," while admitting candidly that he had always been afraid to ask questions about what his father did in China as a soldier.[5]

Postmemory is the broader canvas on which biographical narratives of the war experience are repaired as an intergenerational project. German psychologist Gabriele Rosenthal explains that biographical repair is an interpretive reconstruction of traumatic experiences across generations that often involve selective remembering, strategies of concealment, and assigning guilt to others so that a victim family biography can be constructed, and recovery from trauma can proceed.[6] As we will see in this chapter, biographical repair is not amnesia but a case of hermeneutical reconstruction that glosses over what is difficult to talk about, and passes over what is difficult to listen to. For example, a family's difficulty talking about the meaningless death of a father in a war of invasion might delegate to the child the task of relieving this misery by imagining the father as an innocent victim. When fathers returned from war resorted to emotional withdrawal, which was not untypical, it would be up to the children to keep their rage, bitterness, and frustration from their consciousness.[7] This kind of family dynamic prioritizes harmony at home over the abstract idea of justice for strangers who were victimized in the larger, faraway war. This tacit understanding of priorities developed across generations lies at the heart of the biographical repair project in postwar families. It is an approach geared to self-protection and to make mundane life livable; it is also a widespread mechanism that engenders perpetrator-victim-hero inversions in everyday life.[8]

This chapter explores the contours of postmemory through the lens of biographical repair and asks how difficult war memory is narrated in the family and with what consequences. This question is crucially relevant to understanding the transmission of political identity and responsibility because how we present our *powerlessness* to ourselves and each other vitally influences our sense of political *efficacy* and empowerment.[9] Sociologist Nina Eliasoph suggests that we cultivate feelings of powerlessness purposefully when confronting difficult situations to enable a smooth working of social relationships. We engage in *emotion work* to mute awkward conflicts, "telling ourselves that we do not care, or by trying only to care about problems that we implicitly assume we can easily address, or throwing up our hands in despair." The repeated narration at home of experiences of powerless in the war invites empathetic *emotion work* to facilitate biographical repair of the family, but it can also cultivate indifference to others. The protection of relationships "close at home" by speaking of the father's, the mother's, and the family's powerlessness is enormously effective in conveying the malicious nature of the war experience for the "little people" and in resisting the authoritarian narrative of the war. However, as we will see in this chapter, it also fosters an ethno-cultural blindness to the injustices inflicted on the powerless victims "far from home."[10]

I explore this underresearched topic of narration in family memory and self-efficacy in political identity by examining the personal testimonies of veterans and their adult children and grandchildren. The testimonies that describe the war's impact on their lives are culled from everyday cultural materials: letters to the editor in national newspapers and anthologies of testimonies published in the last 30 years. To look at the patterns by *generations,* I constructed *synthetic age cohorts* by calculating the birth years of the narrators, and then divided their testimonies into two categories: those of the wartime generation, and those of the postwar children and grandchildren. Taking advantage of the large number of personal testimonies that are publicly accessible, I constructed a data set comprising a total of 430 cases: 390 wartime generation, and 40 postwar children and grandchildren, sampled for the years 1986 to 2013.[11] The primary data derive from the readers' page of the left-of-center *Asahi* newspaper, and to interpret them in broader sociological context, I compare them to a subsample of 20 testimonies by children of wartime elites published by the conservative monthly *Bungei Shunjū* in 1989 and 2007.[12] I therefore assess the general trends of memory making by juxtaposing grassroots testimonies with elite testimonies.

Japan's war testimonies are available in many different types of publications, coinciding with the popularity of writing personal history (*jibunshi*) as a practice of autobiographical memoir that flourished since the 1960s and 1970s.[13] An estimated 30,000 self-published wartime memoirs had been deposited in the National Diet Library alone as of 1999.[14] War testimonies proliferated especially since the 1980s as taboos began to break down.[15] They are written by survivors as "witnesses": veterans who fought in vast regions of Asia and the Pacific; civilian survivors of the atomic bombings and air raids on the home front; refugees from Manchuria, Korea, and other territories; civilians and orphans who survived displacement and poverty; and indicted war criminals. Psychiatrist Robert Lifton has suggested that such witnesses can forge a "survivor mission" that gives meaning to their survival after traumatic encounters with death;[16] it is such "missions" that have coalesced into waves of testimonial activities as aging survivors felt the need to speak up as the last witnesses alive. Together with the oral history collections that also exist in large numbers, some of which will be discussed in chapter 3, the testimonials of the wartime generation have created massive records of war experiences in volumes and series of publications, in print, and in digital archives.[17] These "witness" accounts have long played a significant role in Japan's memory culture, and have contributed to the diffuse transmission of war stories in postwar society.[18]

To be sure, those personal testimonies are subjective cultural constructs, not exact factual records of the past. Psychologist Jerome Bruner says of autobiography that "the lives we construct are outcomes of this process of meaning-construction" and that we also make such meaning in the historical circumstances through which we express ourselves.[19] Here, writing self-narrations is an attempt to repair and validate the self by framing the experiences meaningfully.[20] It is therefore not surprising that many testimonials encode messages that assuage the burdens of survival with the hope for a more enlightened future. Many in the *Asahi* sample conclude their descriptions of harrowing war experiences with a statement that war is wretched. Directly or indirectly, they convey the conviction that no part of the war experience was worthwhile or redemptive. The testimonies make no claims to intellectual sophistication; their contentions published year after year and decade after decade nevertheless culminate into an insistent moral sentiment: war, sacrifice, and blind trust in government leadership are dreadful, irrevocable mistakes.

This message embedded in the "survivor mission" helps explain why war testimonies and oral histories have flourished in the last decades, even though dreadful war experiences are admittedly painful to remember and articulate. The testimonies are part of the democratization and popularization of war memory, and an opportunity for the masses to speak up and be heard. The dominant narratives of powerless victims among them have served to keep alive the pacifist sentiment that the suffering should never be repeated. Less dominant are perpetrator narratives and heroic narratives that also comprised some portions of the *Asahi* testimonies. Most in these latter two categories described memories of early war experiences when there were more victories than defeats. Fewer still were testimonies that portrayed moral complexities in different shades of gray. All in all, however, the preponderance of testimonies shows an antiheroic Japan at war: virtually no participant comes out looking good in these *Asahi* testimonies.

Testimonies of the Wartime Generation

Veterans of World War II, whether American or Japanese, are usually called the "reticent generation" for their reluctance to talk about what they saw and did as soldiers.[21] These veterans often explain their reserve by saying that "people who didn't experience it just can't understand it." This claim is also shorthand for saying that the experience is ultimately indescribable. At the same time, it also serves to discourage further questions about something too painful to recount. This undiscussability of the experience is not surprising when we think of the intensity of traumatic experiences which are often near-death encounters. What we know of post-traumatic stress disorder (PTSD) today helps us recognize that shock, grief, and guilt had to be suppressed, and took a long time to work through, digest, and own. Although the difficulties of postwar civilian life—grieving, guilt, self-protection, loss of innocence—seem alike in many ways among Japanese, German, or American veterans, the cultural options that these men had at their disposal to cope with the damage and injury for recovery were not alike.[22]

For many Japanese veterans, the desire for catharsis and self-validation came with the passage of time, and in the 1980s took a turn toward self-expression in memoirs and testimonial writing. It was an attempt to find meaning and healing in an era when there was limited understanding of mental health care. They penned their personal narratives of war for complex motives: they wrote to mourn the dead, to heal through mourning the dead, to alleviate their own burden of having survived, to revisit the trauma so as to overcome it, or to seek social recognition in a society that no longer valued their war experience. This led them to hold their stories in check—leaving out crimes, withholding names, attributing deeds to others and so on—especially in the immediate postwar decades. Those taboos began to weaken slowly when more candid accounts of invasion and confessions of guilt and remorse were made in public. With the passage of time, taboos arising from the veterans' desires to protect themselves, their comrades, and the honor of the war dead gradually relaxed.[23]

Given the unprecedented scale of destruction in the first-ever national defeat, it is not surprising that the repatriated soldiers were devastated men; they were also stigmatized for having waged an unjust, "wrong" war, and for having lost.[24] Sociologist Yoshida Yutaka describes the veterans' identity as dominated by a sense of futility, helplessness, incompetence, and despair, and also mistrust toward the Japanese military strategists and operators. Their postwar lives were not, for the most part, happy: they harbored deep anger and bitterness toward the wartime leaders and felt a grave sense of guilt and indebtedness toward the dead soldiers. They also had reservations and ambivalence about their lives in the moral order of "postwar democracy." There is no question they came home with biographies that needed repair and healing, yet each was left to his own wounds, conscience, anger, and remorse without the social support necessary to bring that healing about.[25]

Open columns for readers to write letters to the editor have a long history in Japanese newspaper publishing; in the *Asahi* newspaper the practice goes back to 1898.[26] In this tradition, the newspaper started a special series on its readers' page focused on the theme of war (*Tēma danwashitsu: Sensō*) in 1986. Following its success, *Asahi*'s readers' page "Voice" (*Koe*) has been regularly carrying individual testimonies of war experiences in groups of eight to ten stories every month. This regular publication continues today in a monthly feature called "Transmitting the War" (*Kataritsugu sensō*)[27] that contains testimonies written primarily by the wartime generation now in their 80s and 90s, but also with increasing frequency those by children who "remember" the war of their deceased parents after discovering some memory objects, like old diaries, photographs, or notebooks. Selections from these testimonies have been published separately in several edited volumes as well, one of which has been translated into English.[28] As a rough estimate, the total number of testimonies on the war published in the daily *Asahi* since July 1986 is over 2,000 cases; it is a treasured archive of popular memory that can be explored alone or in juxtaposition to other types of memories.[29]

As we trace the development of testimonies from the 1980s through the 2010s, some important trends emerge: (1) memories of violence and near-death have lifelong impacts on the survivors, regardless of the age when they write their biographical stories; (2) memories of perpetration do not fade, but they can take on a renewed significance as the aging veterans face their own mortality; and (3) the emotional imprint of the wartime experiences like abandonment, betrayal, fear, guilt, and shame remain indelible.

On the whole, trauma dominates the near-death experiences in far-flung locations where the soldiers fought. The excerpts below describe the experiences of three men writing in the late 1980s when they were in their early 60s. The first veteran describes his flight on Negros Island in the Philippines after the American forces landed, where overwhelming starvation befell his troop. The second veteran, a former schoolteacher, survived the war despite his resolve to die for the Emperor, and now feels deeply resentful about what he was taught to believe. The third veteran was taken prisoner at age 16 in New Guinea and lived through shame and horror among other prisoners who cajoled their comrades to commit suicide.

> One after another, my buddies [died] . . . We were left with many heavily wounded soldiers. Maggots hatched in our bandages, writhing on our flesh and exuding a foul stench . . . Food supplies were cut off. Having eaten up all the stalks of grasses and plants, and all the insects and reptiles, we became malnutrition cases . . . Hunger gnawed at people's spirit . . . There were those who despaired so much that they killed themselves. Their gunshots echoed in the valley . . . Some deserted . . . or fought against other Japanese soldiers to obtain food.[30]

> I only thought about "dying for the Emperor." When I went into the army, I told people who sent me off that "I'll be sure to return home dead." From that moment, I never thought about my parents or brothers . . . [But] his majesty was not God after all. The War was an act of aggression. For me, the Imperial Army was God's army, but then it actually turned out to be a miserable story. I promised myself never to sing the *Kimigayo* [national anthem] again.[31]

> I didn't want to die. I was scared of death; I wanted to live. It was a tormenting agony . . . Death, death, death. Death had a cruel whisper. This is what war did to us.[32]

These testimonies of defeated soldiers (*haizanhei*) reveal what it was like to be reduced to naked self-preservation and to be on the verge of physical and mental collapse. When the dominant memory is overwhelming exhaustion and despair, it overwhelms all other experiences including earlier acts of perpetration. The tales of suffering invite sympathy and effectively focus the attention to the soldiers' plight, cancelling, in a sense, whatever violence they committed as war participants. Presenting powerless suffering as the main event of one's war experience is, then, a defensive stance, a re-rendering of personal memories in light of the transformation that occurred after the defeat.

This self-protective stance, however, can slowly give way to the desire to speak up about guilt.[33] Twenty-five years later, veterans of the same age cohort, now in their 80s and 90s, picked up the torch in the *Asahi* series, penning testimonies that speak of their guilt and responsibility.

These recent testimonies also focus on the last years of war nearing defeat, but they are more inclusive about *whose* suffering they describe. The first soldier, 93 years old (writing in 2012), recalls his harrowing retreat over the 4,000 meter Mount Sarawaged in East New Guinea. They were first ordered to commit collective suicide (*gyokusai*) rather than surrender when they lost their camp, but then reordered to abandon the wounded and retreat. The second soldier, an 85-year-old veteran, expands his empathy to the suffering of Asian victims. He confesses that his unit tortured local civilians on the Nicobar Islands (in the Indian Ocean), who were suspected of sending signals to the British fleet poised for invasion toward the end of the war in 1945. His group killed them and covered up the evidence. The third testimony is from an 85-year-old who remains anonymous, writing about his early experiences in China. Like many other conscripts, he killed Chinese prisoners in Luòyáng, China, and makes clear that this was one instance out of many, presumably more gruesome, acts of perpetration.

> We left the wounded behind, and gave them hand grenades . . . The retreat over Mt. Sarawaged (East New Guinea) was a battle against hunger and exhaustion, and we had to sleep on the jungle trees tops. . .
>
> Some went down the valley to get water, and never returned; others couldn't walk anymore and shot themselves. Their numbers grew. No one claimed "Long Live the Emperor" . . . We were in Wewak when the war ended. War is hell.[34]

> I could hear the screams from the torture. I saw them. The interrogation was haphazard; the only words that anyone knew to communicate were yes and no. We executed them just on suspicion . . . When we found out that the war was over, our superiors told us to go retrieve the bodies in the ditch, and burn them. They were afraid of getting caught for war crimes.[35]

> You don't know when it's going to happen, so you better kill before you get killed. That was the only thing that made sense. . .
>
> I killed a Chinese soldier on the run with my sword . . . I never, ever, want to see his agonized face again . . . Many of our side got killed, too. And when your buddies die, the desire for revenge is tremendous. . .
>
> This is just the tip of the iceberg. The battlefront is nothing but a repulsive encounter with life and death. I am still haunted in my dreams to this day.[36]

Understanding the testimonies of the wartime generation requires recognizing that war experiences were different by age and the year of draft. Their stories tell different types of experiences, depending on where the soldiers were, what they did, at what age, and with what outcome. Those over age 90 today were old enough to have been drafted at the outset of the conflict in China; as a result, they experienced the entire war as adults. Those a decade younger went to war when the Pacific War started in the 1940s; this group has a limited sense of having been part of the invasion of the continent. Those yet another decade younger grew up at the height of the repressive wartime system and underwent an intense indoctrination before the war ended.[37] Even though Japan never set up its own systems of prosecuting war crimes—in stark contrast to postwar Germany—the testimonies of perpetrator deeds are still expressed anonymously.[38] There were pressures to protect the families of the war dead and others implicated in guilt exerted by veterans' groups (*senyūkai*).[39] In this vein, family objections are sometimes considered the biggest obstacle for perpetrators to speak out.[40] Defamation lawsuits of well-known cases could have also inhibited more confessions.

Innumerable war stories have also been told by women recounting experiences on the home front, which also typically focus on the trauma of near-death experiences. Women are a significant part of Japan's memory culture, and many of the women's testimonies are about powerless, broken families. As stories of civilians they exuded certain innocence, virtually never expressing a sense of remorse for having supported the war effort or having been part of a nation that started the war. They claim to bear the brunt of the violence at home as victims of everyday torment. The following two testimonies of women in their mid-70s writing in 2012 and 2007 share different war traumas they experienced as young girls. The first woman describes a perilous evacuation from Naha city (Okinawa), and her trauma of witnessing her mother and grandfather killed violently before her eyes. The second woman describes becoming an orphan instantly when her parents were killed in the Tokyo air raid. Many decades later, the latter became one of the plaintiffs to sue the Japanese government, claiming compensation for their suffering.

When the bomb dropped in the back yard, the house [where we took shelter] turned into a hell of fire. I shook my grandfather but he was dead. My mother lay flat on her face with her legs blown away. They died instantly. . .

I learned that when there is nothing left, you can't even cry. I cut bundles of hair from them to take with me in my emergency bag.[41]

Life turned to hell on March 10th 1945. My parents and my brother were killed in the Tokyo Air Raid. My father was a lawyer, and both of my parents were kind pacifists . . . My body lost all five senses, and I couldn't even smell the stench of the dead bodies. . .

I was straitjacketed in this "war trauma" all my life and could never talk about my fears and anguish to anyone . . . It took 60 years for us "terrified" children to open our "Greater Tokyo Air Raid Exhibit" . . . and sue the state for not even helping us. . .

Our Constitution Article 9 comes in exchange for those 3.1 million deaths. It is our legacy of peace for posterity.[42]

The excerpt below, from a third woman also in her mid-70s in 2012, recalls a heroic memory of a righteous kamikaze pilot who was a martyr in her eyes. She was a proud imperial subject and hers was a vicarious trauma of violence. Just like the two earlier women, she makes no mention of, nor hints at any feelings of, Japan's guilt as a perpetrator nation.

Our teacher told us to write essays praising the first kamikaze pilot from our prefecture who sacrificed himself . . . Many came to the ceremony (to honor the lieutenant as a "war god" [*gunshin*]. We declared from the stage: "We will protect the home front! We will absolutely win the war!" The lieutenant's last poem was so gracious, it deeply moved me . . . Our school set up a memorial on the roof top . . . and portraits [*irei*] were added as more people died.[43]

The women's testimonies focused exclusively on their own trauma and hardship. I suggest that many testimonies of the war generation are predicated on the belief that if trauma is kept alive vicariously, the aversion to war may also stay alive. To be sure, more testimonies in the *Asahi* offered stories of aversion to military authority and repression than those in conservative publications like *Bungei Shunjū*,[44] but the focus on describing hardship is common across the political leanings of the publications. Part of the reason has to do with editorial discretion in collecting and publishing war stories. When editors of publications called for readers' testimonies, they often encouraged certain types of stories in their announcements. For example, when the *Asahi* paper solicited testimonies of war experiences in 2002, it asked for stories from the wartime generation "to reflect on the misery of war, and to transmit the lessons of peace," and called for stories that described "the loss of family members and war buddies, and the miserable and cruel experiences on the battlefield."[45] Similarly, an editor of the monthly *Bungei Shunjū* described the sort of memory they were looking for in their 1995 feature: "Remember our fathers, mothers, brothers and sisters, our own journeys, or those of unforgettable relatives. Japanese families started the journey of postwar in utter despondence, in the summer heat of August 15th. Poverty, hunger, and devastation . . . Then a historically unprecedented chaos assaulted us. After 50 years of postwar, it seems meaningful to trace the road that we Japanese families have traveled from destruction to prosperity."[46] There is a sense of mission in this effort to transmit war memory, a desire to conserve knowledge and understanding as a lasting connection to the war generation. These hardship stories, and perpetrator-victim inversion, have come to comprise a key feature of Japan's memory culture, which might be called a discourse of powerlessness in a defeated society.

Stifled Dialogues between Generations: Filling the Gaps and Healing the Wounds

For Japan's postwar generation, remembering the soldiers in postmemory is a complex undertaking because the men were also perpetrators of the war. The military was guilty by international law for carrying out a war of aggression, including atrocities and myriad brutalities across Asia and the Pacific. Yet, even if they were killers and plunderers, they were also our fathers who loved, fought, killed, and died "for us." They cannot be disowned. The tension between the personal family logic and the political logic is inescapable and overwhelms postmemory. "What did my family do in the war?" "A dirty father is still a father." "Protect grandpa!"[47] With the urge to defend one of your own on the one hand, and the desire to know the authentic family biography on the other hand, the dilemma between personal loyalty and biographical knowledge lies at the heart of the war legacy of the postwar generation.

Postmemory is also a complicated project for Japan's postwar generation because of *generational proximity* and dependence. Families have long been patriarchal institutions, and in Japan, they have been linked specifically to primogeniture and authority relations defined by gender and age.[48] Age hierarchies and age norms therefore played a significant role in postwar family relations that continued to prescribe filial obedience as virtue and criticism of parental authority as anathema, even after the legal structure of the family democratized in 1947. Family norms changed slowly, and for decades after the war, most men of Japan's wartime generation retained authority as heads of households, living in extended families with their married children and grandchildren.[49] Those intergenerational households were also deeply financially interdependent in a society that offered limited pensions in old age and limited salary in young age under a seniority-based wage system at the time. In this milieu, emotion work to smooth family conflict often involved obedience to authority defined by age and gender.[50] In this milieu, family heritage was a vital source of identity, especially in a world that seemed to offer limited religious, philosophical, or other moral authority. Perhaps it was to be expected, then, that youth "revolts" of 1960 and 1968 were short-lived as social movements and limited to small portions of the generation: sociologist Oguma Eiji has estimated that only 5% of the youth cohort joined the 1968 protest movement, and none of them later entered politics.[51] Partly for these reasons, Japanese postwar generations did not develop their own "new memory profiles" about the Asia-Pacific War, and for the most part inherited the war memory of the preceding generation as part of their family history.[52] Although one of the most salient shifts in the postwar decades has been changes of lifestyles in a bourgeoning consumer society, changes of *political* values have not been part of that trend.[53] This generational proximity persists today to a large extent: One in every five Japanese teenagers today still grows up living in three-generation households with parents and grandparents, by far the highest proportion of co-residence in postindustrial societies.[54]

This historical context of generational proximity is especially pertinent to understanding family memory in postwar Japan because it speaks to the effectiveness of transmitting emotional memory. We can trace several significant trends in the testimonies of adult children who remembered hearing war stories when growing up: (1) children tended to fill in the gaps and ambiguities in family biography with positive images of their fathers and mothers; (2) they tended to describe their fathers and mothers in wartime as powerless, and therefore mostly innocent; and (3) the emotional imprint of the wartime experiences like abandonment, betrayal, fear, guilt, and shame remains indelible in family memories.

"He Was a Good Father"

Exploring the strategies of postwar families to negotiate dark history and forge postwar identity, German psychologists Harald Welzer, Sabine Moller, and Karoline Tschuggnall introduced the notion of a *family album*, referring to the positive image of the family that people construct to serve as defense against exposing negative family history. In this protective dynamic, illuminated in their book *Opa war kein Nazi* (*Grandpa Was No Nazi*), children and grandchildren fill the gaps of knowledge to heal the wounds, stressing the suffering of their own family members in wartime as well as their courage and virtue. This syndrome, operating independently of the official narrative of war in society applies similarly to Japanese families that placed a high premium on biographical repair.[55] However, family albums are not all alike. Many imagined war stories aligned with those of family members; others were repulsed by their parents' helplessness but identified with the hardship; still others felt that they needed to make up for the parents' distress and injury. Welzer and his colleagues posited that grandchildren were more susceptible to "heroize" the wartime generation, but little evidence on Japanese grandchildren is available to date on that score.[56]

In the following three examples, adult children of the baby boom generation (*dankai no sedai*) reveal what they heard about their fathers' wartime career while growing up, and how they themselves viewed their fathers' postwar lives. They did not escape hearing that their fathers' war had been a shameful event, but claimed not to know much about the extent of their fathers' guilt. They speak protectively of their fathers' suffering and point out how the fathers tried to live uprightly after the war.

> When I was 20 years old . . . I was shocked to find out what the Japanese army did on the front. I remembered that my father had been to Manchuria and asked my mother about it. She told me what he said: "the Japanese army boasted a lot about the great Yamato spirit . . . but what it did was worse than beasts. They raped innocent women all over the country. . ." She said he was angry with himself and humiliated that as a low-ranked soldier, he couldn't stop it. When I heard this, I was grateful to be his child. (Kuroki Hiroko)[57]

> I never heard my father talk about the war when I was small. If something came on TV like war film footage, my mother would

quietly turn it off. Things like that told me that the war must have impacted my parents' lives deeply in the prime of their lives.

My father forswore all forms of killing when I was born in 1951. He never went back to work at the prefecture's department of stockbreeding where he worked before the war. My mother never went back to teaching either.

Just once, my mother told me in tears that my father was deeply embittered by betrayal in his own battalion. My father used to smile quietly. (Iwasaki Mariko)[58]

My father was a career officer in the former Imperial Navy. My grandfather was also a career officer in the former Imperial Army. Both were purged after the war and had some hardships.

My father did not talk much about the war, but at one point it looks like he was in charge of guiding the *tokkō* [kamikaze] warplanes from [Chiran city in] Kagoshima. He was pilot of a reconnaissance plane but was shot down by the Americans in Kagoshima Bay . . . He escaped the sinking aircraft with a broken hip and was saved by a fishing boat. I think he tried hard afterwards to live [as a decent person]. (Sakuma Yōichi)[59]

The "silent transmission" of traumatic memory in the family required the children to fill the gaps with hopeful, positive images of their fathers: The first woman Hiroko hoped that perhaps her father never joined the "beasts" in the rape, plunder, and killings in China. The second woman Mariko hoped that her father's decision to foreswear violence relieved him from his bitter suffering. The last narrator Yōichi does not quite seem to acknowledge his father and grandfather as "perpetrators" 60 years after the war, although both were purged by the US occupation. The extent of his father's responsibility in sending the pilots on suicide (*kamikaze*) missions is unknown and unresolved. The stifled dialogue between generations allowed the son the hope that his father was somehow more innocent than guilty, and perhaps redeemed by living uprightly after the war. All three children emphasized their fathers' *powerlessness* in some form: as "a low-ranked soldier," "deeply embittered by betrayal," and "shot down by the Americans." The vulnerability and injury that come across in these testimonies echo exactly those of the veterans introduced in the previous section.

The "good father" is another theme that surfaces in many children's testimonies that speaks to the ongoing biographical repair in the family. Writing about their fathers as adults now in their 60s, the two sons below portray them as decent men who were changed by dreadful encounters in the war. The first narrator Takao is aware that his father was in Nanjing city at the time of the infamous mass slayings but does not know the extent of his father's involvement in the crimes. The second narrator Kiyoshi had held his father in awe for being a devoted hard worker while he was growing up, realizing that his father had vowed to make up for lost time in military conscription. But his father started to suffer nightmares and breakdowns, haunted by the memory of ferocious battles, and also started to beat his wife.

> My father was transport personnel at the time in Nanjing. I hear he was a good father, but after hearing and reading testimonies of former soldiers about all the plundering, arson, rape, executions, and biological experiments, I have to wonder if he took part in them . . . I feel ambivalent about it.
>   We must never allow our children and grandchildren to be taken away to war again. Taking a firm stand [in protest against war] is the memorial for my father. (Sakurazawa Takao)[60]

> My gentle father who never even drank became a completely different person. Home went to shambles. My mother suffered from emotional distress. My father was never freed from the war, and died years later.
>   There must be many veterans who suffered from deep physical and mental scars like my father. Everyone who was embroiled in the war was a victim. (Oikawa Kiyoshi)[61]

The sons claim to know little about their fathers' life-altering encounters with violence but have held their inquiries in check. Across the span of 60 years that separates the war and the sons' testimonies, the wounds have not healed, and the gaps in the family album remain open. The vision of the "good father," however, sustains the humanized ideal that these fathers were victims of circumstance as men who were forced to go to war: it suggests that they were vulnerable and powerless to act in any other way than they did.

"We Must Never Go to War"

War memories are difficult to communicate; yet, even if they are suppressed, they are never really "forgotten"; and even if they are shrouded in silence, they are nevertheless transmitted in the family.[62] The silent transmission of war memory is a complex socio-psychological phenomenon surrounding traumatic experience, which has been studied carefully for Holocaust survivors and their descendants, and for the wartime generation and their descendants in Germany. These studies have found that for the traumatized, silence is not "amnesia" but a phenomenon of concealed grief that attests to the enormous time, energy, distance, and self-awareness required to process difficult experiences before they can be communicated.[63] Veterans are also reluctant to disclose possible suggestions of culpability and stigma, partly to protect the family from losing innocence and from guilt by association. This aversion to admitting information damaging to their kin is common among war veterans, not only among the defeated but also among the victors of war.[64]

But it takes two to maintain a silence—one not to speak and the other not to ask. Silence requires the cooperation of the children who are complicit in the legacy of silence. Israeli psychologist Dan Bar-On has aptly described this rift between nonspeaker and nonlistener as the double wall of silence.[65] Children may adopt a "veil of forgetting" out of self-protection.[66] "It is as if, within the families and among friends and neighbors also, an unspoken agreement existed not to talk, not open up, not to make any of the connections clear, and thus to protect each other. After all, an exacting inquiry and an honest search for answers could lead many to lose face."[67] The children are complicit in the pact because they sense from their parents, nonverbally, that those memories are bearable only if they are reduced to a minimum. It creates a mutual protectiveness between parents and children.[68]

After the Japanese fathers came back from the war, their children also grappled with stifled dialogues. Across the double wall, many questions remained unasked and ultimately remained unanswered. To resolve the unresolved questions, many took to short-circuiting the causal link, reasoning that none of this suffering would have happened without the war, and therefore we must never go to war again. In short, never again. The renunciation of war, together with the postwar constitution Article 9, would resolve the problem of sending good fathers to bad situations. The three adult children's testimonies below short-circuit the family silence and channel the family secrets into an antiwar resolve. The first woman, Kyōko, wished her father hadn't been so reluctant to talk about his experience as a prisoner of war in Siberia. However, that curiosity seems restrained when it comes to his role as a colonial administrator in Japan's takeover of Manchuria. The link between the early powerfulness and later powerlessness of his wartime experiences is compressed in Kyōko's conclusion about the importance of taking an antiwar stand.

The only thing I know is that my father, who was an official at the Mint [in Manchuria] . . . had to work on construction sites in Siberia. Once, he fell from the scaffolding, and was seriously injured . . . There are hardships that can't even be told. We must never ever go to war. (Ōtake Kyōko)[69]

Mayumi, in the second testimony, never heard her father talk about the war either. She claims to know about her father's military life only from her mother. She knew his body was riddled with bullet injuries, and she remembers vividly how he surprised them with his horse-riding skills when they were on a trip and how he spoke Chinese to someone who happened to ask him something in Chinese. Mayumi wonders about the meaning of his father's antiwar message when he refused a military pension and repudiated military songs.

My father never said a word about the War. The only things that taught me about his war were the bullet scars on his thigh, and the eerie darkness in his heart. Now as a parent, I don't want my son to carry my father's burden.
  I want to convey to my son what that burden and darkness mean. He would have wanted to meet his grandfather. (Kishida Mayumi).[70]

In the third testimony Ken mourns his father who died a month before the end of the war fighting in Luzon Island (Philippines). His father was conscripted first in 1937, but Ken makes sure to mention in his testimony that his father was a noncombatant in China as a non-commissioned officer in the Shanghai commissariat and therefore innocent of the killings.

When the second draft came, he said to my mother that he might not make it back this time . . . I can't forget what he must have felt. Father, you abhorred the war and despised the military. I will make sure to pass on your diary to your grandchildren and great-grandchildren. We will not waste the sacrifices of the several million. (Kumakawa Ken)[71]

Ken's memory of his father comes entirely from his mother and his father's diary, and it is fully aligned with their script. He is faithful to the narrative that was laid out for him and vows to carry it forward to his own children. The antiwar message is an important aspect of this "inheritance" from his father, and Ken believes he is carrying out a mission that his father could not continue. Ken has become a postmemory carrier who fuses the pacifist message with his father's memory. Ken is making a family album using his postmemory; it is now integrated in the family heritage and identity.

Japan reproduced many postmemories of war experiences like Ken's and Mayumi's, fueled by their "duty to remember" and pledges of antiwar resolve. Many postwar children "remember" their parents' powerless experiences of the air raids, atomic bombings, hunger, and poverty in this way. Other national tragedies have come and gone—some directly affecting the postwar generations more than the Asia-Pacific War—but "that war" and 1945 remain *the* referent for gauging moral rectitude and a deep-rooted anchor for postwar moral identity.[72] This antiwar message has become consistently the most coherent and ennobling lesson espoused in the family album. It offers coherence, integrity, and closure to a dreadful event; and converts memory into a meaningful family credo.[73] The parents' and grandparents' narratives, once integrated into the family heritage, are seldom questioned for accuracy of historical details. The postmemory of postwar generations represents an affirmation of family solidarity and moral commitment to the heritage rather than a faithful account of historical facts.

The theme of powerlessness resurfaces in the next testimonies of two young women of the third and fourth generations who describe the moral heritage that their grandparent and great-grandparent passed onto them. The first woman Sachié heard about the war in the Philippines from her grandfather before he died and illustrates the dire predicament of defeated soldiers on the run, almost exactly like the testimonies of the veterans themselves earlier in this chapter; her story also echoes their focus on fear and helplessness in their near-death experiences. The second woman Hiroko is a teenager who fondly remembers her great-grandmother; she tells us that she heard from her great-grandmother about the hard journey back from Manchuria. Although Hiroko does not remember much detail, she recalls vividly the emotional memory, her great-grandmother's tears and regrets.

> My grandfather saw death all around him, and despaired in his own powerlessness. On the run, they ran out of food, and even ate the maggots growing from their buddies' corpses . . . How they must have feared death, and thought about their life, family and friends . . .

War is built on all these sorrows and tears. We need to elim-
inate wars that make humans inhuman . . . If each one of us
prays for peace, I'd like to believe that peace is possible. (Amino
Sachié)[74]

I always looked forward to visiting my great-grandmother, and
she used to tell me about her war experience. I didn't pay much
attention . . . and only realized after she died, how precious those
stories were . . . I can't recall the details, but clearly remember
that she cried softly every year, saying we must never go to war.
I am etching her message in my heart to help build a peaceful
society. (Matsubara Hiroko)[75]

It is easy to see the strong, emotional identification that these women
feel for their family's war stories, in spite of their limited direct knowledge. Japan's grassroots pacifism can be understood better if we take
account of these uncritical, emotional dimensions of family memory,
and how effectively they shield the future generations from believing
in their own potential for hurting others. Over the decades, peace has
become personal identity for those who internalized a family album
that buffered them from violence. Looking closely at the claims of
powerlessness and abhorrence of war in these testimonies, it is possible
to see that "the courage not to wage war" has become a moral ideal by
default through personal emotional reasoning rather than through
rational philosophy. This ideal does not imply assuming responsibility
for the deeds of forefathers but for *not* waging another abhorrent war
in the future.

"He Was Such a Bully"

Many of the adult children's testimonies focused on the destructive
impact of the war on their personal lives and their families. They illustrated problems of growing up in broken families with absent fathers,
distressed mothers, and many strained, dysfunctional relationships.
Especially intriguing among them were those who disclosed their
deep conflict with the fathers whose authoritarian military values
seemed destructive to the family relationships. In these cases, truthful
communication was thwarted at home not because of awkward silence,
but because the fathers insisted on imposing their own autocratic
values that their postwar children rejected. The mutual apprehension between the generations is obvious, and, for the most part, the

children felt it safer to *disconnect* from the world of their fathers who could not adapt readily to peacetime.

In these cases, the returning veterans held fast to their heroic self-image as military authority, and, probably feeling threatened by losing that authority after defeat, they seemed to try to reinvent their power base at home. Rather than present themselves as powerless, defeated soldiers like the veterans discussed earlier in this chapter, these men saw themselves as people in positions of power and privilege in the military hierarchy. For them, military life was not a disgrace, although they might have kept their boastful thoughts within relatively safe confines. They did not see themselves as perpetrators with questionable moral character, but as competent soldiers who fought gallantly. Japanese sociologist Takahashi Saburō has illustrated the sentiments and unique bonds among those men who were deeply invested in their past military life. They formed veterans' group networks (*senyūkai*) to maintain ties and became active in them as postwar life stabilized in the 1960s and 1970s.[76] They met regularly, mourned the war dead, kept up their directory and their contacts with the bereaved, and typically published newsletters and some historical records of their unit. These groups were not uncontroversial: there were quite a number of veterans who shunned them, abhorring the memories of violence and hazing they experienced in their units. Veterans were therefore by no means a monolithic group.[77]

In the following testimonies, three women of the baby boom generation tell us their memories of growing up with fathers who relished their exploits of the war and military glory. The daughters were openly critical of their fathers' inability to reflect on their deeds in humanitarian terms, oblivious to their guilt as perpetrators. They do not hide their disdain toward the war generation. The first woman, Hiroko, is incredulous about her father's inability to move beyond his fixation with military life, bragging about his exploits and even about criminal acts of killing civilians. She does not hold back her criticism of her father. Nor does the second woman, Atsuko, hide her antipathy for the put-downs directed to her and "the youth today" who were "weaklings" because they had not experienced the war. The third woman wished to remain anonymous to divulge her scathing criticism of her father and the people in her hometown who stroked his megalomania.

My father is singing military songs again. He is in an awfully good mood. I cover my ears. I get irritated whenever I hear that unique rhythm. He boasts a lot about his army life . . . He says he wasn't in combat, but brags all the same about his so-called heroic exploits . . . Once he got so excited [elated] talking about local slayings in the Philippines. I couldn't help screaming at him. (Watanabe Hiroko)[78]

All the bragging and the same old sermons about the war—they were disgusting . . . They never searched their conscience . . . and claimed we had to be grateful for the sacrifices they made for the war. The conceit! If it weren't for the war, we wouldn't have all these people grieving; we'd have lower inflation, better welfare, and happier lives. . .

Shouldn't they talk more about war responsibility than war exploits? (Suda Atsuko)[79]

My father came from a poor family so he must have been really happy to throw his weight around as an army captain. Not a day went by that I didn't hear his high and mighty war stories when I was growing up. He said he beheaded Chinese enemies; he said he made a dog eat a prisoner . . . He talked gleefully, with no shred of soul-searching. He was such a bully, but my hick town respected him all the same for having been a military officer. (Anonymous)[80]

Japanese Sociologist Fukuma Yoshiaki has shown that the practice of transmitting war experiences (*keishō*) comes in several varieties, some of which involve painful self-criticism, but others are nostalgic, feel-good reminiscences.[81] In that sense, transmitting war memories does not, in and of itself, ensure shared regret; it can provoke loathing instead of bonding and drive a wedge (*danzetsu*) between generations. The foregoing cases reveal a disconnect between the generations as the children came to detest the parents' inability to reflect on and regret their wartime violence. These intergenerational frictions also peaked around the 1960s and 1970s, especially among the youth involved in student and pacifist movements opposed to the Vietnam War, who saw the parallel between an imperialist incursion in Vietnam and Japan's aggression in Asia.[82]

Finally, another set of cases that offer a contrast to the above testimonies are the writings by adult children of prominent wartime leaders whose comments appear in commemorative issues of monthly magazines like the conservative *Bungei Shunjū*. Those private accounts of public figures tended to underplay the fathers' structural positions of power to describe a kind of "dignified powerlessness." The tone was consistently empathetic, and sensitive not to inflict hurt on the surviving family members: A loving father who was killed in a war he opposed

(Yamamoto Yoshihisa); a thoughtful father who had hoped to stop the war and always mourned the subordinates who died (Imamura Kazuo); and an adorable, dashing father who had to fight a tragic war that was impossible to win (Nishi Yasunori).[83] The brutal violence that is the main feature of warfare is effectively hidden from the spotlight on the heroic fathers. The accounts insinuate that the military establishment included decent men who opposed the war and convert its powerful leaders into a group of loving, family men—profiles of heroes that fit well into the values of postwar society.

Family Belonging and Structured Powerlessness

"The world does not present itself in the form of 'well-made stories' " and, as such, we must recognize that the war testimonies in this chapter are only partial, even contradictory, accounts of what happened.[84] What they do communicate are selective war memories, organized in ways that are meaningful and coherent to the narrators. They are not factual representations of reality but reformulated narratives that make our self-knowledge coherent and emotionally resonant.[85] Therefore, it is easy to point to the self-serving biases of the narrow, inward-looking accounts excerpted in this chapter that remember the pain of family members without thinking of the pain of the tens of millions of Asian victims in the larger war. These one-sided stories can be recognized, however, as tangible personal stories that help anchor and stabilize individual and collective identity while repairing biographical wounds, and avoid threatening political entanglement with the outside world.

Close attention to the testimonies in this chapter shows that what is threatening for the postwar generations about engaging in the broader vision—which they are perfectly capable of doing—is a deep sense of inefficacy, or powerlessness, that they have internalized from the family war stories. The war would have been overwhelming for them too, in the same way that it was for their parents; it is threatening, because they are discomfited by the realization that if they were put in the same situation in a totalitarian militarist society identical to their parents, *they would not have, in all honestly, had the gumption to act differently.*[86] A studied indifference can therefore be motivated by a sense of helplessness that people adopt when they feel they cannot change anything.[87] A pervasive sense of inefficacy, shaped by accounts of defeat, is part of what forms the narrow apolitical vision of the postwar generation. They are in a zone where information is only partially registered to protect them from uncomfortable knowledge.[88] The difficult knowledge, in their case, is not so much the actual war of 70 years ago, but the realization that they would not know what to do themselves if presented with the same dilemma of "kill or be killed."

This problem of inefficacy also makes sense when we realize that postwar pacifism failed to train postwar citizens to think about, or even imagine, the legitimate means of resistance to a military machine at war, such as conscientious objection to serve the military, disobeying illegal orders of superiors, questioning the use of excessive military force, and protecting the rights of civilians and soldiers guaranteed by international conventions in times of war. Instead of building social mechanisms like these to *regulate* military power, the defeated society offered a social prescription to *avoid* building military power. This prescription to delegitimize aggression and belligerence declawed the citizens, and also deprived them of the legitimate means to act *against* state authority when needed. It was a prescription that ensured a deep level of structural disempowerment in Japanese society.

The significance of structural powerlessness can be seen more clearly when we compare Japan's war testimonies to those in Great Britain that describe an entirely different kind of self-efficacy.[89] Compared to the Japanese counterparts, the BBC testimonies collected in the 2000s from people of all walks of life are characteristically stoic, determined to carry on, and optimistic about victory. Even when they talked about enduring air raids, the hardship is understated, recounted without drama or self-pity, and united in the support for the nation at war. There are also no vows for peace or claims about never going to war again. Evidently, victors do not seem to be encumbered by a sense of disempowerment about the war.

In the last decades, each new generation in Japanese society has emerged with a lower sense of self-worth and self-efficacy than the previous generation. The majority of high school students (84%) today report feeling inadequate (*damena ningen*) and are critical of themselves for not being smarter, more lovable, principled, and self-sufficient to a greater extent than their counterparts in the United States, China, and South Korea.[90] The young also show a great deal of ambivalence about the meaning of being Japanese and report being largely undecided (47%) about their love for their country.[91] Raised in a society that relies heavily on authority-obedience and conformity norms, the young generations in postwar Japan have mostly had little encouragement and room to transcend their ascribed social and family boundaries.[92] Their self-actualization within this social order has been, then, to create their zone of ambiguity, an amorphous zone between yes and no, and between black-and-white morality to deal with the social problems inherited from their parents. It is a phenomenon that is akin to what psychiatrist Noda Masaaki calls the making of "conflict free" citizens who, intimidated at the prospect of criticizing authority, are blocked in their ability to think about conflict.[93]

Child and human development experts have shown that children who see their fathers as powerful tend to be more informed and interested in political matters, while children who do not see their fathers that way tend to acquire fewer political attitudes, not develop political orientations, and give more "don't know" responses.[94] Thus parental mentoring matters in developing political character, and the same might be said of its influence on developing moral character. In both Japan and Germany, fewer parents tend to be involved in the moral instruction of children such as teaching them not to lie, compared to parents in the United States and South Korea.[95] The low moral authority for truthfulness is especially notable in Japan (whose figures are about half of Germany's). Children who receive little guidance and mentorship in this way are clearly at a disadvantage in learning to grow up with confidence and take the risks of transcending their family and national heritage.

In 2006, more than half of the Japanese felt that there had not been enough debates and actions regarding war responsibility and felt that efforts should continue.[96] In many ways, the intergenerational project of biographical repair has amplified the unfinished moral and political responsibilities of the war. There are notable pioneers, however, who are breaking out of the cycle of structured powerlessness as activists and volunteers toiling to help bring justice to the Asian victims of the war, like "comfort women" and forced laborers. Many work as volunteers in NGOs and support, for example, the lawsuits of Chinese and Korean plaintiffs[97] reminiscent of the erstwhile volunteers who supported the Ienaga trials discussed in chapter 1. There are also descendants of perpetrators who take personal quests to make amends for their forefathers, and some have discussed their work publicly like Kurahashi Ayako, Ushijima Sadamitsu, and Komai Osamu.[98] As the witness generation passes away, war stories of key individuals are now retold to successive generations who have their own needs for reshaping and recycling war narratives. As the task of carrying memory changes hands, the shape, scope, and intensity of memory narratives will also change. These new custodians of the national trauma may do their best to take critical ownership of their own history and excise the tendencies for self-exculpation, and, with those efforts, they may gain the strength and security to rework Japan's ambivalence about its past.

3

Defeat Reconsidered

Heroes, Victims, and Perpetrators in the Popular Media

Every year on August 15, Japan commemorates the end of World War II with events that have become fixtures on the national calendar. On that day, government leaders and dignitaries, veterans and bereaved, media commentators and observers participate in annual rituals of commemoration to remember the lost war and to "renew the nation's vow for peace." Citizens can turn on the television at noon to watch the state-sponsored Memorial Service for the War Dead broadcast live from Budōkan, one of Tokyo's largest arenas. It is the focal official event of the memorial day, attended by the Emperor who formally conveys words of mourning for those who died in the war, followed by a brief speech by the prime minister. The choreography of the one-hour ceremony is solemn, centered on a soaring tablet representing the souls of the war dead displayed in the middle of the stage and surrounded by a twin-peak sculpture of yellow and white chrysanthemums. Many participants are attired in funeral black, including representatives of all branches of government and over 5,000 representatives of bereaved families from all over the nation. Every year, this ceremony takes place at the same time and place, using the same stage, the same protocol, the same address, and with the same funerary effects. This sameness year after year brings a certain familiarity and indelibility to war memory, as it reiterates an official memory that promotes a continuity of collective mourning. At the same time, it allows the state to reiterate its discourse of war, reconnecting it to the private narratives of loss, and superimposing it on cultural templates of funerary dramaturgy.

On the same day, citizens can find commemorative editorials in their daily newspapers, usually recounting some tragic experiences of national failure and vowing to overcome them with pledges of peace. The somber themes of war and peace appear in most major national and regional papers, urging readers to carry on the war memory by never forgetting the hardship, passing on the painful lessons, confronting the difficult history, and more with varied emphasis according to the paper's political persuasion.[1] In the evening, and throughout most of the month, audiences can find similar themes on television that feature commemorative documentaries, live debates, oral history interviews, live-action drama and reenactments, or feature films. Media war discourses have thrived especially during this month in the past decades as the memory boom flourished: scores of nationally circulated magazines offered commemorative features molding and remolding the collective memory of war; major book publishers competed to sell war memory books and special editions that bring back memories of events and experiences, like oral history collections; film producers competed for audiences for their latest "commemorative" feature films. The mass media were apt to draw attention to the negative legacy with sensational headlines: "Japan was Defeated," "Japan's Failure," "Causes of Japan's Defeat," "Why Did We Lose That War?"[2]

These concerted acts of commemoration show how deeply war memory is still embedded in contemporary life in Japan. At the same time, they show that the cumulative effect of reproducing familiar war memory over and over in a concentrated timeframe—recounting suicide missions, deadly bombings, mortal danger, fear, starvation, violence, killings, deaths, and more—also situates the hateful events in the past, on the other side of ruptured time symbolized by August 15, 1945. In a broader sense, August 15, 1945, has come to represent not strictly the end of a military conflict but the cultural trauma of a fallen nation, the collapse of the nation's social and moral order, and the failed aspirations of an East Asian empire. Epitomizing a rupture of national history rather than a strictly military event, Japan's notion of "August 15, 1945," has come to represent an idea similar to the German "May 8, 1945" (the "Zero Hour"), that also emphasizes a radical departure from a stigmatized past. Japan's commemorative performances and debates are discursive tools that set off the failures of 1945 from the present, while reinforcing the events as a cultural trauma for successive generations.[3] Those commemorative events also conceal wide dissension among the populace, a trend common to national remembrances elsewhere.

The establishment of August 15 as the commemorative day was many years in the making. As in most cases of "invented tradition," what appears today to be a long-standing custom was not, in fact, determined by historical imperative but constructed over time to symbolize, reinforce, and reinvent the political meaning of defeat. The official date of commemoration could have been August 14 (the date of signing the acceptance of the Potsdam declaration) or even September 2 (the signing of the instrument of surrender), but August 15 ultimately carried emotional resonance because it represented the ritual between the Emperor and his subjects, mediated by the radio broadcast, when the surrender was announced and emotionally accepted as final. At the same time, there were other coincidences for August 15, like *obon*, the day for honoring departed souls.[4]

During the US occupation (1945–1952), no commemoration of August 15 took place. The occupation had officially banned the Shinto memorialization of the war dead and commemorated Japan's surrender on VJ Day, September 2. It was only in 1952, after regaining sovereignty, that the Japanese government held a memorial service for the departed soldiers for the first time. This commemoration set in motion a process of memory making focused on the Emperor's announcement of the end of the war rather than the capitulation to the victors. In 1963, the government began the memorial service as an annual ritual broadcast on both radio and television, and, by 1965, when the secular service moved to the Budōkan arena, the construction of war memory was in full swing, establishing the association between the deaths of *obon* and deaths of soldiers, fathers, and sons all merged into one. Films, novels, television programs, and other cultural media dramatizing the events of August 15 rather than September 2 also accentuated it as the end of the imperial era and the war.[5]

Underneath this ritualization of the war's end, however, lies deep social discord over the assessment of Japan's war. Some have resisted and protested the annual state commemoration by holding their own countermemorial for Asians victimized by Japanese aggression, as the socialists did until 1993. Others have long attempted to elevate the status of annual commemoration beyond the state ceremony by agitating for prime ministers to officially honor the war dead regularly at the controversial Yasukuni Shrine. Because of this dissonance over the commemoration, different groups have come to attach different meanings to August 15: for some it is simply a day to pledge never to wage war again, for others it is a way of mythologizing the Emperor's connection to the people or to purify the tainted war, and for still others it is an angry time to remember the untrustworthiness of the military and the evils of authoritarian leadership.[6]

Scholars have observed that commemorations severely test a society's ability to cope with multiple versions of the past.[7] Ritualized commemorations can rejuvenate the values of a moral community and bridge cleavages of political conflicts and debates, but they can also become catalysts for dissent and acrimony.[8] A growing cacophony of views and voices has grown up around Japan's August 15 anniversaries in the last two decades, igniting criticisms, conflict and animosity, and, to a lesser extent, forging common ground in recounting cautionary tales about past traumas. In this time, official government statements changed, as did the symbolic political performances for mourning the war dead. Commemorative television programs burgeoned, newspaper editorials intensified their claims, and major media corporations launched commemorative projects that revisited and probed war responsibility. Museum exhibits strained to find common language to represent the meaning of the Asia-Pacific War, with different degrees of success. Underlying the diverse views on the growing controversies of the war were two fundamental questions to be answered: *Why did we fight an unwinnable war? Why did they kill and die for a lost cause?*

These long-standing questions strike at the heart of troubling concerns over war responsibility and national belonging, which ultimately probe the relations between the individual and the state and between the living and the dead. People may bring different narratives to bear, debate different rational positions in the controversies, and opt for different solutions, but, ultimately, the answers are formed by personal and political reactions to knowledge of failure, injustice, and suffering. The moral doubts are numerous and run deep: Was it legitimate for the state to wage war and mobilize its people to die for the nation? If the war was wrong, did our people die in vain? Is it right for the living to change the war dead from heroes to perpetrators when the war is lost or wrong? Why didn't the leaders stop the war, and who takes responsibility for the mass deaths and sacrifice? Questions like these, however, go against the grain of everyday habits we construct to avoid knowing what we do not want to know; they defy our desire to protect ourselves from information that is too disturbing and threatening. These direct questions therefore take people out of a comfort zone, which British sociologist Stanley Cohen calls a simultaneous state of "knowing and not knowing," a condition of self-protective denial that is always incomplete because some information is always registered in the mind. When people attempt to formulate narratives of what happened, they are jolted out of complacency to recognize the knowledge of distant suffering they had safely tucked away in the back of their consciousness, to give some answers to questions that they have suspended but can no longer avoid.[9]

Controversies at commemorations discussed in this chapter, like the Yasukuni Shrine, are explosive precisely because they disturb this state of "knowing and not knowing" and reveal the dark side of the country's history and its people. Carrying unresolved legal, religious, philosophical, and historical complexities as they do, the controversies themselves are in a sense epiphenomenal in terms of the underlying questions about the dark side of "our" moral identity as Japanese people. This chapter examines the struggles over public memory that force people to probe their moral compass, and rework their memory, in the face of an uncertain, changing memory culture. I will explore the layers of narratives offered to answer the fundamental questions, focusing on the interplay of political performance and media discourse during commemorative moments. I will trace how memory struggles served to remold the cultural trauma in the search for a more agreeable and less tarnished national identity.

The Political Performance of Commemorations

Modernity, Benedict Anderson reminds us, has been characterized by the emergence of nation-states that can mobilize the passion of young men to "die for the country" on a mass scale.[10] Once mobilized, nationalist passion allows a soldier in modern wars to believe "he is dying for something greater than himself, for something that will outlast his individual, perishable life in place of a greater, eternal vitality."[11] But after demobilization, this passion withers, no longer fed and needed for everyday combat. For those on the losing side of the war, this passion no longer has any social and moral legitimacy. Justification for violent deaths on a scale of millions is especially hard to summon in a lost war.

The tension between recognizing the futility of war and seeking something meaningful in the deaths has remained an unresolved dilemma after modern wars that called up millions of conscripts. The tension is especially acute in vanquished nations where, as Schivelbusch asserts, the desire to search for positive meaning in the defeat by seeking a progressive narrative of the loss is a common and powerful need. So strong was the impulse for making meaning that it led to the myth of the "lost cause" among the American Confederacy after the Civil War and also to the myth of the "fallen soldier" among the German soldiers who died in World War I.[12] Among the victors, too, mass deaths have called for moral justifications, the most famous of which was calling World War I "the war to end all wars" in Great Britain. Attempts to look for a "silver lining" force the momentous question of the ultimate value in national sacrifice.

These conflicting desires and contradictory reasoning lie at the heart of efforts to make sense of the Asia-Pacific War in Japan's public discourse. If Japan embarked on an unwinnable war, as most would now agree, then efforts to give meaning to the catastrophic losses that followed run into enormous problems of comprehension and justification. At the turn of the twenty-first century, these questions were raised by a new generation of politicians, public intellectuals, journalists, teachers, and families further removed from the reality of the war in time and space. These questions "refused to go away" and had no easy answers.[13]

In the past, the political schisms were described in dichotomous categories in the public discourse: reactionaries versus progressives, right versus left, Liberal Democrats versus Socialists, and so on. However, as political parties reconfigured and realigned after the end of the Cold War, these dichotomies had less descriptive power. The end of the Liberal Democratic Party's (LDP) monopoly, the Gulf War, and the North Korean missile launches all conspired to shake up the long-secure national self-definitions based on pacifism. The complexities lurking underneath the old dichotomies began to show. The political performances and the disputes invoked today come with new scripts, interests, alliances, and agendas, partly hidden even as they are encoded and recoded in the discourse of war memory by new and old players.[14]

Why Did We Fight and Die for an Unwinnable War?

In 1985, the same year that German President Richard von Weizsäcker made his definitive speech on German guilt to the Bundestag on the 40th anniversary of the end of the war, Prime Minister Nakasone Yasuhiro broke with postwar political practice and paid an official visit to the controversial Yasukuni Shrine on August 15. It was the first time in postwar Japan that an incumbent head of government paid homage in his official capacity to the century-old Shinto Shrine, built to honor the nation's soldiers who fought and died for the Emperor, which today enshrines the war dead of the Asia-Pacific War, including Class A war criminals indicted for crimes against peace. This highly visible performance met with a storm of protests from the Chinese government, vexed at the symbolic act of legitimating the war in which China had suffered severe casualties and destruction. Nakasone, recognizing that his action had deeply strained Japanese–Chinese relations, refrained from making visits in subsequent years. This moratorium on an incumbent prime minister's visits to Yasukuni on August 15 was to last for another 20 years until 2005.[15] During this interval, Japan's war memory landscape would develop dramatically.

The developments in subsequent decades had much to do with changing political and government leadership, increasing transnational scrutiny, and the growing public consciousness that the time had come to bring closure to the unfinished business of war before the wartime generation passed on. The death in 1989 of the controversial Shōwa Emperor who reigned during wartime Japan opened the discursive space to address some old taboos; the trouncing of the LDP in the election of 1993 made room for others to seize the official narrative for the first time in 55 years. With a socialist prime minister leading a coalition government, the 50th anniversary of the end of war in 1995 offered Japan a chance to break with the practice of articulating ambiguous messages of remorse for the war in the international arena. Prime Minister Murayama Tomi'ichi sought to move beyond the domestic political impasse by defining Japan's war responsibility in a resolution of remorse in the national parliament. The effort was hardly a success; 241 members of parliament walked out, some claiming that Maruyama went too far, and others accusing him of not going far enough to express "deep remorse." The resolution that ultimately passed in the Diet was a watered-down version that hardly met the high expectations for genuinely addressing the wrongs of the imperial past.[16] Then, two months later, at the August 15 commemoration, Maruyama raised the stakes by issuing an official statement recognizing Japan's wrongdoing as perpetrators in the Asia-Pacific War. It prefigured the increasing diffusion of perpetrator awareness in the 1990s and 2000s.

> During a certain period in the not too distant past, Japan, following a mistaken national policy, advanced along the road to war, only to ensnare the Japanese people in a fateful crisis, and, through its colonial rule and aggression, caused tremendous damage and suffering to the people of many countries, particularly to those of Asian nations. In the hope that no such mistake be made in the future, I regard, in a spirit of humility, these irrefutable facts of history, and express here once again my feelings

of deep remorse and state my heartfelt apology. Allow me also to express my feelings of profound mourning for all victims, both at home and abroad, of that history.[17]

This statement—approved by his cabinet—has proven to be surprisingly durable as *the* referent for his successors, in spite of the ideological discord it still generates. Recognizing perpetrator acts and responsibility for past wrongs has been an integral part of Japan's contentious war discourse since the Tokyo War Crimes Trials (1946–1947), and especially since the antiwar movements of the 1960s and 1970s, so in that sense, the acknowledgment itself was nothing new.[18] An explicit expression of state responsibility in the *official* national narrative of the war, however, had to await the advent of this coalition government in 1995.[19] Once officially articulated, this perpetrator narrative was continually adopted by successors, which include some conservative politicians in coalition governments.[20]

The next shift in the official national narrative came during the 60th anniversary in 2005, when Prime Minister Koizumi Junichirō, like Nakasone, seized the commemorative moment to make an official visit to the shrine. He then introduced significant victim sentiments into his commemorative statement. Koizumi declared:

> On the sixtieth anniversary of the end of the war, I reaffirm my determination that Japan must never again take the path to war, reflecting that the peace and prosperity we enjoy today are founded on the ultimate sacrifices of those who lost their lives for the war *against their will*. More than three million compatriots died in the war—in the battlefield thinking about their homeland and worrying about their families, while others perished amidst the destruction of war, or after the war in remote foreign countries.[21] (Emphasis mine)

Koizumi would reiterate this notion of unwilling sacrifice in six successive anniversaries during his tenure as prime minister.[22] While presupposing that people died in a war "against their will," Koizumi also regretted the pain inflicted in Asia through Japan's "colonial rule and aggression," using Murayama's phraseology. Put together, the two sentiments blurred and contradicted the demarcations of guilt and innocence, and merged the transgressions with national sacrifice. Speeches such as Koizumi's readapted the script of national sacrifice to contemporary society where willingly dying for the state was now logically incompatible with the ideal of the "peace-loving" nation.

This sentiment that national sacrifice was forced on people "against their will" has now become a hallmark of recent victim narratives in the memory culture from films and documentaries to novels and manga books, although it does not necessarily mean the same thing to everyone. Here, the powerlessness of forced sacrifice has become an "organizing metaphor" for explaining and understanding the terror of war, giving vocabulary to the experience of overwhelming fear, and emphasizing the suffering of immediate family and friends over the torment inflicted on distant others.[23] At the same time, the retroactive claim that people did not want the war also legitimates a self-serving "victim consciousness" that obscures the larger perpetrator guilt as well as the empirical evidence that many fervently supported the war especially at the beginning.[24] To complicate the story, official narratives of the 2000s also proved to be more multivocal and mixed as other LDP members such as Speaker of the House Kōno Yōhei voiced dissent. He used his office to call for a moratorium on visiting the Yasukuni Shrine (2005) and for more elucidation on Japan's war responsibility (2006).[25]

The official narrative was to take yet another turn in the next decade when Prime Minister Abe Shinzō aligned his official commemorative statement on August 15, 2013, with his keen nationalist beliefs: he *removed* the now routine "remorse" for Japan's "colonial rule and aggression," and the *involuntary* nature of the soldier's national sacrifice, as well as the customary "vow never to wage war again." These modifications in an official national speech were significant. In a stroke, he ennobled and "heroized" the fallen soldiers by omitting the implications that they were perpetrators or involuntary warriors.[26] Then, four months after modifying the national narrative, Abe performed another highly visible political act by paying tribute to the Yasukuni Shrine on the anniversary of taking office (December 26, 2013, rather than August 15). He did this fully aware of the symbolic implication that an official visit would have, because Yasukuni has enshrined since 1979 Class A war criminals indicted and executed for crimes against peace, including Tōjō Hideki, the prime minister and the army minister.

Political performances like these—paying or not paying tribute to a controversial shrine that includes war criminals, or redefining the meaning of national sacrifice—attempt to rebrand the national symbols of war and, by extension, Japanese national identity. They are significant performances, because rituals, speeches, tributes, and worship can dramatize social relations and affirm carefully crafted meanings.[27] Knowing that carefully calibrated semantic changes can alter the meaning and moral status of the national story, successive prime ministers used their office to champion their moral view of the cultural trauma of defeat. Nakasone and Abe promoted the narrative of the fallen heroes and fostered the lore of the fortunate fall: the nation is indebted to the noble sacrifices of the war dead for the peace and prosperity it enjoys today. By contrast, Murayama asserted the perpetrator narrative in the national narrative, acknowledging Japan's dark descent in the past, and pointed the way toward a deeper reconciliation with former adversaries and former colonies. Koizumi expanded the victim narrative and affirmed the solidarity of the people that shared the catastrophe: the nation will never forget the suffering inflicted by the war.

The Yasukuni Shrine, historically a critical social device to legitimate the war dead and national sacrifice, no longer has the symbolic power to turn the next generations into believers of dying for the fatherland or the Emperor. As more wartime generations aged and died in the twenty-first century, the stakeholders of the shrine have dwindled dramatically, while those who venerate the Emperor are also now a small minority.[28] The intense emotional logic of the controversy surrounding Yasukuni for the neonationalist advocates, according to Japanese philosopher Takahashi Tetsuya, can be characterized as an "alchemy of emotions," a problem of transforming the moral status of the dead by transposing rhetoric of the war dead back to the prewar context of national mobilization.[29] For its proponents, Yasukuni is the epicenter for meaning making for the lost war and for the fallen soldiers. Those wishing to keep the dead soldiers innocent, however, must then necessarily bracket out the Asian victims they killed.[30] This way of remembering the soldiers as victims has protected many Japanese from confronting the meaninglessness of the war deaths of loved ones and from disrupting the tacit practice of "knowing and not knowing" the dark side of their past, while depriving them of "acknowledging responsibility for their own roles" in supporting the war.[31] This "Yasukuni problem," then, embodies the deeply personal conflicts and contradictions of mourning *and* self-protection, complicated by the politics of today.

Discourses of War Responsibility and Sacrifice in
National Newspaper Editorials

In both positive and negative ways, mass cultural media like newspapers, television programs, films, and novels have played a significant role in bringing about a broader awareness of war memory in the 1990s through the 2010s. If the ceremonies of August 15 are like annual funerals, newspaper editorials of August 15 are a cacophony of reflections on mass deaths. Although national newspapers are generally circumspect in reporting politically sensitive issues like perpetrator guilt, they do stake out the paper's political position in their editorials. The commemorative editorials published on August 15 have become effective vehicles to articulate their stance on the legitimacy of war, national sacrifice, and war responsibility. In this section I illustrate the polyvalent arguments they publish using different threads of perpetrator, victim, and heroic narratives.

Riding the wave of a "memory boom" nationally and transnationally, the commemorative editorials of the national newspapers in the 1990s and 2000s grew more candid in expressing perpetrator guilt than in earlier years.[32] In tandem with the political shifts in the 1990s, Japan's perpetrator narratives in the public discourse deepened, coinciding with fresh political developments like the Murayama statement in 1995 and Chief of Staff Kōno Yōhei's statement of apology to the "comfort women" in 1993 in which he expressed "sincere apologies and remorse to all those, irrespective of place of origin, who suffered immeasurable pain and incurable physical and psychological wounds as comfort women."[33] During this time, the plight of wartime "comfort women" came into the media limelight through new historical research.[34] Feminist movements also helped bring attention to the women's lawsuits against the government over sexual forced labor. The Asian Women's Fund was established to extend compensation to the "comfort women," although it stopped short of becoming an official government fund.[35] New lawsuits from wartime prisoners, forced laborers, and other victims of maltreatment also kept perpetrator narratives in the public eye during this time. A research group called War Responsibility Center opened in 1993 and began to publish a journal dedicated to war responsibility issues. The progressive weekly *Shūkan Kinyobi* was inaugurated also in 1993 to give voice to independent journalists reporting on politically volatile issues including redress for wartime injustices. This constellation of developments in the public sphere helped raise awareness of Japan's perpetrator acts among the broader population, who also began to hear the testimonies of victims through the global media in a democratizing Asia.

A backlash to this trend materialized quickly.[36] In 1997, an assortment of nationalist academics and reactionary public intellectuals formed a coalition known as Tsukurukai (Atarashii rekishi kyōkasho o tsukurukai, Committee to Write New Textbooks) to insert their revised version of history to the popular discourse.[37] The first Abe government introduced patriotic education in the curriculum in 2006.[38] Other new legislation mandated the use of the national anthem and national flag in schools over the vigorous protests of progressive schoolteachers objecting to their association with the war.[39] This radical-right populist backlash attracted the support of the socially disenfranchised against the backdrop of economic stagnation in the 2000s.[40] The populists wanted to repair and restore the innocence of wartime heroes and challenged the outcome of the Tokyo Trials which defined Japan's defeat and war crimes. In their eyes, the moral and political crusades to promote state officials' visits to the Yasukuni Shrine were projects to cancel the stigma of defeat and an effort to decontaminate the "dirty" national identity.

All five national newspapers' commemorative editorials of August 15 consistently adopt the notion that the national sacrifice is "our bedrock for peace" as a normative framework, mourning the dead with a determination to make something meaningful from the lives that were cut short.[41] Most editorials echo the themes of damage, loss, and mass death, inviting the readers to remember, directly or indirectly, the enforced national sacrifice. Although the affirmation that the millions of war dead were an honorable "national sacrifice" is to this day an essential trope, the logic has always been strained, since much of the death, and even the war itself, might have been prevented with more prudent, courageous, and far-sighted decision-making. The need for this validating rhetoric in the editorials is nevertheless so strong that readers of national newspapers across the political spectrum—from *Asahi, Mainichi,* and *Nikkei* to *Yomiuri,* and *Sankei*—can usually find some version of it. This focus on the trauma of young lives cut short, then, usually leads papers to point the finger to the *shadow perpetrators* who wrought the catastrophe on their own people.

The idea that the national sacrifice has contributed to peace and prosperity in a narrative of the "fortunate fall" is articulated in this editorial in the *Yomiuri* newspaper (circulation ten million): "No one should forget that Japan's peace and prosperity today are founded upon the death of 3.1 million Japanese in the war."[42] Layering this tribute to the dead with outbursts of mourning is also common, as in this editorial by the *Asahi* newspaper (circulation eight million):

> There are 3.1 million of them—the number of military personnel and civilians who died in the last war. Who were they? How did they lose their lives?

Iga Takako (age 68) has been searching for the names of individuals who died in the fifty air raids of Osaka through the summer of 1945 . . . It's taken her sixteen years to register 4,817 names from Osaka city and 914 from Sakai city. These are only half of the 15,000 or so who are said to have perished . . . Iga was thirteen years old when she ran to the water pool to escape the burning. Her mother died instantly. Her brother, a first grader, was burned severely and died three days later. Alone with her father, she buried the remains in a hole they dug up in the ruins. There were many scenes like that . . . For many people like Iga, the war dead are still alive.[43]

This despair then turns to fury toward the Japanese leadership who are the shadow perpetrators, as in this editorial by the *Mainichi* newspaper (circulation four million):

Japan's military went over [to Asia], took over [their land] for selfish reasons, and then killed mountains of people. The prime minister must not worship in a shrine that enshrines Tōjō Hideki and other wartime leaders who ordered [the war], failed to stop it earlier, failed to instruct soldiers about international rules of treating war prisoners, forced mass suicides under the no surrender policy, and took decisions that incurred millions of deaths.[44]

In the 1990s and 2000s, the political differences in the treatment of perpetrator guilt became ever more salient even as the papers shared the similar intention of mourning the dead.[45] Three national papers—*Asahi*, *Mainichi*, and *Nikkei* (circulation three million) newspapers—began to run regular commemorative editorials that defined Japan's past as a perpetrator nation. The largest newspaper *Yomiuri* (circulation ten million) and the smaller *Sankei* (circulation two million) differed, taking a defensive, nationalist stance on war responsibility and claiming that guilt was framed unfairly by the victors.[46] (*Yomiuri* was to change its position in 2006.) On August 15, 2005, at the 60th anniversary of the end of war when Koizumi visited the Yasukuni Shrine, all national newspaper editorials except the *Sankei* newspaper focused directly on the question of war responsibility. This consensus of the four papers was in remarkable contrast to earlier years. The pacifist *Asahi* newspaper has been particularly vocal in claiming that peace is Japan's atonement for the war; the way to repair moral identity and attain the respect of the world.[47] *Asahi*'s antiwar narrative originates in remorse over its history of war collaboration, the stain of having incited the mass readership to join the war effort and misleading them with distorted reportage.[48] Given this sense of their own war responsibility, their demand for state accountability and indictment of wartime leaders and bureaucrats is particularly fierce.

The *Nihon Keizai* (*Nikkei*) newspaper, an elite business paper directed to a pragmatic, internationally minded readership, adds direct, lucid, and also practical editorials to the fray. In contrast to *Asahi*, *Nikkei* presents memorial editorials with ideological detachment but unreserved opinion. Taking a clear stand against Koizumi's repeated visit to the Yasukuni Shrine, for example, *Nikkei* offers scathing, unsparing criticism of wartime leadership. "The responsibility of the wartime leaders who brought the nation to ruin and caused the tremendous damage to Japan's neighbors should never be obscured . . . The terrible diplomatic ineptitude of the Japanese leaders that delayed the end of the war added to many more casualties."[49]

The *Yomiuri* newspaper's turn to directly tackle war responsibility came after 2005 when it carried out its own "reexamination" of war responsibility by the wartime leadership, independent of the judgment of the Tokyo Trials. Acknowledging that their own findings in the project were similar to those of the Tokyo Trials, *Yomiuri* ceased to defend the Yasukuni Shrine and Class A criminals. This turn will be discussed in more detail in the next section.

Comparing the editorials of the *Mainichi* newspaper, Japan's oldest daily paper,[50] and the *Sankei* newspaper is a study of contrasts. They are furthest apart in political ideology, while both take the tone of the political as personal, so to speak. War responsibility is a matter of "we," not "they"; hence *Mainichi's* embrace of war responsibility and *Sankei's* rejection of war responsibility are about accepting or refusing the dark side of history as their own identity. *Mainichi's* insistence on assuming perpetratorhood as part of "our" national identity also comes with ambivalence and complexity, however. In the 2005 anniversary editorial, the Japanese are perpetrators *and* victims; the Japanese military and Class A criminals are perpetrators, and the three million Japanese people who died were victims.[51] For the *Sankei* newspaper, the most reactionary of the five national papers, Japan was victimized by the victors who stigmatized the nation, so the priority now is to fight those claims and take back the heroic narrative of the nation's history from the West's hegemonic discourse.[52]

Notwithstanding the inclusion of Asian victims in recent editorials, critics have often admonished the complacency of Japan's narratives for settling too easily in a comfort zone without deeply probing the political and historical causes, and the structural violence and military abuse, that perpetuated the victimizers' power in the first place.[53] Sociologist Nina Eliasoph probes the question of how "perfectly capable people can keep misrecognizing themselves as innocent victims, seemingly blinded to the harm they've done, seemingly so myopic," not because they are stupid, but because it is a means of social bonding.[54] Sharing the generalized victim's voice also serves to promote structured helplessness, and becomes a vehicle for legitimating victimhood.[55] This recurring dynamic of self-pity partly explains why Japan's victim consciousness has been so durable over the decades and so effective in reproducing the culture of defeat.

The enormous concern for the damage inflicted on one's own people over any injury they wrought onto others permeates many mnemonic narratives, including the American memory of the Vietnam War.[56] Japanese narratives of victimhood also demonstrate a narrow, ethnocentric vision of the war dead. The proclivity to care about those "close to home" over distant others, discussed earlier as part of the struggle to find redemption in the death of those who never returned, will be discussed further at the end of this chapter. As the meaning of national sacrifice shifts and shuffles during the long defeat of a now pacifist nation, the answers are often ambivalent and contradictory, leaving space for multivalent interpretations of victimhood.

The Cultural Media Productions on Commemorations

Memory culture produces what historian John Bodnar calls "tangled versions of what actually happened and some mythical or hopeful view of what the world was like before and could become again." They do not represent the past perfectly but "fuse the real and the mythical, driven not simply by a need to remember, but also by a desire to forget."[57] Japan's commemorative publications and programs, television documentaries, and feature films are such memory culture products. They depict wartime Japanese soldiers and civilians in narrative plots as heroes, victims, and perpetrators—and in shades of gray; the protagonists' experiences and actions vary as do their relationships to the military state. They describe the different images and embodiment of war and defeat in individual lives, fusing different meanings, actions, and consequences. This section describes cultural memory projects that produce those "tangled versions" in the mass media.

Commemorating the war and deaths in a defeated nation that professes pacifism is a morally and politically complicated operation.

Whether documentaries or dramatic enactments, memory products do not escape moral evaluations: stories of violence and danger, humiliated masculinity, helpless destruction and loss, liberation from state oppression, anger toward leadership, and the callous regression of human decency tend to be framed as morality tales for a wider audience in the present. The recent media productions, far from bridging disparate memories, fail to bring collective closure or renew national solidarity, and reinforce the deeper separate preoccupations of the trauma of defeat. They have managed the complex requirements of remembering a difficult past—redressing injustices and past wrongs, healing ruptured wounds, and restoring a positive moral and national identity—but do not coalesce into a neat "collective memory."

Broadly, three preoccupations have dominated this memory landscape of the 1990s through today. First, there was a sense of urgency that the "witness generation" was passing on and that time was limited to seek more clarity from them about what happened in the war. The aging of this war generation reenergized efforts to disseminate victim narratives of how "little people" suffer in war, and this reinforced the pacifist, antiwar message. Second, there was at the same time a deepening awareness of the injustices committed against individual men and women in the war, which sharpened the perpetrator narratives that were then spread more widely. The growing recognition and claims of the Asian victims of the war for redress over the past decades has also been infused with a sense of urgency to resolve them while those victims they were still alive. Third, attempts to rehabilitate Japan's identity that had been sullied by the war and defeat renewed a furious politics of identity. Partly in response to the deepening awareness of Japan's history of perpetration, new heroic narratives emerged, conveying, directly or indirectly, indignation over the deviant identity imputed to Japanese men who fought the war. These nationalist efforts aimed to revise the vilified image and "restore the dignity" of these men. These trends are discussed below as they intersected with the concerns of different generations.

The Misery of Our Dreadful War

Recognizing a dark history of perpetration does not come easily to any nation. The self-protective impulse to suppress, overlook, or reinterpret the guilty, shameful past tends to prevail over the inclination to acknowledge it. Illuminating dark national history and questioning the political and moral responsibility of the war in Japan build on efforts of the wartime generation who became educators, intellectuals, journalists, and activists who insisted on accepting the offender's identity, facing the responsibility, and redressing the injustices that were unleashed. Prominent public intellectuals of this generation played a critical role in articulating these concerns and influenced progressive elites for decades. In this effort crucial leadership came not only from historians like Ienaga Saburō (discussed in chapter 1) but also from intellectuals in diverse fields, for example Maruyama Masao, Tsurumi Shunsuke, Oda Makoto, Ōe Kenzaburo, and others. Best-selling investigative journalism on the military's brutal transgressions in China also emanated from well-known writers like Honda Katsuichi and Morimura Seiichi who wrote in the 1970s and 1980s. Social groups and movements such as the teachers' union, peace movements, and human rights movements were all firmly engaged in keeping the perpetrator narrative alive and voiced their concern over redressing the injustice in different ways and with different degrees of success.[58]

Building on this work, mainstream journalism at the turn of the millennium produced high-profile war memory projects to reassess the state of the field as anniversary specials. They were intended for a wide popular audience: published in serials spanning days and months, then reproduced in books, television programs, and websites. One example was a long serial reportage on war responsibility published by the *Yomiuri* newspaper, designed as a countertrial to the Tokyo Trials, by the Japanese for the Japanese. This year-long (August 2004 to August 2005) independent inquiry over the conduct and responsibility of wartime leaders culminated in its own list of "who was responsible" for the failed war. The list had much overlap with, and was actually even longer than that of the Allies' trial in 1948–1949, but like the Allies' trial, it exonerated the Shōwa Emperor of war guilt.[59]

After this "reexamination," *Yomiuri* was to switch its position to anti-Yasukuni, spearheaded by the well-known octogenarian editor-in-chief Watanabe Tsuneo. Watanabe's anger is not unlike others of his generation who knew many lost in the war:

Nothing shows the utter cruelty of the Japanese military more than the kamikaze suicide missions (*tokkō*). The soldiers didn't go willingly [as officially claimed]. They were ordered to go by the higher-ups, orders that were tantamount to orders from the Emperor...

Military Headquarters also forced the soldiers [in the battlefront] to commit collective suicide (*gyokusai*). They sent no reinforcements, and then ordered the soldiers there to kill themselves [rather than surrender]. These were acts of brutal murder.

The irresponsible, sloppy war plans also forced countless "martyrs" of the nation to die of hunger—especially in the South Pacific. Mountains of them starved to death . . . To claim that they died "for the nation, hailing the Emperor," is a complete distortion of history. We have to demolish that [myth].[60]

Similarly, the·*Asahi* newspaper's project to examine war responsibility in the "past that will not go away" culminated in a serial that spanned four months in 2006.[61] Its approach to reexamining the Tokyo Trials was transnational, investigating the viewpoints from the United States to India, whose judicial representative issued the sole dissenting opinion finding all defendants not guilty. It also questioned the war responsibilities of the Emperor and the mass media (including *Asahi*'s own war collaboration) but not that of the masses. Showing how other nations mourned their war dead and overcame the past, the project also investigated international cases in Germany, France, Great Britain, South Korea, South Africa, Chile, and the United States. Unlike other commemorative projects, *Asahi*'s international approach necessarily entailed an examination of Japan's colonial past in Korea, Taiwan, Manchuria, and the scheme of the Greater East Asia Co-Prosperity Sphere. Investigating the injury wrought in annexing Korea and seizing China's northern provinces, the project invited commentaries of international experts and interviewed Asian victims. This approach showed that the blame for war and colonial oppression cannot be confined to a handful of "reckless military leaders"; however, the project stopped short of pointing fingers and leaves readers to draw their own conclusions on the collaborative responsibility of colonists, business leaders, and the military administration in the occupied territories.

The sense of urgency to record and archive wartime experiences also led to an oral history project called *Testimonial Records: The Soldiers' War* (*Shōgen kiroku: Heishitachi no sensō*, 2007–2011) produced by NHK television (Nippon Hōsō Kyōkai), Japan's national broadcasting station.[62] Like the BBC's oral history project *WW2 People's War* in Great Britain, NHK's project serves as a digital depository of war testimonies made available on the web. The project researched, recorded interviews, and produced programs over several years, starting in August 2007 and ending in 2011 to commemorate the 70th anniversary of the start of the Pacific War. It offers forceful accounts, in the words of the soldiers themselves, of what it was like to live through and survive the war. The programs reveal these veterans as unhappy men when they are recounting painful events, bitter about their brutal experience, mortified by their own desperate acts of self-preservation, ashamed of their degraded behavior, and haunted by their acts of violence.[63] Their testimonies are infused with self-loathing for what they were reduced to do for naked survival and loathing for their superiors who reduced them to pitiful beasts and expendable pawns. The Asia-Pacific War looks anything but heroic in these vivid testimonies of dehumanization and degradation.

As the veterans reflect on the meaning of their experience, it is evident that most do not find any redemption in this suffering. They carry frustrations, anger, mourning, guilt, and repugnance that remain unresolved and unanswered. The audience, however, must rely on their own reflections to draw conclusions as they read and hear what it is like to kill your own wounded before retreat;[64] rob the local peasants of their food;[65] obey incompetent commands to charge ahead without any strategy or tactics other than wasting life after life;[66] recognize the worthlessness of human life for the military command;[67] feel haunted by survivor guilt;[68] mourn[69] and vent anger at the meaningless loss and suffering;[70] remember the men who lost their minds[71] and men who killed themselves to seek relief from the suffering;[72] kill the enemy;[73] and even resort to cannibalism for naked survival.[74] The only positive aspects that comes through in these testimonies are examples of men of integrity (such as a commander who killed himself to save his subordinates[75]) and the compassion that men felt for each other.[76]

The intellectual monthly *Sekai* featured a project about Japan's perpetrators in China tracing their emotional reckoning with their brutal crimes while incarcerated in Chinese reeducation camps as war criminals. Psychiatrist Noda Masaaki examined the impact of perpetrator trauma in the emotional journeys of dozens of former soldiers in the serial over the course of a year and a half in 1997–1998.[77] Like American psychiatrist Robert Lifton's study of Vietnam War veterans,[78] Noda Masaaki unraveled the veteran's arduous path to emotional recovery, from gaining the ability to recognize and feel pain, developing empathy with the victims whose lives and families they had destroyed, to recognizing abuse, accepting guilt for their crimes, and regaining a sense of humanity. After repatriation, these former war criminals went on to form a moral witness movement, in which they lectured, published memoirs, and even began their own journal in 1997.[79] Noda's study not only made their stories accessible and understandable to a general audience, but it also shed light on the profound psychic numbing and inability to feel guilt under the imperialist ideological indoctrination that these men had experienced. Such psychological study of perpetrator profiles by professional psychiatrists has been largely absent in Japan until recently.

One of the cases that Noda illustrated was Yuasa Ken, an indicted war criminal who spent years in Soviet and Chinese prisoners' camps and, on return to Japan, became an activist in a veteran's movement dedicated to atoning for Japanese war crimes. For decades he has been speaking out about the crimes he committed as a medical doctor in an army hospital in Shanxi, China, where he killed 14 prisoners for "surgical practice." As difficult as it is for him to confess over and over to the wrongs he committed, he does not mince words. He spoke candidly to a journalist in a 2000 interview and makes his testimonies publicly available on the movement's website, among those of his colleagues:

> The goal of the Japanese army's invasion in China . . . was to plunder their resources. So, it was basically, robbery. . .
>
> None of my comrades will speak up . . . so, I will say this to rest the souls [*kuyō*] of the Chinese who were killed. . .
>
> I did . . . live dissections . . . 7 times . . . on 14 Chinese people . . . I still remember . . . their faces. . .
>
> When I remember those times, I am filled with remorse, bitterness, and regret.[80]

Works such as Noda's have led the way to exploring anew the dark side of memory buried in the zone of "knowing and not knowing."

The Folly of Our Father's War

In his classic study of postwar television documentaries on the war, Sakurai Hitoshi is self-critical of the early efforts as "closed circuit monologues." Working in isolation, he remembers that the producers' efforts to articulate victimization actually only made sense to those inside Japan. By the 1990s and 2000s, however, the uncomfortable themes of war guilt and responsibility for Japan's perpetrator past had become inescapable subjects of anniversary television broadcasts. Documentaries today typically involve extensive investigative reportage tracking down evidence and witnesses abroad, and incorporating archival work in the United States and Europe. These critical documentaries and action docudramas have become mainstays of August broadcasts and garner high ratings. In particular, *NHK Special*, a prime-time documentary series broadcast twice weekly, has long been a wellspring of award-winning investigations. It played a significant, sometimes controversial, role in shaping and transmitting war memory, including perpetrator narratives, to an intergenerational audience, although its general political orientation remains within the confines of a state-funded public television station.[81]

NHK Special, produced entirely by the postwar generation today, has offered some of the most in-depth investigative journalism on the Asia-Pacific War. The documentaries have uncovered many subjects of the war, especially the military organization and its conduct: the systemic cover-ups of the wartime navy's blunders and crimes (*Japanese Navy's 400 Hours of Testimonies*, 2009);[82] the opportunism, negligence, and collusion of the military, government, power elite, and media that collectively failed to stop the war (*Why Did the Japanese Go to War?* 2011, a four-part series);[83] the opium trade that the Japanese army dabbled in to finance the war in China (*Investigative Report: The Japanese Army and Opium*, 2008);[84] and more.

On the 64th anniversary of the end of the war in 2009, for example, NHK devoted prime-time programming over three days (August 8, 9, and 10) to a documentary series based on recently uncovered records of former Imperial Navy officers discussing what went wrong in the war. These men met 163 times from the 1970s through the 1990s to exchange their frank thoughts; those exchanges, recorded in 400 hours of tape, were the basis of the program and revealed candid confessions of efforts to shield their leaders at the Tokyo Trials, the crimes committed by the navy in the Philippines, and even a frank discussion of the Emperor's war responsibility.[85] The project also sought to contextualize those former officers' behavior and motives by interviewing their children (now in their 60s and 70s). Those children seemed to suggest that the hint of guilty conscience redeemed their fathers: "Father never spoke about it." "It was guilty silence [*yamashiki chinmoku dana*]." "He prayed for the lost soldiers every day." "He said he was powerless to stop what he opposed."

Piling up the evidence of incompetence and irresponsibility has a powerful cumulative effect, even as the program stops short of criticizing these officers directly. However, by revealing their collective loss of nerve, not having the courage to confront difficulty, and looking to others for approval, the program lets the data speak for themselves that the Imperial Navy was as guilty and self-serving as the Imperial Army.[86]

Six years later on the 70th anniversary of the start of the Pacific War in 2011, *NHK Special* produced a four-part series that asked why Japan decided to enter an unwinnable war against the United States.[87] The series, broadcast early in the year and then rerun during the August commemoration, probed the historical circumstances that led to Japan's plunge into the Pacific War in 1941. The NHK journalists targeted four culpable parties: the diplomac corps, the army, the media, and the state and military leadership. Individuals are not singled out for blame, but the sense of doom is pervasive. The series covered the enormous mistakes made, and the tragic consequences that ensued, emphasizing the deep sense of irresponsibilty permeating all four parties collectively. Of special note was the candid indictment of the mass media that manufactured the will, enthusiasm, and exaltation to fight, in lock step with state censorship. The moderator's commentaries suggest that there is a morality tale to be learned from this history by the postwar generation:

> Most important is to realize that they went to war, even while knowing well that war was a foolish choice. We can't just say it was insanity of the moment when so many perished because of Japan. We can't stop asking why we chose to go to war when so many sacrificed themselves.[88]

This theme of the folly and pity of war was repeated in an *NHK Special* called *The Red Papers Were Delivered to the Village: Who and Why They Were Sent to the Battle Front* (August 1996) about the destruction of life and livelihood of an entire village.[89] It traces the conscription records of a village in Toyama prefecture over eight years when 246 men were drafted to the war, receiving their conscription orders printed on red paper. The narrative alludes to the state as the shadow perpetrator that victimized the villagers and presents an obliquely negative view of how villagers and the village economy were killed in the name of the state. Muted resentment runs through the interviews with survivors who returned and labored to recover their tulip farms. A farmer who was conscripted at age 15 recalled how he was meant to dedicate his life to the state: "it was absolutely cruel." Some of the men had been drafted three or four times, even at age 44. Ultimately the enormity of these deaths cannot escape the verdict that they were futile, because that is the only assessment consistent with the widespread perception that the public was duped by wartime leaders—duped into making the mistake of going to war.[90] This awareness of coercion, exploitation, and betrayal by the state is not easily placated by government speeches such as Koizumi's.

Although NHK often presents new evidence and revelations for investigative documentary programs, it also courts its share of political controversies: one such case came in 2001 when NHK's educational station ostensibly gave into political pressure to modify its depiction of the International Women's Tribunal that highlighted the crimes against "comfort women." This independent people's tribunal, designed as women's countertrial to the Tokyo Trials, was held on Pearl Harbor Day in 2000 and indicted the Shōwa Emperor among several others for their wartime crimes of sexual forced labor. Organized by the well-known feminist journalist Matsui Yayori, the ensuing lawsuit over the "edited" NHK program fortuitously brought further publicity to the "comfort women" issue and the television program itself than the producers had probably originally envisaged.[91]

These recent accounts of Japan's wartime perpetration have not gone unchallenged. Some have criticized these perpetrator narratives as overly "politically correct," staying on the level of rhetoric, and never reaching a deeper understanding of the perpetrators motivations and sentiments.[92] For these critics, mostly from the political left, deepening consciousness requires a public recognition that the perpetrator past is an irrevocable part of national history to be accepted as national identity. The ritualized pledge for peace that usually accompanies the narratives often leaves ambiguous the roles of the perpetrators as colonizers, military aggressors, war criminals, and "ordinary" soldiers, not clarifying whether they are meant to be "us" or "them." From a critical memory perspective, this ambiguity of the audience's relationship to the perpetrators leaves much room to draw self-serving conclusions about Japan's war responsibility: a handful—especially a limited group of leaders defined guilty by the Tokyo Trials—can be made to bear the brunt of responsibility for the war, while the rest of the military, bureaucracy, government, power elite, and civilian population can remain comfortably "innocent" or even consider themselves victims.

By contrast, others from the opposite end of the political spectrum have criticized those perpetrator narratives as overly "self-loathing" and "biased"; such critics have challenged *NHK Special*'s coverage for going too far rather than condemning it for not going far enough.[93]

The Gallantry of Our Grandpa's War

Since the prevailing worldview of the West is that good triumphed over evil in World War II, coming to terms with the past in Japan has as much to do with addressing stigmatized deviant identity as making sense of gruesome losses. The instigators of the mass carnage have been demonized as fanatical, barbaric, and backward, and diminished from normal to deviant; the very moral fiber of the nation's inhabitants is called into question. Sociologist Erving Goffman defined stigma as "an attribute that is deeply discrediting" that diminishes the bearer "from a whole and usual person to a tainted, discounted one."[94] This deviant identity does not fade easily; it thrives as caricatures and stereotypes on the broad canvas of global mass culture that can still make Japanese viewers wince and cringe. It has also been internalized by many Japanese over the course of the long defeat.

It is not surprising then that this diminished, discounted identity has strained the national sense of self-esteem over time and across generations, much to the consternation of Japanese neonationalists. Attempts to restore the tainted image of patriotic heroes discussed in this section cannot be understood without taking account of this bitter resentment. Here I discuss efforts to reimagine the "deviant" Japanese military to counteract the images of misery and folly that became the mainstay of the cultural media in the 1990s and 2000s. Suggesting kinship as well as temporal distance from the imagined past, these stories are framed as narratives of our grandfathers' war. Often they are about war heroes of one's family who fought gallantly but did not return. Recently, however, these grandpa stories probe different outcomes, to make up for the flaw in the plot that war heroes of a lost war have to die to become war heroes: they show grandpas who survived the war—survived to help others live, survived in spite of the flawed military plans, and survived for the future of their families. Plausibly glamorizing those who survived life-changing carnage is not easy. Nor is it easy to depict them as kinder and gentler warriors, looking to save their lives rather than sacrifice themselves, so that they may return to their loved ones.[95] Yet this effort tries to turn the whole war into one fought to protect their loved ones, not to sacrifice for the fatherland or the Emperor.

These images of war and family are, of course, updated to fit the ideals of the twenty-first century and to resonate with young audiences who were raised in an era of romantic love. The wartime generation had a generally weaker emotional attachment to family life compared to now: they did not generally have romantic love marriages but had arranged marriages; they also gave up children for adoption when desired for primogeniture;[96] and in the wartime state Shinto ethos, mothers were congratulated when their sons died at war and were expected not to grieve their deaths. But family love has grown more important now and offers revised heroic role models for the young audience; it makes possible a new and improved image of Japanese military men to look up to even if they are fictive.

Thus, in a significant shift from martyrdom, the new and improved heroes do not always die at war. In the new feature films and novels about the war, Japanese soldiers are no longer willing to fight and die for the Emperor or the state but only for their "loved ones," that is, their parents, spouses, children, siblings, and friends. The greater cause has changed: they reject dying for the nation at war and cherish survival. Heroes are therefore not warmongers but peace seekers.

Even with this crowd-pleasing bent, recent feature films released to coincide with the August 15 commemorations still represent different meanings of war and defeat, a variety of real and fictive situations, and an assortment of diverse characters. Recent protagonists are an imprisoned dissident tortured to death by the military police and his widow; an indicted war criminal who pursues exoneration; a navy captain who defies the call to sacrifice his men in suicide missions and then happily marries his sweetheart after the war; a decorated soldier disfigured and limbless from combat injury and haunted by the memory of the rapes and atrocities in China, who callously and sadistically abuses his wife; a civilian shopkeeper who upholds a moral conscience to guide his children through wartime chaos; and a dreamy civilian engineer single-mindedly pursuing his childhood dream of building the best aircraft in the world, completely oblivious to the carnage it would cause as a weapon of lethal destruction.[97] These war stories are less about staking contentious truth claims than they are about illuminating different pieces of a larger whole that yet remain in tension. It is left to the audience to stitch the pieces together, recognizing that the characters are morally complicated and multidimensional and that our understanding is imperfect and incomplete.

Recent films like *Last Operations under the Orion* (2009) are inspired, written, created, and acted by postwar generations that never experienced the war but have grown up with an understanding that Japan's defeat and practices in World War II have left an indelible stain on the military. However, in *Orion*—and others of the same genre—military protagonists neither die tragic deaths nor become victims of the war but survive with daring and tenacity. This particular story revolves around Captain Kuramoto, played by the heartthrob Tamaki Hiroshi, who runs a submarine charged with thwarting the operations of American destroyers in the Pacific Ocean. Reversing the image of the fanatical Japanese military leader, Kuramoto is a kind, courteous, courageous, smart, and decisive leader who sees that his mission and responsibility are to save his men from needless death. So, he coolly refuses repeated pressures to send his men on suicide missions as human torpedoes (*kaiten*) that would help save ammunition. He counsels the four zeal-ous *kaiten* volunteers on board with reason and compassion: "Listen to me. We're not fighting to *die*. We are fighting to *live*. Humans are not weapons. We only have one life. It's too precious."

Although his best friend dies in a downed submarine, Kuramoto survives the war, marries his childhood sweetheart, and lives long enough for his granddaughter, who is now discovering his past military life, to remember his family life. While it is easy enough to criticize this entertaining action film as a prowar and promilitary tale, it should be recognized that the film also repudiates the erstwhile practices of kami-kaze missions and suicide charges that were valorized by the pre-1945 military. The audience finds moral dignity in a sanitized, revised past that is inhabited with Japanese men who treat each other with respect and resolutely refuse to sacrifice subordinates like dispensable pawns. This new and improved image allows the young audience to identify with and applaud the captain when he refuses false bravery, just as they can identify with and applaud American captains like Tom Hanks in *Saving Private Ryan*. *Orion* attempts to overcome the deviant "Jap" label in a growing genre of what might be called "grandpa" stories that refashion the armed forces into one that Japanese could become *proud* of.

To be a good soldier today, then, is to have a warm heart and good family values. Similar heroic grandpa stories are making their mark as a new popular fantasy genre in which the postwar audience can identify with brave and honest military heroes in a reimagined world. In the million-seller novel and feature film *Eternal Zero* (*Eien no zero*) a jobless, wayward grandson goes on a journey to discover his grandfa-ther's life, and along the way discovers the true meaning of life—love for the family and *not* dying for the state and Emperor. The courage of his grandfather to stick to this principle even as he serves as a phe-nomenal ace zero pilot for the Imperial Navy is the key to this story. The protagonist Miyabe is a cool flier, caring officer, smart strategist, and loving family man who is forced to become a *tokkō* suicide pilot by the navy and dies at the end of the war. The mixture of valorizing zero pilots and lamenting the *tokkō* system that killed those talented young men in the name of the state, defines the moral scope of this story. It keeps the empathy and respect for the sacrifices intact, but the purpose of those sacrifices has been switched from nation, Emperor, and fatherland to family and home.[98]

These stories work as entertaining fantasy for the young audi-ence, resonating with notions of "loved ones" and "family values" now saturated in the global entertainment media. Furthermore, *Zero* expresses a selective antimilitarist streak in denouncing inept petty bureaucrats in the navy, self-serving and cowardly military upper brass, and other reckless war mongers, all of whom are blamed for the tragic deaths of young Japanese men. In this worldview, the *tokkō* men are not zealous ultranationalist suicide bombers, but good men in bad situations who had no other choice. They wanted to live for their families but died. Depicting these men as "good ordinary men," however, also has major limitations: the stories must start after 1941 and depict the war against the United States rather than China. If Miyabe's story had started before 1941 during his deployment in China, he might well have had to be shown as one of the pilots carrying out vicious, indiscriminate bombings, like the infamous air raid of Chongqing city. The message from this fictive genre is disregard the inconvenient memory; there is something worth cherishing about the wartime heritage that can and *should* comprise the backbone of positive national and moral identity.

Ironically, the fictive grandpas reimagined by postwar authors and producers today actually adopt the norms and moral boundaries of the global Anglo-American popular culture. Courage, principle, skills, loyalty, and dedication indeed comprise the backbone of positive moral identity for Hollywood models. Japan's wartime ideal of ultimate courage and loyalty—a willingness to sacrifice one's own life for the sake of the Emperor or fatherland—is entirely incompatible with peacetime ideals to live for family, love, and happiness in a "peace-loving" nation. Grandpa's war stories in the commercial media have to overcome this cognitive dissonance by modifying the past.

How does the young audience today react to these tales of national sacrifice? On August 15, 2001, on the 56th anniversary of the end of the war, another *NHK Special* aired at prime time asked three dozen young participants in the studio to share their thoughts and perceptions of wartime Japan, especially of the young soldiers who fought to their death as suicide pilots. The majority were critical of their grandparents' war, though the views were far from uniform.

"I couldn't do what [the kamikaze pilot] did. How could anyone young do that for a cause? Was it because he didn't have a choice? I don't understand it."

"I don't get it. Did they go out to die because there was no other way? How could a cause [*taigi*] sway so many young people? I couldn't do it."

"I think it was convenient for them to say they couldn't help it."

"I sort of get it. I may have done the same thing. We're a bit similar to prewar Japan now: No principles or integrity"

"To say they couldn't help it must have been frustrating. It's resignation, accepting what they couldn't control."

"I also like to say that I can't help it. I'd say it one hundred times. But I'm not going to think about the public good. I'm only going to think about myself. I don't want to try too hard."

"To switch perspectives like that after the war . . . that was so spineless [*darashiganai*]."

"The negative legacy isn't over. I can see in my Korean friends that they are still carrying the anger [*kuyashisa*]. New ties can begin with apologies."

"I do feel the weight of [being part of] a 'nation,' but I'm not sure how to integrate [internalize] it in myself. I don't know what to believe, which makes me nervous."

"I don't know. I don't know what it means to 'take responsibility.' What am I supposed to do?"

"I think keeping peace is the best way to take responsibility."[99]

Neither uniform nor consensual, these young people are different from one another in how they feel about and understand the war, and what they take away from it. And yet, there are some discernible common sentiments among them: a thinly veiled contempt for the war generation for having completely switched their moral identity after the war; some anger that there are no moral principles besides "no more war" to guide their thinking about the future of Japan; and care about peace as a worthy goal.

National Belonging and Blocked Empathy

Critical of the perpetrator narratives in today's media, Japanese sociologist Fukuma Yoshiaki has argued that they have become overly politically correct and self-satisfied. He also takes issue with victim narratives that are used as a refuge from exploring perpetrator guilt. Fukuma reasons that to probe both positions in depth, we would inevitably have to understand the connection between the two, create a circuitry between understanding perpetratorhood and victimhood and bridge them at a deeper level of awareness. A deepening consciousness of perpetratorhood-cum-victimhood would lead us to an understanding of the complex sentiments of perpetrators themselves. It would also ultimately force us out of a safety zone of "knowing and not knowing" where we shield ourselves from accusations of wrongdoing. It would force us to examine whether we would or could have done differently under the same conditions. Deepening perpetrator-cum-victim consciousness should ultimately take us from the depths of the inexpressible, unutterable sentiments to recognizing the political structure in which the victimizers abused the victims. The quest is therefore not to abandon the comfortable victim's sentiments but to weave them into a more inclusive imaginative circuitry.[100]

This new circuitry requires a deeper *imperial consciousness* (*teikoku ishiki*), as historian Arai Shin'ichi maintains.[101] Without that imperial consciousness, the Japanese are blocked from empathizing with the Asian victims, insisting instead that they themselves were innocent bystanders caught up in an undeclared war. To gain an imperial awareness, however, it is important to reach a deeper level of awareness about the collusion of the masses in the war effort, whether as collaborators or bystanders. That this is both difficult and painful is evident in the words of this war-timer:

> After all, everyone older than my age had war experience of one kind or another regardless of gender. We all lived through the war, pulling each other's legs, and helping ourselves. So, thinking about war responsibility means we'd have to be critical of ourselves, and admonish ourselves . . . It's hard for us . . . If we tried, we'd have to tear ourselves from within; [we] are not mentally strong enough to bear that.[102]

This complex approach to remembering embraces a trend toward identifying an integrated "good-and-also-evil" narrative. It attempts to move beyond the split between good *versus* evil by identifying the perpetrators as victims of military abuse, while, at the same time, condemning their actions as perpetrators. These attempts are efforts to move beyond the impasse that has stagnated Japan's culture of defeat for some time and has contributed to a weak sense of responsibility for the victims "far-from-home" in Asia.[103] Among others, public intellectuals Oda Makoto, Tsurumi Shunsuke, Kato Norihiro, Oguma Eiji, and Yoshida Yutaka have attempted to break through this impasse, to suture the different horizons of meaning.[104]

Historian Hyōdō Akiko suggests a framework that conceptualizes the intersection of perpetrator and victim as two sides of the same coin.[105] While desensitization to violence is imperative to carrying out violent warfare, it can also lead to desensitization to violence directed at oneself. In a sense, Hyōdō calls for empathy for those who were trained and conditioned, and thereafter compelled, to carry out atrocities, without excusing those atrocities. This is an approach that calls for a level of empathy for the soldiers who turned into killing machines and who had to make a pact with the devil to survive in hell. It is no longer as easy to identify with them as classic heroes or villains, but some level of understanding the perpetrators-cum-victims as vulnerable and flawed men is necessary for an empathetic understanding that "it could happen to me, too."

The postwar generation seems to be taking heed. Recent surveys show that more Japanese of the postwar generation than the wartime generation think that they should bear responsibility for the war.[106] Nearly half (47%) think that the Japanese should continue to feel responsible for the enormous damage they brought to the people of China.[107] More than two-thirds (69%) thought that postwar Japan has not sufficiently examined what Japan did in the war and should debate the problem of war responsibility.[108]

This search for an integrated, coherent approach to heroes, victims, and perpetrators may allow postwar generations to evaluate individuals participating in the war as neither all-perpetrator nor all-victim. Contradictions abound in this way of looking at the realities of life: accept viciousness in kind people, and expect meanness in nice people. The approach ultimately reaches a zone of ambiguity between good and bad, or what Primo Levi has called the gray zone.[109]

Narratives of heroes, victims, and perpetrators coexist uneasily in part because different elements are embodied in the same people simultaneously: victims of one story can be simultaneously perpetrators of another story, and yet be cast as heroes of yet another story. A given family may be remembered at once as ardent supporters of military aggression as well as victims of indiscriminate aerial scorching, yet also saviors to local neighbors. As individuals, a Japanese soldier may be remembered at once as a perpetrator of illicit invasion and also a victim of army maltreatment, while also unwilling to kill a POW as ordered. Adding more complexity, a given family may remember several members in different hero/victim/perpetrator roles, like a dissident, a war dead, and a war criminal. The moral complexity is especially poignant for kamikaze pilots who embody this moral dilemma of simultaneous role assignment: although a "victim" of senseless orders, he makes a "heroic" sacrifice, which turns him into "perpetrator" of a military that committed war crimes.

Public intellectual and peace activist Oda Makoto articulated his vision of the integrated perpetrator-cum-victim already in the 1970s stemming from his experience of surviving the meaningless Osaka air raid on the eve of Japan's surrender and involvement in Japan's anti–Vietnam War movement (*Beheiren*). He suggested that the separation between perpetrator and victim is an artificial construct of moralities that are actually intermeshed. Perpetrators are born when people are turned into killing machines, which is enforced by the military state. Insofar as that turn (to perpetration) is enforced by a military system of authority that people had no option to refuse (by conscription), the perpetrators, before becoming perpetrators, are victims of the military state. This does not exonerate the perpetrators of atrocious crimes or of the need to take responsibility for them, but it means that perpetratorhood originates in another kind of violence done to them by the state. The original victimhood cannot be denied, though it does not cancel out their perpetratorhood.[110]

Without a more complex imaginative circuitry connecting victimhood to perpetratorhood, Japan's national attempt to keep its dead soldiers innocent will continue to require the bracketing out of other Asian deaths. Stories of Japanese victims, mobilized for many purposes and feeding into the larger cultural trauma of defeat, tend to push the distant Asian victims largely out of the official narratives and the public media. When empathy for the Asian victims seemingly falls off the radar of the postwar generation, we tend to attribute this behavior to apathy, small-mindedness, or amnesia. But prioritizing concerns about issues "close to home" is not unusual, and this apparent apathy may not be different from the ignorance of and indifference to the enemy dead in wars from the Vietnam War to the Iraq War. It may have to do with the feeling of powerlessness to address sufferings "far from home" relative to sufferings "close to home," or a sense of resignation on the part of people who feel disempowered to voice their concerns.[111] War responsibility, however, never ceases, so long as the same nation-state remains in place.[112]

Comparative studies scholar Nakamasa Masaki points out that the limited scope of national discussion about the culpability of the civilians and the suffering of distant victims lies at the heart of Japan's ambiguous self-understanding as perpetrator-cum-victim. He argues that self-understanding has been seriously compromised for political reasons: the situation derives from the collusion of convenience between the political left and the right for whom suppressing the discussion served different purposes. For the left, it helped ensure that they did not have to antagonize the general public whose political support they were seeking. For the right, it helped deflect possibly endless presumptions of guilt, including that of the Emperor. This protection of bystanders with silence became a diffuse practice as the sacrifice discourse solidified. Leaving the war dead unscathed became a national imperative.[113] This ambiguous self-understanding also derives from the salient memory of Hiroshima, framed and diffused as a massive victim story in the public discourse. This narrative, effective for peace education and pacifist socialization of children, can reinforce the vision that war's lethal violence is random and arbitrary instead of recognizing the human agency that makes that violence possible.[114] I turn to this problem of transmitting war memory to children in the next chapter.

Pedagogies of War and Peace

Teaching World War II to Children

Every May and June, the school trip season begins in Japan when many children go on tours to visit Tokyo, Kyoto, Hiroshima, Hokkaido, Okinawa, and other places for a few days of sightseeing and study. On a radiant afternoon in spring 2010, such a group of school children were visiting the Kyoto Museum for World Peace as part of their elementary school trip excursion. About 80 boys and girls dressed in brightly colored shirts and blouses wandered through different sections of the spacious museum built in 1992. They were led by volunteer guides ready at hand to take them through the exhibits. Many museums like this, and others around the country, are sites of "peace education" where intergenerational memory of the war is forged and reproduced. At this exhibit on the Asia-Pacific War, children listened to their elderly guides who patiently described the displays, taking in explanations of tattered military uniforms and flags, the mock-up of a sparse and dark living room prepared for air raids, the austere food-rationed menu, the model of a nuclear bomb, and photographs of student soldiers and annihilated cities. Some children listened raptly, absorbing the story of how everyday life was controlled in wartime, from food and clothing to beliefs and ideology; they jotted down their impressions in the notebooks that were given to them. Others showed no interest in taking notes; were more interested in hanging out with their friends; and wandered about freely from display to display, glancing, staring, reading, or pondering whatever sights or objects that caught their fancy.

"Three million Japanese died. And twenty million Asians also died. You see, we killed more people than we lost people. You see, we killed six or seven times more than we lost." A volunteer guide speaks in the tone and style common to elderly grandparents telling stories to their grandchildren. But unlike everyday family talk, the topic here is nothing less than brutal mass death: "Half of the soldiers died of starvation when all the supplies were cut off." "They fought until they were all annihilated [*zenmetsu surumade*]." She continues matter-of-factly exposing the young children to the lethal violence that took place in her lifetime. Another elderly guide introduces the children to a simulated wartime family room, and takes pains to explain why people couldn't stop the war: "They said you were unpatriotic if you didn't cooperate with the neighborhood war effort." Sitting with the young visitors around a small dining table in the sparse room, she tries to bridge the gulf that separates her childhood from theirs by describing how her mother prepared for the night air raids by darkening the windows and lights. A third guide, speaking much like an elderly schoolteacher in a classroom, points to the broader relevance of war and peace in the children's lives as he holds court in front of large photo displays of Hiroshima after the bomb: "There are people meeting right now at the United Nations to talk about the Nuclear Non-Proliferation Treaty. Japan doesn't want nuclear weapons. This goes all the way back to 1945. Hiroshima was hit around a two-kilometer radius. But today, just three bombs could annihilate all of Japan." Introduced to the possibility that all of Japan could be obliterated like that, the young listeners were motionless. This was an early exposure to the idea that they themselves, children, were not immune from nuclear threats and that they too could easily die from just one of those bombs.

A few days later, in a different peace museum in central Japan about 50 kilometers northwest of Tokyo, another group of children on a school trip were also learning peace education. The Saitama Peace Museum, established in a municipal park in 1993, was hosting a large group of local elementary school children, dressed in bright red school caps on a rainy day. The museum staff was standing by ready to offer them a simulated air raid experience complete with an evacuation drill. The supposed "attack" takes place while the children are in a mock classroom watching an authoritarian teacher (shown in film) extolling the virtues of the fatherland. As the air raid siren interrupts the class, the children are ushered into an "air raid shelter" filled with simulated smoke and the sights and sounds of aerial bombardment for a few minutes. Some children reacted with anxiety and nervousness, while others seemed bewildered. They had been primed for this experience beforehand in the auditorium where they were treated to an animated film *The Last Air Raid—Kumagaya*

(*Saigo no kūshū—Kumagaya*), based on the real air raid of Kumagaya city of Saitama Prefecture on the night before the war ended in August 1945. It is the story of a seven-year-old girl who was evacuated to Kumagaya to stay with relatives after she lost both of her parents in the Tokyo air raid. Orphaned, she tries hard to adjust to her new life and home, only to perish in yet another air raid there. This gloomy theme of abandoned children dying in war is common in a range of Japanese war stories for small children. The most well-known of this genre is the *Graves of the Fireflies* (*Hotaru no haka*) created by the animation tsar Miyazaki Hayao's in Studio Ghibli, based on a real air raid experience, and also shown for peace education in Japanese schools. *Fireflies* is again a story of orphaned children who struggle to survive after losing their mother in a devastating air raid and their father in war; they are then abandoned again by uncaring relatives and finally die of starvation on the street, ragged, penniless, and alone. The young audience can identify with these children and develop gut awareness that something can go terribly wrong in war which can reduce them to sheer helplessness: they too could really lose their parents, their family, their friends, and everything else that they depend on for protection and survival. It is not uncommon to find in peace education the use of narratives that encourage negative emotions: pity, horror, and visceral fear of abandonment and violent death.

In *Ethics of Memory*, Israeli philosopher Avishai Margalit argues that memory of negative emotions is a very powerful motivator of moral conduct.[1] Peace museums exemplify this idea as sites of memory that retell the painful past and evoke strong antiwar sentiments in visitors. A growing number of cultural institutions like these play a pivotal role in producing generational memory as the wartime generation passes on and stories of direct war experience become less available at home. Drawing on the emotions of cultural trauma to forge a pacifist moral trajectory is a common technique of transmitting memory in such institutions. The effectiveness of transmitting war memory, often call *keishō*, relies on the symbolic weight of that cultural trauma, and the ability to keep the crude emotional memory alive for future generations.[2] The narratives chosen are often compelling for remembering the war with emotions of horror and fear. Thus peace education tends to encourage the moral sentiment of pacifism based on gut survival instincts rather than on judicious reasoning about just and unjust wars. In this respect, it is not surprising that Japanese sociologist Murakami Toshifumi found in his recent survey that no more than 13.1% of Japanese middle school children support the idea of "just war"—a war of self-defense to defend the nation—compared to the 44.5% in an

English sample.[3] Young Japanese students who develop an early moral awareness that "something dreadful happened in Japanese war history" may not always know or understand the full picture of the events, but they can nevertheless act on the accrued negative emotions that encourage them to turn their back on the violent legacy.

Such peace museums are quite distinct from war museums that offer narratives of patriotic valor to remember the past. War and military museums around the world—far more numerous and long established than museums for peace—are designed to venerate past wars and events by showcasing the heroic martial achievements of historical figures. For the most part, exhibits in those museums tend to valorize military tradition by offering accounts of campaigns, displays of weapons, and stories of leaders and soldiers, while limiting attention to the lethal consequences. The Imperial War Museum in London and Les Invalides (Musée de l'Armée of Hôtel National des Invalides) in Paris are examples of such repositories of military accomplishments and celebrations of a heroic heritage. However, the weight of moral persuasion there rests on the premise that the wars waged were fundamentally just and legitimate, and it is this premise that distinguishes the battles from unruly carnage, and the combat from arbitrary rampage. This premise is harder to establish in defeat cultures, where military failures do not lend themselves readily to triumphant narratives of a just and valiant war. It is therefore not surprising to find many more peace museums than war museums in Japan where the former have grown exponentially especially in the 1980s and 1990s.[4] Of all peace museums around the world today, almost a third of them (65) are located in Japan, spread across the nation from Hokkaido to Okinawa.[5]

Yūshūkan in Tokyo is an example of a war museum—privately run by the controversial Yasukuni Shrine that honors the war dead and was a state institution until the end of World War II as discussed in chapter 3—that attempts to buffer the stigma of defeat and failure in order to promote the narrative of patriotic valor. It revives the story of the "Greater East Asia War" as a just and necessary war by referencing the hostile geopolitical environment of the time and symbolically equating the value of patriotic feats to samurai gallantry in feudal society. Moral indebtedness to the war dead is built into such a story, aided with displays of photos, personal effects, personal letters, and even the last wills of suicide pilots of the Asia-Pacific War.[6] By putting a human face to the ultimate sacrifice, and ignoring the violent repercussions, the emotional narratives strike a tone that encourages the viewers to feel beholden to the dead and perhaps even protective of their honor. However, portrayals of tragic death for an unsuccessful war can inspire as much pity as admiration, and stir as much aversion as passion to follow suit. Even as the portrayals of these "heroes" may shock and awe young visitors, it seems questionable that those tragic figures would arouse in many the desire to emulate their actions, especially when there seems no evident or compelling reason why the state would be worth dying for again today.

As German memory scholar Aleida Assmann argues, we are today at a critical time in the early twenty-first century when the historical memory of the war is translated into cultural memory in the public sphere.[7] As the wartime generation passes away, the postwar generations with no war experience have taken over as carriers of that memory together with the injunction to "never forget." This translation work—in museums, cultural media, and educational material—is an ongoing process of *culture work* where the narrative of the nation is remembered, reoriented, and reproduced. In the Japanese case, the transmission of generational war memory, *keishō*, attempts to transform the culture of defeat into a culture of peace, not a culture of contrition as in the case of postwar Germany. The legacy of cultural trauma is amply evoked in this process, often emphasizing the emotional memory of suffering at home more than the guilt of having inflicted even more suffering in colonized and occupied Asia. The triad of hero/victim/perpetrator narratives discussed in earlier chapters is deployed in this process, in museum exhibits, textbooks, anime films, and popular comics for children. They comprise the cultural material that will be explored in this chapter.

Plural and heterogeneous memories of a traumatic past thrive side by side in society, especially when what is remembered is a global multidimensional war. As a nation, Japan remembers itself at once as a perpetrator nation that was also victimized by the atomic bombings, yet capable also of fighting daring battles. A given family may be remembered at once as ardent supporters of military aggression as well as victims of indiscriminate aerial scorching, but also as saviors to local neighbors. An individual Japanese soldier may be remembered at once as a perpetrator of illicit invasion and also a victim of army maltreatment, while also unwilling to kill a POW as ordered. Adding more complexity, a given family may remember several members in different hero/victim/perpetrator roles, like a dissident, a war dead, and a war criminal. Thus, a mixture of hero, victim, and perpetrator roles and memories coexist uneasily from one situation to another in a state of moral indeterminacy that defies easy categorization. The contemporaneous, diverse memories often remain morally incompatible, especially when the larger picture of the Asia-Pacific War remains contentious and elusive.

Carriers of divided memories nevertheless operate within a horizon of shared meaning that is more or less contained in a normative frame that renders social solidarity possible.[8] In a divided and defeated nation, the normative frame using a broad umbrella construct like "peace" or "contrition" allows the incongruent narratives within public and private lives to coexist within a common structure of meaning.[9] Thus, even when "multiple forms of remembering are operating at once," common ground can be negotiated and tenuous bonds forged.[10] In this dynamic, what changes with ongoing memory work, then, are not the claims to historical truth, but the *salience* of some cultural narratives over others that prevail at given times in given places in describing the contentious past. If some eclipse others at different times, however, none really disappears altogether. Thus, "coming to terms with the past" is not a tidy, linear project, but a messy undertaking that is subject to recurrent waves of different historical tales that are incompatible, contradictory, and contingent on particular conditions and constraints.

History from Above: War and Peace in Social Studies Textbooks

The problem of narrating contentious national history is not unique to Japan as we know from copious examples around the world. Difficulties of recounting painful pasts abound, like the Vietnam War in the United States, the Cultural Revolution in China, and Stalinism in Russia, or the Rabin assassination in Israel.[11] People are apt to disagree on how to recount traumatic pasts not only because the actual interpretations diverge, but also because the dominant accounts shape the national legacy for future generations. In the education field, the history problem is further compounded by the national project to use school instruction to shape national identity. From Turkey to France and Greece, social studies and history education have been vehicles for fostering positive identification with the nation by highlighting heroic national achievements.[12] In the United States, too, history textbooks in the past have been a compilation of morality tales and proxy ideological battles such as during the Cold War.[13] To be sure, textbooks are *malleable* in the hands of the carriers of historical knowledge and have long been subject to the ebb and flow of political tides and institutional interventions.[14]

In Japan, the added complication is the fact that social studies education was originally introduced by the US occupation (1945–1952) as a tool to reeducate Japanese citizens in *its* image, under neocolonial conditions. The occupation banned history, geography, and moral education from Japanese schools, recognizing them as the prewar instruments of mobilizing nationalist prowar sentiments. The old ideological canon of loyalty to the imperial state was supplanted by the new ideals of human rights in the democratic state, framed as the "correct" ideas for new citizenship in the new society. Thus in 1947, social studies replaced the prewar nationalist instruction and introduced American democracy in occupied Japan.[15]

After this inauspicious beginning, social studies turned into one of the fiercest political battlefields following the occupation.[16] Although welcomed by those who wanted to see Japan move away from the prewar structure of authoritarian education, it was fought by those who feared the erosion of their political authority, and became the most intensely contested site of ideological struggle over citizenship education. Like the ferocious contest between the creationists and evolutionists in American education, the battle over war history has been a long, explosive culture war in Japan for decades, vying for the hearts and minds of the next generation. Many Japanese schoolteachers would attest that the struggle for control over narrating modern national history became so politically charged with the question of the guilt and shame over the stigmatized past that it had become "a dreaded subject."[17]

Here at stake is the legitimacy of regulating national history to cultivate "desirable" national identity and solidarity, as the wartime regime and the US occupation had also done. The proponents—mostly the state and state bureaucracy—legitimated positive framing of the past by separating the pedagogical and the academic aspects of history. They argue that in history education, national stories of accomplishment should foster national belonging and confidence in the nation's future citizens.[18] To this end, the autonomy and freedom of education is necessarily diminished and secondary to national interest. The opponents—mostly the teachers and teachers' unions—maintain that education should be based solely on academic historiography without state interference; history education should ensure both the rights of teachers to teach the truth and of children to learn the truth.[19] Accordingly, Japan's dark past must be taught in all its facets, including inconvenient truths like colonial oppression, wartime atrocities, and war crimes, whether it is the Nanjing massacre, the biological experiment Unit 731, "comfort women," or the Three-Alls campaign.[20]

The discord is therefore not only about the accuracy of the historical record but also a proxy battle about the value of teaching critical history to future generations.

Teaching of perpetrator history to future citizens has been even more problematic. Representing Japan in textbooks as the perpetrator of an unjust war has been at the center of long-standing, ideological, and deeply painful discord precisely because of the inherent stain on national identity and pride. From the 1960s, the problem of portraying candid perpetrator narratives stood at the core of the Ienaga textbook lawsuits against the state's demands to change his depictions of Japan's aggressive role in the Asia-Pacific War. Those lawsuits spanned over 30 years through the 1990s, the longest in Japan's modern history. The question of critically depicting perpetrator conduct has also been at the center of the international textbook controversies since the 1980s, which resulted in the "Neighboring Country Clause" policy in 1982 that requires the textbook certification process to take account of the concerns of neighboring countries that were victimized in the war. In the late 1990s, the increasing perpetrator descriptions that resulted met with a backlash in a renewed textbook controversy mostly among postwar intellectuals. The neonationalists among them published a series of controversial books and articles attacking the emergent perpetrator narratives (e.g., the "enslavement" of "comfort women," forced laborers, etc.) and sought to replace them with their own heroic narratives in "alternative" textbooks. These volatile swings through the decades represent the pendulum move through the processes of reckoning, backlash, provocation, and entrenchment that are part of the ongoing work of coming to terms with tainted war legacies and guilt.[21]

Beyond their political symbolism, observers have also pointed to the limitation of textbooks as effective instructional tools for aiding the interpretation of history. Thomas Rohlen, for example, noted almost 30 years ago that most high school textbooks in Japan offered "a march of events" that explicitly avoided interpretations, passions, judgments, and evaluations. In his view, they were textbooks of the traditional mold that presented a menu of facts without a clear narrative frame that invited meaningful interpretations of events.[22] Since then, however, textbooks have expanded their coverage of contemporary history and have made their war content war more explicit, while still remaining within the parameters of successive Ministry curricular guidelines. Thus it is misleading to think of Japanese school textbooks today as all alike. Although Japanese textbooks are packaged to appear similar—in size, length, format, style, semantics, coverage, and price—they differ in their perspectives on the events they describe. Carefully choosing words and phrases, they differentiate themselves in their emphasis on different intent, motivation, and locus of power and responsibility in describing the war. They differentiate themselves by deploying dissimilar frames to interpret the "perpetrators of an unjust war."

For example, all history textbooks cover the "Manchurian Incident," the Japan-China War, and the Pacific War, but they vary in how they characterize the state's intent in invading or occupying the neighboring Asian countries: the territorial expansion was intended to secure strategic resources that would facilitate war or to overcome the economic crisis in the world depression; the military was deployed to China in order to gain territories or to thwart belligerence toward Japan; the rogue army garrison (of Japan's Kwantung Army in Manchuria) defied orders, policies, and agreements in order to expand colonial territories, or to secure the borders. Different emphases and justifications implicate the wartime Japanese state in the war of aggression to different degrees of illegality, which, in turn, implies different levels of responsibility, blame, and guilt. Because such differences can literally hinge on a few choice words or phrases in the short segment on the Asia-Pacific War, they are easy to overlook in a quantitative content analysis. However, they unmistakably convey different meanings of war and peace to their young readers.[23]

The 15 history and civics textbooks selected here for discourse analysis, published by five publishers, are widely circulated textbooks for high school students in those classes. The sample is made up of the *top three* textbooks in *each* of *five* social studies subjects: Japanese History A, Japanese History B, Contemporary Society (*Gendai Shakai*), Politics/Economy (*Seiji Keizai*), and Ethics (*Rinri*).[24] I use the 2014 edition of those history and civics textbooks that ranked highest in market shares in those subjects. There were a total of 59 texts on these five subjects published by 11 publishers.[25] To help contextualize and verify the trends found in those texts, I compare them additionally with a secondary sample comprising the *previous* editions of those same texts, as well as the *alternative* texts published by the same publishers in the same subject categories. With 31 additional texts assessed in this secondary sample, I assess a total of 46 social studies textbooks for this analysis.[26]

These texts are usually written by teams of 6 to 12 scholars and teachers, and tend to keep the same "mold" through successive editions and Ministry curricular guidelines; thus they often develop their distinct narrative idioms that articulate preferred orientations. Such orientations often cut across social studies subjects. Partly for that reason, students and teachers usually refer to their texts by the publisher's name rather than by the individual titles, authors' names, or teams of authors, (e.g., "we use the Yamakawa text in history class"). I will follow that custom here as well. Japanese History A is designed to cover mostly modern and contemporary history; Japanese History B covers the entire history chronologically. As an elective, Japanese high school students can opt to take one or the other, but not both.[27]

Accounts of War and Peace in High School History Textbooks

Hayden White observed that historical narrations involve ethical judgments embedded in a moral framework, and the same holds for historical narrations in school textbooks.[28] History texts cannot merely impart empirical "truths" to students as if they exist in a moral void. Word choices and frame choices influence the writers' and the readers' interpretations of the events, consciously or not. As history texts choose their language carefully, cognizant of the full political meaning and impact of the choice, some descriptors become de facto code words to signal messages to the readers. Careful attention to such "code words" that attribute meaning to military and state actions, and the legitimacy of the war is needed to decipher these ethical judgments: words like "invasion," "advance," "occupation," "colonization," "annexation," and so forth (*shinryaku, shinshutsu, senryō, shokuminchika, heigō*) are politically, morally, and legally loaded, and therefore distinguished carefully by the authors and publishers. The same care applies also to phrases that imply different moral responsibility for the war: while phrases like "there was no choice but to go to war," and "the conflict escalated unexpectedly"[29] signal a lack of malicious intent on the part of the Japanese state, phrases like "Japan then escalated the war without declaring war,"[30] and "it was part of the Japanese Army's scheme to spread the war"[31] signal precisely the opposite.

All in all, the history texts describe the 1920s and 1930s as a violent, turbulent era that sent Japan spiraling down a wretched path to war. Japan's plunge was marred by misjudgments, missteps, misguided expectations, and misdirected ambitions that ultimately brought Japan into a high-stakes confrontation with Western powers. National strategies proved ineffective in the unpredictable early twentieth-century world of revolutions (China and USSR), wars (Sino-Japanese War,

Russo-Japanese War, and World War I), and shifting international pacts and alliances. National policies also proved exceedingly unstable as leaderships changed, political rivalries intensified, and nationalist violence escalated. The world was infested with racial prejudice, oppression, menace, suspicion and colonial ambitions, not all of which were Japan's making. But the fact remains that Japan was signatory to the Nine-Power Treaty of 1922 (the treaty affirming the sovereignty and territorial integrity of China), as well as the Pact of Paris of 1928 (the General Treaty for the Renunciation of War, or the Kellogg-Briand Treaty), and stood in violation of those international agreements by waging war in the Asia-Pacific region.

Origins of the Asia-Pacific War

What, then, do students learn about the fundamental justifications for the Asia-Pacific War? The high school history texts offer two different broad frameworks: (1) it was a war of choice, an intentional invasion driven by imperialist ambition and carried out by unjust military aggression, which ultimately escalated into a bloody war of attrition; or (2) it was a war of necessity, an expanded occupation of the continent compelled by economic and political pressures that ultimately developed unexpectedly into a prolonged, large-scale conflict.[32] Students are exposed to these different frameworks according to which texts they use, what type of supplemental material they are offered, and what kind of teachers they are assigned. The ultimate moral message taken away in both cases is that the Japanese state acted recklessly at a crucial time in history and failed its people monumentally.

Four of the six widely circulated texts use the first framework.[33] In one of them, Japan is an ambitious state that entered into the conflict with China fully intending to gain power and strategic resources. The nation competed with the Western superpowers over political influence and control of China's material resources, and believed in the legitimacy of these colonial acts as a pathway to becoming a world power. Japan was therefore not *forced* to wage war; it proactively sought to colonize and exploit the land and resources of East Asia.[34] This argument is echoed by another: "The real intention behind the New World Order was not peace in Asia, but the establishment of Japanese hegemony; accordingly, Japan expanded the invasion in Asia to seek strategic resources for continuing the war."[35] This type of textbook has consistently taken the position that the war waged against China was a war of aggression spanning 15 years (1931–1945) to gain strategic resources and territories on the continent.

The other two texts describe a "war of necessity" that ultimately developed into a prolonged, large-scale conflict. In a text with a very large circulation in the Japan History B market, Japan in the 1920s was in a dysfunctional state, unable to resolve the crises of governance emanating from the conflicts among political parties, military rivalries, competing strategies, ideologies, and social movements. It was also burdened by a flawed system of governance that crucially restricted civilian control over the military. National leaders failed to respond effectively to explosive international crises and were incapable of coordinating and controlling the country among internationalists and nationalists, progressives and reactionaries, communists, loyalists, and peace seekers/conciliators. These texts emphasize the significance of perceived international threats, especially from China, the USSR, and the United States. By this account, Japan's colonial ambition is primarily a defensive one. Ultimately, there was "no way other than resort to war" in a world dominated by hostile, imperialist Western powers.[36]

Of these top-selling history texts, the former group narrates Japan as the perpetrator of the war, while the latter tends to narrate Japan as the reluctant belligerent; thus neither group promotes any heroic narratives of the war. These "camps" comprise legitimate weight and counterweight in the history textbook market, although the latter lead the former in total circulation figures.[37] The narrative of the heroic "war of liberation" is offered only in one neonationalist textbook that has a limited and inconsequential circulation in the high school Japanese History B market.[38]

Since Western media reports have for years totalized and stereotyped Japanese textbooks to sensationalist effect,[39] it may be surprising to some that on closer look the recent history texts actually vary in content and coverage. The range of texts used in high school Japanese History A and B merit closer attention for that reason. I review here three "war of choice" texts and one "war of necessity" text from the sample of top-circulation texts to assess their different positions and approaches on the meaning of the war and the messages they send to young readers.

1. *Kōkō nihonshi B* (*High School Japanese History B*) by Jikkyō Shuppan publishers has long taken the position that the war waged against China was a war of aggression to attain strategic resources and territories in the continent. The Asia-Pacific War was a long war spanning over 15 years from 1931 to 1945 that was out of step with the international pacts concluded with the world's military powers after World War I. Japan was an ambitious state that competed

with the Western super powers over political influence and material control of China's resources and believed in the legitimacy of its colonial acts as a pathway to become a world power. It was therefore not forced into the war but actively aspired to colonize and exploit the land and resources of East Asia. The text describes the state and military actions leading up to war by referring to a wide cast of enablers. For example, the Emperor plays an explicit role in both starting the war and delaying the end of war. He is portrayed as the final arbiter to go to war with the United States and as rejecting the idea of surrender in the early months of 1945 that would have saved many lives. The text describes a range of perpetrator acts by the Japanese military, especially in Manchuria, Southeast Asia, and China, including the Nanjing massacre, use of poison gas, and the 731 biological warfare unit. It also lists the estimated death toll country by country, from China and Korea to Taiwan, Vietnam, Indonesia, Philippines, India, Malaysia, Singapore, and Burma.[40]

2. Daiichi Gakushūsha publisher's *Kōtōgakkō nihonshi A* (*High School Japanese History A*), the top-selling text in the Japanese History A market, offers a relatively balanced account of the war, cautious of imputing blame to individual perpetrators, while illustrating the illicit wartime conduct by the Japanese military and also showing the significance of claims for compensations by Asian victims today. The text stands out for showing everyday life in wartime as experienced by well-known persons like an Olympic swimmer, award-winning cartoonists, critical academics, a dissenting legislator, and a defiant diplomat. Using text boxes effectively, the book informs young readers that popular responses to the war were neither completely uniform nor totally complacent. Although the recent 2014 edition moderates somewhat the language that describes Asian suffering as a consequence of Japan's action, the volume mentions Japan's war crimes against civilians in the Chongqing air raids, Nanjing massacre, use of poison gas, forced labor, "comfort women," and the 731 biological warfare unit. Unlike the Jikkō textbook, however, it omits the larger picture, that is, the estimated total deaths that would give the students an understanding of the destruction that continues to reproduce the cultural trauma.[41]

3. Tokyo Shoseki's *Nihonshi A: Gendai karano rekishi* (*Japanese History A: Contemporary History*) is creative in taking and illustrating a critical perspective from outside Japan. The text stands out for its international outlook, attempting to open up the question of what the

war *means* for Japan and East Asia today, taking stock of the enormous damage and casualties and their long-term consequences. It features text boxes written by distinguished international scholars like Andrew Gordon, Sun Ge, Tessa Morris-Suzuki, Lee Yeounsuk, Brij Tankha, Wolfgang Seifert, Mahdi Elmandjjra, and others who offer critical views on imperialist war legacies today. Readers are encouraged to consider questions posed by these contributors (who are American, Chinese, Australian, Korean, Indian, German, and Moroccan) on the consequences of national pride, ethnocentrism, colonialism, war compensation, and colonization in the Third World. This innovative text also suggests—along with Jikkyō's and Daiichi's—that Japan had designs to control resources in China and East Asia and implicates all who were involved, not merely a handful of Kwangtong Army leaders.[42] Thus "Japan escalated the invasion in Asia, searching for more resources to carry on the war" that resulted in "Japanese conscripts experiencing not only fierce combat, disease and hunger, but also slaughter and torture of prisoners and violence toward civilians."[43] The text is also notable for highlighting issues of war responsibility and war compensation in postwar Japan, especially the international disputes in the 1990s and 2000s.[44]

4. Yamakawa Shuppan's *Shōsetsu nihonshi B* (*Japanese History B in Details*) has dominated the Japanese History B market for some time, reputed to be the source book for the university entrance examinations. Of the top-circulation textbooks, Yamakawa's text consistently stands out for its relative restraint from taking a critical perspective on the war. The text is carefully worded regarding the question of the war's legitimacy; it neither valorizes nor criticizes the state's conduct. The 2014 edition describes the nation in the 1920s and 1930s in a dysfunctional state. Burdened by a flawed system of governance that leaders failed to maneuver effectively, Japan responded to multiple international crises haphazardly. The Japan-China War originated in an independent military action of a defiant garrison force, stationed in Manchuria to protect Japan's strategic interests and security. The actions by the Kwantung Army led to an expanded occupation, which then escalated unexpectedly, through a series of provocations, into an all-out war. Emphasizing the significance of perceived international threats, the Japan-China War was not a premeditated invasion but a set of poorly handled conflicts that escalated. The accounts and explanations of Japan's war conduct, as well as the death tolls and the extensive suffering inflicted on Asian victims, tend to be limited compared to other texts.[45]

Conduct in the Asia-Pacific War

The history textbooks sampled here describe the conduct of war and its consequences along similar fault lines. Working within the limited space of thin paperbacks, most of the "war of choice" texts describe Japanese acts of perpetration on civilians, including slaughter, plunder, and arson (the Three-Alls campaign); maltreatment of "comfort women," forced laborers, and prisoners of war; and the biological warfare experiments—in Shanghai, Nanjing, Chongqing, Manila, Singapore, and elsewhere. The largest circulation text in Japanese History A illustrates, for example, the illegal injury and killing of civilians from the Chongqing air raids and the Nanjing massacre to the use of poison gas, forced labor, "comfort women," and the 731 biological warfare unit.[46] Such texts follow up these descriptions with brief statements on war compensation and responsibility as well. However, only few offer the total scope of the Asia-Pacific War by indicating estimates of the total death and injuries.[47]

These "war of choice" texts also make use of photos that visually communicate Japan's acts of perpetration and oppression. One text, for example, shows photographs of Korean forced laborers toiling at a stone quarry, and Chinese civilians being inspected in occupied Guangdong.[48] Another text shows photographs of requisitioned local laborers slogging at the Burma railway construction site and a Shinto shrine in colonized Korea that local people were forced to revere.[49] Still another text displays a photo of the derelict building that once housed the biological warfare experiment Unit 731 where it says 3,000 Chinese and Russian captives were killed.[50]

Young readers are also exposed to illustrations and photos of Japan's own experiences of annihilation, from battlefronts like Guadalcanal to home fronts like the air raids in Tokyo and Osaka and the atomic bombings in Hiroshima and Nagasaki.[51] As the texts chronicle the lives of people under duress, the subjugation of Japanese citizens by their own state and military also becomes evident: the hazing of military conscripts,[52] enforced deaths of Okinawan civilians,[53] abandonment of Japanese immigrants in Manchuria after the Soviet invasion,[54] and military suicide charges that cut many young lives short.[55] Implicitly, they call into question the performance and trustworthiness of the Japanese authorities in protecting their own people.

By contrast, the "war of necessity" texts tend to tell history from above and to focus the narratives on international politics shaped in the world of political elites like diplomats, ministers, and military leaders. Illustrations of perpetrator acts tend to be generally peripheral in these texts which are relatively circumspect in critically assessing

Japan's actual conduct of war and its human consequences. In one text, perpetrator illustrations are confined to brief mention of the "Nanjing Incident" that killed scores of Chinese civilians, mass executions in Singapore, and slaughters of Filipino civilians.[56] No illustrative photographs or accounts of Korean forced laborers or the biological warfare Unit 731 are offered. In another text, critical assessments of the state tend to focus somewhat more on domestic repression like suppressing popular dissidence and less on destroying the lives and livelihoods of Asian victims.[57]

Observers who take issue with Japanese history textbooks for not going far and deeply enough to describe perpetrator history—especially the damage and injury to tens of millions of Asian victims—render an important service in drawing attention to the inward-looking nature of Japanese war history instruction. Flawed as the texts are in many respects, however, what is easily overlooked in the focus on shortcomings is the significant impact that these types of war stories can still have on young readers by helping them grasp the monumental scale of state betrayal that Japanese subjects witnessed, not only in bringing the nation to defeat but also in sacrificing its people's lives. Regardless of which causal narratives they hear—whether Japan was an aggressive state or a dysfunctional state—young Japanese cannot escape learning in one way or the other that their country, at a crucial time in modern history, failed to protect its people. Men, women, and children who entrusted their fate to the state as "subjects" were betrayed massively by the state that was in the end ready to sacrifice them. The chilling morality tale learned here is therefore that when push came to shove, the state abandoned its own people. The message of *broken trust* between state and people is here one of the most powerful historical lessons that underlie the postwar national identity of peace: for as long as Japan is at peace, the state cannot play roulette with people's lives again. This deep anxiety embedded in the victim narratives is part of the drive that continues to render Japanese war memory into a cultural trauma. The cultural trauma reproduced in the texts serves not only to inform and educate but, latently, also to warn and question.

Accounts of War and Peace in High School Civics Textbooks

In contrast to high school textbooks for history, civics texts focus mostly on the foundations of Japanese society and the civic character of its people in the postwar years. It is in these texts that the moral values of peace come into clearer focus, especially when pacifist principles are presented as consequences of war and defeat and democratic governance as a result of the postwar political reforms. Here, pacifism and democracy are set up as core civic values of postwar Japan and framed specifically in *negative contrast* to the previous dark history. Contemporary Japanese identity is therefore given special positive meaning and legitimacy through its difference from the past—which is described as authoritarian, militarist, repressive, and violent—and which culminated in the "wretched experience of war."[58] Japan's national story told in the school civics texts is therefore by and large the story of a pacifist nation founded on a *repudiation* of its militarist, violent history.

This "pacifist nation" embraces a range of meanings in different arenas for varied purposes: it is, by turns, a civic identity, a guiding constitutional principle, a secular moral order, a national security policy, an antinuclear ideology, a norm against military violence, a declaration of repentance, and a vow not to repeat the mistakes of the past.[59] The array of meanings is evident across the civics textbooks: for example, in one *Contemporary Society* text, peace is a universal right, as "Japan embraces unequivocal pacifism by confirming the rights of all peoples of the world to live in peace."[60] In another, peace is a symbol of repentance: "based on regrets about the past, Japan vowed never to invade another nation and never to wage a dreadful war again."[61] Pacifism can also be a veiled rebuke at having been destroyed by nuclear bombs, such as in the claim about the Japanese that "as citizens of the only nation in the world that experienced destruction by atomic bombs, we have taken on a special mission to promote the message of world peace."[62] Although the narratives' emphases vary and shift over time, it is hard to miss that traumatic war memory is the *referent* from which desirable morality tales are produced for consumption by the next generation.[63]

This multifaceted definition of pacifism is based on Article 9 of the constitution whose weighty meanings must be unpacked and explained in the civics textbooks. The article—which renounces war, possession of arms, and the right to belligerence as a means to resolve disputes—is celebrated for its unequivocal stance that is "meaningful for world history" and "with few precedents in the world."[64] The broad outline of the stipulation for peace is straightforward enough in the texts like *Contemporary Society* and *Politics/Economics*; where they differ, however, is in the way they address the complexities that arise from piecing together different interpretations of peace, possession of arms, and right to belligerence. These go straight to the heart of Japan's political dilemmas about the exercise of self-defense, collective self-defense, and people's sovereignty.[65] When is self-defense justified? How can the Self-Defense Force be deployed legitimately? Can state and military authorities be trusted to command the armed forces again? The moral legitimacy of the "pacifist nation" is implicitly called into question beyond strategy and tactics, whether discussing deployment of the Self-Defense Force or cooperation with the US armed forces or the UN Peacekeeping forces.

Over the decades, interpretations of the constitution have evolved contentiously with the ebb and flow of geopolitics in East and Southeast Asia. Initially imposed by the American occupation to arrest wartime militarism, and then soon redefined by it to support the US military presence in East Asia during the Cold War and the Korean War, Article 9 has been at the center of contention over Japan's rearmament for 60 years. The ensuing schism is usually represented as a struggle between two camps on opposite sides of the political spectrum. The proponents of "armed peace" have typically supported a strong security alliance with the United States who has strategic military bases in Japan and invest full legitimacy in the military role of the Self-Defense Force. These realists—typically reactionaries who tend to claim that war is a necessary evil of the last resort—emphasize Japan's vulnerability in being surrounded by powerful, nuclear-arms-owning neighbors such as Russia, China, and North Korea. For them, exercising force for the purpose of self-defense is a legitimate and appropriate action within the stipulation of the constitution. The proponents of "unarmed peace," on the other hand, have typically supported a stringent interpretation of Article 9, cautious of Japan's dependence for security on the United States, and wary also of trusting the Japanese government with the power to command a military force like the Self-Defense Force again. These idealists—usually progressives who tend to consider war as unmitigated evil—see Japan's peaceful relations with its powerful neighbors as sustainable within an international security framework. For them, exercising force even for the purpose of self-defense is a dubious proposition under the strict reading of the constitution. Neither side, however, resolves the fundamental political contradiction that Japan's quest for peace is basically untenable, armed or unarmed, without the US security umbrella or another collective security arrangement, when nuclear weapons are stockpiled in neighboring countries.[66] Nevertheless, this broadly defined fault line goes some ways toward accounting for the divergent views on the policy changes in the 1990s and 2000s—such as the emergency bills in case of an armed attack, law for antiterror measures, the UN Peacekeeping Operation (PKO) law, and others—that responded to drastic shifts in post–Cold War geopolitics.[67]

Civics: Contemporary Society and Politics/Economy

Civics textbooks—which are charged with explaining the complex, contradictory, and evolving ideas on sustaining peace—cannot escape these fault lines, even as they claim to practice studied neutrality. The most widely circulated high school texts used in two civics subjects—Contemporary Society (*Gendai Shakai*), and Politics/Economy (*Seiji Keizai*)[68]—tread carefully around the politics of constitutional pacifism, framing the dispute around specific policies, legislation, and legal interpretations rather than tackle the broader question of what is a morally justifiable "self-defense" for a pacifist nation. The national narrative framework of peace is precarious, constructed from the fabric of traumatic war memory, held together by a brief article in the constitution, and sustained by dependence on the world's largest military force with stockpiles of nuclear weapons. The textbooks charged with articulating Japan's civic identity based on these contradictory premises also navigate between the reality of "armed peace" and the ideal of "unarmed peace." One text, for example, considers the constitutionality of an armed self-defense: "The legitimacy of Japan's militarization has been strenuously debated in relation to Article 9 of the Constitution that renounces war and prohibits the maintenance of military force . . . to date, the Supreme Court has not reached a definitive judgment about the constitutionality [of the Self-Defense Force]."[69] Another text considers the serious need for restraints on state power for exercising armed self-defense: "The provisions of the Contingency Bills [of 2003 and 2004] were welcomed to prevent possible human rights violations by the government in an emergency; at the same time, however, the provisions are themselves being criticized for their incompatibility with constitutional pacifism."[70] Misgivings and apprehensions for exercising "armed peace" are evident, even as texts strive to be as uncontroversial as their counterparts in other countries strive to be.[71]

In civics, the long shadow of the war is also visible in the treatment of Japan's relations with East Asia in the current globalizing world. The widely used civics textbooks on Politics/Economy all take up the issue of war compensation in these relationships and use the repudiation of the past as a common launching pad for discussing them. However, the texts—designed to survey introductory politics and economics for both Japan and the world in about 200–220 pages—only briefly cover the basic concerns without elaborating on the specific wartime deeds that precipitated those claims by "comfort women," forced laborers, and others. As one text notes, reconciliation is an appropriate issue for sustaining future relations because "having wrought so much damage by invading the Asian and Pacific countries, Japan must . . . promote the understanding that it embraces the principles of pacifism . . . and respond sincerely to the compensation issues raised as a consequence of Japan's deeds in World War II."[72] Another text is even more circumspect: "The government's position is that these compensation problems have already been resolved by state-to-state compensation. But it is also incumbent upon the government to treat with sincerity the former prisoners of war and comfort women who were treated inhumanely."[73] Thus young readers are introduced to the idea of unfinished business harming international relations that harkens back to Japan's dark history but without concrete information on how "so much damage" came to be and why. The strategy of staying above the fray by muting controversy common in civics texts is even more salient for the currently explosive territorial disputes that also derive from the imperialist past—with China (*Senkaku*/Diaoyu Islands), South Korea (*Takeshima*/Dokdo Island), and Russia (*Hoppō ryōdo*/Kuril Islands). Although defeat and loss of empire are here the historical referent from which the disputes arise, this link is unarticulated.

Civics: Ethics

Ethics (*Rinri*) is another subject in high school civics that covers war, peace, and social justice in an introductory survey of moral values and social thought.[74] The Ethics textbooks describe key ideas, values, and beliefs in both Eastern and Western civilizations, drawing from subjects like moral philosophy, history of social thought, psychology, religion, and civilizations. This task is accomplished also in a limited space of about 200 pages, with the contents abridged, condensed, and packaged succinctly for young readers. A cursory count suggests that the number of thinkers crammed into each text is about 120–150, making brevity of the essence, and allowing precious little space for elaboration.

The texts are designed to survey the history of moral values and norms within the overall context of civics education to facilitate understanding of peace and democracy.[75] Within these parameters, and the curricular constraints of coverage and length, the variation among the Ethics texts is relatively small but still notable. The allocation of space and choice of tone to illustrate different public intellectuals and their ideas offer some clues on the different texts' priorities. One, for example, rather than focusing solely on orthodox thinkers, also illuminates dissenters who dared to challenge prevailing views, risking their careers and lives.[76] In such a text, young Japanese students will find surprisingly little information on the substance of Japan's warrior philosophy and culture (*Bushido*), despite the significance of the military elite during seven centuries of feudal rule, but more focus on pacifists and humanists.[77] In another text, the specific content of particular ultranationalist ideologies that provided the backbone of authoritarian military society in prewar and wartime Japan is relatively scant, yet a full page is given nevertheless to describe Japan's orientalist prejudices toward Asia that wrought repressive colonial practices.[78] Notable again in the three top-selling Ethics texts—which together comprise two-thirds of the market share—is the repudiation of the "abhorrent Asia-Pacific War" as the referent from which they narrate the dramatic transformation of the moral order in postwar society. The quandary of teaching Ethics remains, however, that, while students are made to wade through the array of Eastern philosophy over the millennia, the narrative of rupture and establishing a new beginning in 1945 interrupts the sense of continuity of moral heritage and leaves the pacifist and democratic ideals of contemporary society disconnected from historical ethnic self-understandings.

History from Below: War and Peace in Popular Comic Collections

In a country where the popular cultural media are ubiquitous in everyday life, it is not surprising that material for learning Japanese history is especially abundant in the commercial media. In Japan 40% of all books and magazines are manga (comic art) publications. It stands to reason that manga has been a popular vehicle for supplemental instruction and education. This genre is called "study manga," or "education manga" (*gakushū manga*), and found readily in school libraries, local public libraries, and bookstores. As informal tools of cultural learning, they are on a par with television and animation films in how they bring cognitive comprehension to children, influencing their perceptions as memory carriers of the next generation. Of the public media that transmit and translate war memory—from newspapers, magazines, books, and novels to television documentaries and films—study manga merits special attention as a vehicle that exclusively targets children at a formative age, when their ethical judgment and moral dispositions are formed.[79]

The moral evaluation of war and peace in pop-history study manga comes into clear focus when we closely examine the content for plot, characters, visual clues, and dramatic style. They are, however, not standardized or uniform within the genre. Study manga can be classified in several categories: "academic" history manga series by professional scholars; "popular" history manga series by superstar artists in the manga industry; manga history "study guides" designed for students preparing for entrance exams; "digest" history manga for quick reference; "biographical" manga of eminent and popular figures; "novelized" history manga for entertainment, and more. I focus in this chapter on the "academic" history manga series and the "popular" history manga series that have proven their staying power as classics, reprinted many times over in the last two decades. They include six well-known history manga series: three are "academic" history manga collections supervised by professional historians, published by mainstream publishers Gakushū Kenkyūsha (referred to by the shorthand Gakken), Shūeisha, and Shōgakkan; the other three are "popular" history manga collections offered by the studios of three phenomenally successful star artists of the postwar manga industry, Fujiko F. Fujio, Mizuki Shigeru, and Ishinomori Shōtarō.

Successful study manga make grim history palatable, with dynamic plots, colorful characters, and humorous asides. The stories, in contrast to textbooks, are often page turners that sustain the readers' curiosity and entice them to imagine and identify with distant, unfamiliar times and places. They also help the reader's cognitive grasp of moral distinctions by showing the ethical qualities of key characters with graphic visual cues like facial expressions, body language, and other signals. For example, if characters are drawn with a menacing grin, harried body language, and in dark silhouettes, the reader readily understands that the plan they are hatching must be of dubious moral quality. Equally significant and captivating in study manga is the view of history from below, allowing readers to see events through the eyes of "ordinary families" that are interspersed in the narration to drive the plot, to comment on the events, and to express feelings about the impact of the events on their everyday life. This sympathy with the "little people" gives these stories an unmistakable populist tilt and an interpretive framework critical of higher authority. The chutzpah and irreverence typical of Japanese comics are perfectly suited to expressing misgivings about authorities like the government, military, and police; and indeed, caricatures are delightful ways to get back at the overbearing bullies who intimidated, oppressed, policed, betrayed, and devalued the masses in wartime society.

"Academic" History Manga Collections

Educational comics about national history, a familiar children's literature genre in many countries, have been popular tools of learning
in Japan since the 1970s.[80] In Japan, they typically come in multivolume collections offered by major publishers in hardcovers and are
purchased by schools and local libraries as well as parents and grandparents for young children to read at home. For example, the well-known
Gakken's series on Japanese history is an 18-volume set in its current
edition, now in its 60th printing since 1982; the Shōgakkan's current
series spans 23 volumes and is now in its 49th printing since 1983; the
Shūeisha's current series is a 20-volume set in its ninth printing since
1998. These educational manga series, supervised by academic historians, are targeted to children of school age, mostly in elementary and
middle schools.[81]

For the most part, the academic manga offer colorful portrayals of
2,000 years of Japanese history from early settlement through the contemporary era in chronological order. The portrayal of the Asia-Pacific
War usually takes up one volume, averaging about 150 pages in length.
As a portrayal of a discredited and disastrous war, there are no gallant
national heroes or enchanting political leaders that brighten up the
pages and dramatically drive the plot. Instead, the stories unfold with
accounts of divisive politics and deteriorating economic life that are
rife with social conflict, unstable governments, an ambitious military,
terrorist violence, rogue actions, and rampant poverty.

The descent into war is rendered into a sobering morality tale of what
not to do again. The pacifist moral frame is consistent: war-friendly
characters and actions are portrayed negatively, and, by contrast,
peace-friendly characters and actions are portrayed favorably. The
antiwar messages of the "little people" are especially striking, from
a grim conscript's claim ("I curse this war")[82] to a stunned mother's
lament ("War—I hate war"),[83] and a grandmother's desperate statement when her grandson departs for war ("Everyone cursed the war,
and prayed their children would come home safe").[84] Even a family dog
bemoans, "I hate war!"[85] Front and back matters of the books also convey moral evaluations, such as a note to the family that pleads, "Please
make sure to let the readers pay attention to Japanese acts of perpetration in China."[86] As war memory is translated into cultural memory
in educational manga, compassion for suffering is now directed to
antiwar pacifism—the desired moral quality transmitted to the young
readers—even though in wartime it was condemned as unpatriotic.

No heroes make their mark in these war stories, but a few villains make unceremonious appearances. None of these villains are American, Chinese, Russian, or anyone else in the enemy camps: they are Japanese. The designated "bad" characters are Japanese men who advocated, instigated, promoted, and then bungled the war. Such "war mongers" are usually officers of the Japanese army, especially those in the Kwantung garrison in Manchuria and the high military and civilian leadership who backed and covered for the rogue army. These loaded characterizations produce a vernacular understanding of Japan's colonial war on the continent in young readers who develop an early moral awareness of "something gone terribly wrong in Japanese history."

To be sure, what went terribly wrong is not only colonial exploitation and military catastrophes but also the massive death toll of over 20 million people in Asia, many of whom were noncombatants. To this end, two of the three study manga series—Shūeisha and Shōgakkan—offer explicit perpetrator narratives illustrating Japan's subjugation of civilians in East and Southeast Asia during the years of war and colonization. One volume describes Japanese atrocities carried out in the "Nanjing Incident," the slaughter of civilians in Chinese villages, recruiting forced laborers in occupied territories, and the biological warfare Unit 731.[87] Another volume gives graphic accounts of civilians slaughtered in Nanjing, as well as villagers slain in rural China in the campaign to kill, plunder, and burn (the Three-Alls campaign).[88] The ferocious Japanese invasion of East and Southeast Asia is also described, including full-page accounts of the massacre of civilians in Singapore and elsewhere.[89] The brutal treatment of forced laborers—locally drafted or captured POWs—by Japanese soldiers and administrators also takes up full pages in both volumes.[90]

As a rendering of a multidimensional war, the portrayal of the violence and dehumanization inflicted *by* the Japanese soldiers on Asian victims is also extended to those inflicted *on* the Japanese soldiers by the Japanese military. Their anguish typically comes from the battlefront, from fighting unwinnable and lethal battles planned by incompetent military strategists in places like Imphal ("Damn! I curse the top brass who planned this . . ."),[91] to dying of disease and starvation in Guadalcanal and elsewhere as supplies ran out ("We can't go on fighting with malaria and malnutrition"),[92] and killing themselves en masse rather than surrender to the enemy ("I can't move anymore. Kill me.").[93] The suffering of Japanese civilians is described with equal candor—deaths by aerial bombings, atomic bombs, and the battle of Okinawa—and takes up an amount of space similar to the illustration of Asian victims at Japanese hands.

In all, these texts offer a barebones synopsis of a war that caused, in their estimates, a total death toll in the order of 20 to 23 million. The underlying causes of the atrocities, however, are not explained in detail to the young readers. Other than the bare outline of events, there is no close reasoning of the causal chain of events. They are tuned to cognitive rather than conceptual comprehension and emotional rather than rational understanding. What is inculcated here is a simple pacifist sentiment that precludes any possibility of a just war: war is bad and unjust, because war kills and makes people suffer; it is an evil that hurts people like you, your family, and friends; the government that wages war is bad and can't be trusted to help and protect you. To be sure, abridged history stories for young children are sanitized cultural products, but they can nevertheless play a notable role in cultivating moral dispositions.

Compared to the foregoing two series, Gakken's national war is visually brighter, shown as an event carried out by childlike, inoffensive protagonists who are muddling through an international crisis. It is largely a "war story lite" about state and military leadership decisions, without showing any bloodshed or dead bodies. The war was instigated by the belligerent Japanese army that amassed power through the prolonged crisis and turned Japan into an oppressive military state. They waged a bad war and created a bad society, but as the plot moves forward, and people's lives deteriorate, not much suffering of Japanese or Asian victims is shown. When no suffering is shown, no one is held accountable for it; when no one is held accountable for suffering, it is possible to take a benign, no-guilt approach to war and colonial oppression. This less-perturbed approach is different from the foregoing two series, but the moral sentiment that "everyone cursed the war"[94] is nevertheless built into the storyline and comes across clearly to the readers. The much simplified, abridged history strives to be unthreatening to children, yet war is anything but glamorous. When historical memory is rendered into long-term cultural memory in this type of no-guilt educational manga, the moral sentiment is nevertheless anything but prowar or promilitary.

"Popular" History Manga Collections

Fujiko F. Fujio, Ishinomori Shōtarō, and Mizuki Shigeru are superstar manga artists who are celebrated for their classics from samurai adventures and space ventures to family stories and ghost stories, and are well-known beyond the manga and animated film industries. Over the years, their imaginary characters have become household names, like the delightful robocat Doraemon who is ubiquitous in popular culture from television shows and commercials, to paraphernalia like guitars, stationery, and refrigerator magnets. Such popular characters that enchanted and entertained successive generations growing up in postwar Japan have also been put to good use for producing popular history comics, rendering complex history into abridged stories for successive young generations. The result is a particular style of documentary history comic stories told by fictional narrators, unfolding with a kind of *Verfremdungseffekt* (alienation effect) of a Brechtian play that tells stories within stories to create a disengaged critical perspective. With commentary from lovable iconic characters, tragic dark history can be rendered into accessible morality tales rich with emotion, irony, and caricature.

These popular stories, produced by the manga artists or franchised by their production companies, are multivolume sets of history manga published in paperback that are less scholarly than the academic series and less constrained by curricular guidelines. These popular study manga take more artistic liberties than academic manga. They are imaginative in rendering war history into entertaining cultural products that are appealing to younger generations. To be sure, the artistry comes at a cost to comprehensive rigor and assessment of history. The complex reality that heroes, victims, and perpetrators are often the same people in defeat culture is left largely untouched. But readers nevertheless take away a cognitive understanding that contemporary Japanese history is a stained legacy and that being Japanese means they are burdened with that stain.

Fujiko F. Fujio Studio's *Doraemon* Series

As a winner of many prestigious awards and a phenomenal merchandizing success, Doraemon is perhaps the most fitting manga icon to entice elementary school children to take an interest in learning dark history. The section on World War II in the Nichinōken series takes up only 18 out of 220 pages, but it takes the readers from the depression and the Manchurian incident through the escalation of war and oppression in society, to the final catastrophic defeat. As the section sketches the main events, young readers are given succinct commentaries about them by the endearing robocat Doraemon and his dimwitted friend Nobita. It is mostly Nobita who conveys the moral evaluation of the war and wartime society through his visceral cries: "Ugh, another war?! I can't take another one." "That's a terrible law [to arrest people who opposed the government]." "I never want to go to war!" "They're even sending students to war." "Someone, stop [the atomic bomb]!"[95] These gut pacifist sentiments are Nobita's response to the violence and authoritarian oppression introduced in the text. Even though the number of pages devoted to the world war is slim, the morality tale to be learned here comes across clearly: the government, military, and business go to war to profit from it. The little people like us are dragged into war and are hurt by it. We don't trust leaders in power who hurt the little people.

To be sure, the ethics of care for the suffering of little people being taught here applies only within the limits of Japan's national boundary. Taking the blame for the horrors of war and mounting casualties are not the enemy forces in China or the United States but Japanese war mongers who instigated and promoted the war. Not even the atomic bombings of Hiroshima and Nagasaki are blamed on the Americans but on the Japanese leadership that missed chances to capitulate earlier, which might have forestalled those tragedies.[96] All told, this domestic perspective on the war depicts the Japanese as *both* perpetrators *and* victims.[97]

Mizuki Shigeru's *Shōwa History* Series

Mizuki's message about the war is direct and consistent: Fighting in the military to die for the country is utterly *absurd*. The powerful message that there is no heroism in fighting and dying in an unwinnable war is grounded directly in Mizuki's wartime experiences—near-death experiences from combat, bombardment, starvation, malaria, and ultimately amputation—which are all depicted in the series. This compelling message also flies in the face of the patriotic mantra of "honorable death" ingrained in his generation of soldiers. Born in 1922 and conscripted at age 20, Mizuki was sent to Rabaul in New Britain, Papua New Guinea, which was a central base of Japanese military and naval operations in the South Pacific at the time. He barely survived combat and repeated bombardment that overwhelmed the ill-equipped and scantily supplied Japanese forces. He survived, thanks to the help of friendly local tribes and was repatriated after the war. He started writing his war stories in the 1970s after garnering success with *Kitarō* in the 1960s and has since remained an antiwar voice, driven by his loyalty to his war buddies who died needlessly, and his indignation toward the military and state leaders who abandoned the soldiers on the battlefront without proper supplies, strategic planning, or compassion—causing preventable disasters and unnecessary loss of life.[98] Both Mizuki and his brother Sōhei survived, but not without sustaining life-changing

traumas like many others of their generation: Mizuki became an ampu-
tee, and his brother became a Class B war criminal for killing a POW
and was indicted and incarcerated in Sugamo prison.

Mizuki's war history, focused on the lowest rung of military life,
is an especially gripping tale that young readers can probably empathize with. The young men in the stories who went to war and died
for the country, however, are not heroic personalities that children
should aspire to. They are unfortunate scrawny characters, beaten
and broken, who succumbed to defeat. To be sure, there are extensive
battle scenes and gallant military encounters especially in the first six
months of the Pacific War—like Pearl Harbor—reminiscent of boys'
war stories popularized in major comic weeklies in the 1960s.[99] But as
losses mount and war prospects turn grim, the battles become more
chilling than thrilling and the soldiers become more pitiful than
brave. For hundreds of pages, readers wading through graphic illustrations of men falling and dying—in Leyte, Guadalcanal, Imphal,
and elsewhere—can recognize the protracted despair. There is no
exhilarating valor.[100]

Mizuki's accounts are largely victim narratives within the triad of
narratives explored in this book. The stories of wrongs inflicted on
Japanese soldiers—whose survival rate was atrocious—overshadow
those inflicted on Asian people whose lands they invaded.[101] This narrow focus on one's own suffering does not necessarily derive from the
intent to whitewash or divert attention from perpetrator history, though
personal narratives focused on local experience can depict a narrow
range of events that often exclude distant suffering. On the contrary, it
is important to recognize these stories as powerful indictments of the
Japanese state and military that dragged people through an unnecessary war, killed them needlessly, and betrayed their trust until the bitter
end. The anguished stories barely conceal anger toward the deception
of the unjust military establishment. War memory here is framed by the
"pent-up anger toward war" that gnawed at the survivors like Mizuki for
many decades.[102] In the final volume, Mizuki takes over as the narrator
to offer his reflections and reminiscences. Here, his indictment of the
Japanese state as the perpetrator is no longer disguised. The antistate,
antimilitary message to the young readers is unmistakable:

> I really hated militarism. People deluded themselves into believ-
> ing that anything daring and brave would bring luck and fortune.
> They parroted all along: "Loyalty to the Emperor. Patriotism to
> the State." . . . We were not supposed to think about "ourselves" but
> be happy to die as "good subjects" when the draft letter arrived.

If truth be told, people who lived through early Shōwa [era] were bullied by the State . . . The "military" was like a cancer that had to be surgically removed [by defeat].[103]

Ishinomori Shōtarō's *Manga History of Japan* Series
In *Manga History of Japan*, the Asia-Pacific War period takes up nearly 300 pages and is presented as a descent into a ruinous war through many ill-fated political maneuvers and erroneous decisions. The dominant story is that of the fierce political struggle among a cadre of elite men in power. In that struggle, the bellicose army leadership ultimately rises to power and recklessly thrusts the nation into a world war that ends in a devastating downfall. The bickering rivalries, mistrust, miscalculations, and miscoordination at the heart of the story are recounted in much detail: the leaders fail to heed warnings, miss opportunities to negotiate, lose strategic momentum, misplace their confidence in wishful thinking, and make incompetent decisions. As the military amasses more power over time through emergency legislation and totalitarian repression, the nation becomes a police state. All told, this is a disheartening history of a nation led by misguided villains without any wise heroes who stood firm enough to foil them.

Ishinomori's comic history, unlike the foregoing examples, does not rely on familiar manga characters for narration but develops the plot solely through authorial narratives and graphic depictions of dynamic events and encounters. Taking a populist approach, a regular cast of seven or eight people appears throughout as ordinary people voicing their thoughts and feelings about the unfolding events. Their commentaries are presented as casual conversations in a mom-and-pop diner, where the proprietor family and regular patrons shoot the breeze over meals and drinks. They are imaginary witnesses and bystanders of wartime Japan: independent-minded people who own small establishments and regular customers who drop in from all walks of life: newspaper journalists feeling the squeeze of state censorship, youths at schools or in show business being called up to military service, foreign ministry workers confessing to being clueless about the ongoing diplomatic whirlwind, blue-collar workers being laid off from struggling factories, and others. As the war escalates, they feel by turns apprehensive and ambivalent, surprised and cheered, ignorant and manipulated, fearful and confused, resentful and weary, and ultimately, desperate and indignant that the war is dragging the country into an abyss with no end in sight.

The Japanese are clearly shown as the aggressors, not pitiful victims. The reasons why this war escalated to such levels of brutality or why the military callously abandoned Japanese civilians in Manchuria, Saipan, and Okinawa—driving them to desperate mass suicides—are never fully explained, however.[104] While young readers are offered insights that this war should have been and could have been prevented, they are given no moral or conceptual means to reflect on practical alternative possibilities that could have been pursued.

Successful pop history projects of manga celebrities like these exemplify the power of cultural memory forged outside the reach of state educational institutions. Phenomenally effective in reaching youths—though much overlooked by scholarship—manga rode the wave of a generational turnover of Japanese youth, for whom it continues to be, with television and the Internet, a compelling, indispensable mode of communication and resource for information. Communicating history stories by manga is a generationally distinct, and decidedly freer, mode of transmitting memory, embraced first by the baby boomers who welcomed the new expressive voice unencumbered by traditional literature, plays, and poetry. Those readers were also happy to turn up their noses at "serious" moralizing work by the wartime generation that controlled the public sphere. Having sensed that those adults had themselves wrought "something dreadful that happened in the past," the younger generation had good reason to distrust the traditional carriers of memory and celebrate an alternative sphere of communication of their very own. Manga stories, then, became *their* stories and allowed them to indulge in subverting the authoritarian gaze while also bonding with their peers. It is therefore not surprising that mistrust of state authority is a salient element of pop history, even if the criticism is often tactfully muted. There is neither glamour nor valor in the way most mainstream manga history depicts those responsible for the war. In this sense, young readers are more likely to come away disheartened and distressed than entertained by the illustrations of the unenviable legacy that they have inherited as Japanese nationals.

Cultural Trauma as Morality Tale for Generations of Postwar Children

British historian Timothy Ashplant once noted that "the past is not automatically passed between generations, but must be actively transmitted so that later generations accept that past as meaningful."[105] In defeated nations, that meaning has been often found in transforming the stigma of the past into a moral quality that helps purge the contamination.[106] In Japan's case, this transformation work is framed often as a moral responsibility to nurture sentiments in young generations to denounce future wars. This is, however, preferably to be done without undermining the moral standing of the parent or grandparent generation who waged the war. Thus the task is often said to be about communicating the "reality of war" to the postwar generations who do not know war (*sensō o shiranai sedai*), who are "blessed in ignorance of one of humankind's oldest, most repugnant activities."[107] This discourse has allowed the wartime generation to keep much control over the mnemonic scripts of the past war *and* the derivative lessons learned from them. It is within this intergenerational power dynamic that the emotional memory of "something dreadful that happened in Japanese history" has been passed on to successor generations. The successor generations have, in turn, confronted that history with a mixture of dread, curiosity, anxiety, and also a desire to decontaminate both their families and themselves.

In this chapter, we have seen that Japanese children are raised in an environment encoded with generational memory that often encourages them to develop negative moral sentiments about the war. The "encouragement" comes in subtle and unsubtle ways, as young children develop gut instincts that "something dreadful happened in the past," even if they don't fully understand what or why. Even when they encounter emotional memory of terror that seems unfathomable, many can still understand that, unlike the wars in video games and television shows, this one *really* engulfed the lives of their grandparents when they were small children like themselves. It was so bad that children like themselves lost their families, friends, homes, then couldn't escape and died. From such "shock and awe" war stories that elicit a visceral response—in animated films, textbook photos, peace education, school instruction, popular history, and more—they may learn to empathize and identify with those war orphans, malnourished children, bombed children, injured children, and abandoned children who lost everything that sustained them.[108] Over time, this kind of emotional socialization that taps into instincts for self-preservation turns into "feeling rules," with which children learn to internalize how they are *supposed* to feel about war in a pacifist country.[109] Clearly, this choice of strategy is not geared toward raising nascent critical thinkers who would assume responsibility for the past atrocious deeds of their forefathers as in a culture of contrition, like Germany, but focused instead on *not* raising the type of Japanese people who could perpetrate another abhorrent war in the future.

The impact of generational memory on the emotional and normative socialization of children that we have discussed in this chapter, however, is not easily measured by robust empirical indicators. How children respond to and internalize messages encoded in their environment can vary depending on different factors and may also change over time. Cross-sectional attitudinal surveys that often serve as proxy indicators of socialization and identity are therefore best supplemented with multiple sources of empirical information, including longitudinal data, toward a method of triangulation. For this reason, I rely in the chapters of this book on multiple sources by, for, and on postwar generations from surveys, interviews, focus groups, and public fora, to blogs, websites, essays, and letters to newspapers in an attempt to build a *collage*. Even so, the effects of generational memory on moral and national identity making are captured indirectly and inferentially based on assumptions about the probable link between cause and effect.

What we learn from surveys, however, shows that transmitting war memory that invokes cultural trauma has probably made an indelible mark on attitudes toward future wars. For decades, the antipathy toward the prospect of exercising military power has been consistently high and especially so among the young. For example, Japan ranks *lowest* among 59 nations in the proportion of people who are willing to fight for their country. Only 15–33%, depending on the survey, are willing to do so; this figure is also lower for younger people in their 20s and 30s, and for women.[110] Likewise, the proportion of those who support the total ban on nuclear arms (the Three Non-Nuclear Principles) has been always high and is endorsed today by as much as 80–90% of middle and high school students.[111] Remarkably, the antipathy toward exercising military force has scarcely fluctuated even in the last decade when nuclear threats from North Korea and China have intensified and people reporting their fear of becoming entangled in a war have doubled.[112] It seems reasonable to say that these antipathies are consistent and are a key part of the moral identity that is diffused with generational memory.

The powerful cultural code that "something dreadful happened in the past" can also signal an underlying apprehension about state power that wrought untold deaths and even demanded "voluntary" deaths from its subjects in the name of patriotic sacrifice. It is therefore not surprising that the antipathy toward military force would extend to a wariness and suspicion of patriotism associated with obedience to state authority. Japan ranks quite low—71st among 74 countries—in level of professed patriotism, with 54.2% of its people claiming to feel pride in their nation.[113] This trend is also especially pronounced for younger people in their 20s and 30s and for women.[114] Among high school students, only a handful claim to take pride in Japan's national anthem and national flag, which are fiercely controversial vestiges of the militarist nation-state. Attachment to those core national symbols hovers around 11–13%, which is much lower than 54–55% in the United States, and 48–50% in China. Japanese high school students also have a high proportion who are *not* proud of their country (48.3%), compared to the United States (37.1%) and China (20.3%).[115] The sense of detachment and skepticism toward the state resonates with the significant destabilization of trust experienced in the post-defeat society. This mistrust of patriotic devotion and loyalty encoded in generational memory has likely helped keep the heroic patriotic narratives out of the everyday cultural material for teaching children like those reviewed in this chapter. This effacement of patriotic-heroic narratives in illustrating Japan's path to World War II has been a long-term project of the proponents of victim narratives as well as perpetrator narratives.

Critics will surely point to the many flaws of the scare tactics applied to children to swear off future wars—for good reason. The pressure can breed insecurity and anxiety in children who deserve a safe upbringing as all children do. Moreover, their exposure to domestic suffering like air raids and atomic bombs can be blown out of proportion, when considering that the deaths that the Japanese inflicted on Asian victims were several times greater. Moreover, the heavy exposure to suffering at home can breed the much-criticized "victim consciousness" that can relegate the understanding of perpetrator responsibility to the sidelines. Above all, it fails to inculcate a strong awareness that the suffering, however painful, was the result of a war the Japanese started themselves and not a calamity that befell like a natural disaster. Most criticisms from the left also make implicit comparison to the "German model" in shaming the Japanese practices of coming to terms with the past as evasive and dishonest.[116] However, critics from the other end, the provocative radical right, charge to the contrary that scare-inducing antimilitarist discourse misinforms and misleads the children into believing that everything and anything about the past war was evil, including the sacrifices of brave soldiers and loyal families who are worthy of respect. In this view, Japanese children are exposed to too many perpetrator narratives that undermine their self-esteem and confidence about being Japanese. It claims that the victor's narrative that Japan waged a "bad" war is dishonest and should be revised, so that children can develop a "healthier" sense of Japanese identity.[117] In many ways, the representations of the war today are caught in the middle of these political perspectives without clear resolution, resulting in a slow, incremental, back and forth development.

As we have seen in this chapter, the museum exhibits, textbooks, and popular history books that young children can access today are actually not *entirely* dominated by victim narratives at the expense of perpetrator accounts. Precisely because such perpetrator accounts had made inroads in the past decades, peace museum exhibits, textbook illustrations, and nonfiction stories were targeted in a round of political backlash by the neonationalist right who sought to "correct" those problems in the late 1990s and 2000s, as discussed in the previous chapter. In this environment, public agencies were pressured into withdrawing funding for municipal peace museums, and textbook illustrations took a conservative turn.[118] New comics appeared such as Kobayashi Yoshinori's *On War* series, aimed to resurrect the popularity of heroic patriotic narratives and supported by neoconservative media and Internet sites.[119] Soon a political movement "Tsukurukai" was afoot, embraced by the malcontent and alienated young segments of society who vehemently protested "bowing" to China and Korea.[120] After this new pendulum swing, the stalemate among the triad of cultural trauma narratives moved to the next round, with new actors and new generations carrying the torch for their teams.

Thus, beneath the broader cultural premise of the pacifist nation, the plural narratives of dark history continue to cast a shadow on the nation's political consciousness. The fault lines found in the history and civics texts are mirrored in the memory politics of the young as they enter the fray to contest issues that impact their generation. In the 2000s when Japan faced a series of critical legislative measures on national defense and education, the youth's responses undoubtedly mirrored those fault lines. Whether or not they favored the controversial neoconservative initiatives to enhance the state's operative capabilities in military contingencies, or its ability to cultivate patriotic instruction, observant young people were evidently aware that these measures would alter the cultural script of the "bad" military in the moral landscape of the twenty-first century. The memory of military violence as cultural trauma remained a common referent for them to gauge the present, even as they were divided in their views. For example, in a recent letter to the young readers' column of the *Asahi*

newspaper, an 18-year-old male student, echoing the antiwar and antistate discourses of previous generations, wrote angrily:

> Now that "patriotic" instruction will be forced on us, isn't that
> like going back to the compulsory education of prewar "milita-
> rism"? Although the Constitution renounces war, [the revised
> Fundamental Law of Education] could eventually send us high
> school students to the battlefront again.[121]

Another 18-year-old female student voiced her concern in the same
vein, referring explicitly to her lessons from school:

> I am tired of hearing the government exalt "Strong Japan" and
> "Japanese Power" . . . it reminds me of the prewar militarism that
> we read about in school textbooks . . . Why do we have to be so
> strong anyway? And what for?[122]

Realists retorted against such misgivings, as a 22-year-old male student
expressed:

> Sentimental chants of "Peace! Peace!" alone can't bring any
> peace . . . We don't live anymore in Imperial Japan under the Meiji
> Constitution. I can't possibly imagine that politicians in democratic
> and pacifist Japan today want to go to war. But around the world,
> there are nations that will violate the peace of others. If Japan is
> invaded, how are we going to confront it? That's why we need the
> contingency law. It's important . . . in order to realize the ideal of
> peace and to maintain Japan's sovereignty.[123]

As we have seen, the moral framework that consigns war to
the category of "absolute evil" derives from negative affect based
on bitter experience, not critical reflections on or judicious reasoning regarding social justice. This approach can be effective in
unleashing popular antiwar emotions, but it also undermines an
understanding of the vastly complicated world of human animosity,
greed, conformity, and self-preservation, muddied by realities that
are never clear-cut or black and white. A casualty of the passionate
project to "Just Say No" to war, paradoxically, is the development of
a clear, expressive vocabulary to articulate feelings and understandings of moral conscience, guilt, responsibility, and injustice that lie
in the gray zone between the binary formula—vocabulary that can

represent the possibility that good and evil actions are not always mutually exclusive and yet demand responsibility for those actions. It is only then that the circle of empathy for the suffering of others can widen and expand toward a universalized understanding of war and peace. Such a project has only just begun.

due to the growing perceptions of threat triggered by North Korea's missile launches in 1998, 2006, 2009, 2013, and 2014;[13] worsening territorial disputes with China and South Korea; and the Abe government's intensified efforts to legitimate rearmament. In 2014, the government introduced a revised interpretation of Article 9 that would allow the SDF to participate in military actions of collective self-defense in limited cases.[14] This move, which the government called "proactive peace," has been largely unpopular in the court of public opinion, where the stalemate remains unresolved.[15] As of this writing, the contentious issues surrounding the use of SDF for collective self-defense has yet to be fully debated in parliament or translated into specific legislation.[16]

Moving Beyond the Culture of Defeat: Three Visions of Moral Recovery

The central idea of this book is that culture is shaped by memories of violent conflicts and their outcomes. I have argued that in defeated societies, this memory work does not produce a monolithic and consensual culture but a divided public discourse. War memories illustrated in this book recount different versions of the past that make the past more bearable and the present more palatable; they also vie for recognition to influence future generations and legitimate their self-identity. Overcoming defeat requires this type of *moral recovery* work which is just as important as economic recovery to revitalize postwar society.[17] The culture of defeat is fueled by a shared desire to recover from the setback even if people's specific visions for the future are not identical. Those visions as expressed in memory narratives are often incongruent—as we have seen in the narratives of fallen heroes, victims, and perpetrators—and prioritize different aspects of moral recovery. Japan's long defeat, then, is a process of moral recovery work, to recover from stigma, to heal from the losses, and to right the wrongs. The long standoff on the question of revising the constitution and becoming a "normal country" is deeply symptomatic of the domestic impasse over the different means of attaining "recovery."

In the post–Cold War world, political dichotomies such as "left versus right," "conservative versus liberal," or "hawks versus doves" pegged to political party affiliations increasingly lost their illustrative power on the map of political culture. As memory politics also cuts across party lines, it makes sense to identify different approaches to moral recovery by orientations within the political culture rather than by party ideologies and affiliations.[18] The three approaches that I outline here are different options for Japan to move forward on the questions of constitutional peace and the "history problem." These approaches—*nationalism, pacifism,* and *reconciliationism*—are direct logical extensions of the three memory narratives discussed in this book and suggest the pathways beyond the long defeat. They are preoccupied with different concerns and visions for the future, and Japan must ultimately find some compromises among them.

The *nationalist approach* calls for overcoming the past by advancing national strength rather than through international reconciliation. It emphasizes shared national belonging and collective attachment to a historical community and derives a social identity from that traditional heritage. People adopting this approach tend to use the language of national pride and resent the loss of national prestige and international standing that came with defeat. They vary along a spectrum of intensity from aggressive hardliners to moderates in their search for respect, and vary from realist to idealist in seeking the competitive edge over other nations, like those in neighboring East Asia. Their use of heroic narratives of the war is consistent with their preoccupation to remove the *stigma* of the past and gain equal recognition from the United States and the West as part of "overcoming" the long defeat.

The *pacifist approach* espouses an antimilitary ethos and a pacifist creed as part of atonement for the Asia-Pacific War. It considers war as the enemy and mistrusts the state as an agent for peaceful conflict resolution. Pacifism is a source of humanist pride as well as a collective identity that allows Japan to recover its moral prestige from the deviant past. This people-centered vision focuses on all victims of war violence and nuclear threats, and uses the language of human suffering and human insecurity wrought by military action. People adopting this approach vary along a spectrum of intensity from aggressive to moderate in their protest of military violence, and from national to international in their images of victims, like those killed by atomic bombs and air raids, and the refugees in Syria.

The *reconciliationist approach* espouses rapprochement in East Asia as atonement for Japan's perpetrator past. This approach prioritizes better relations with Japan's regional neighbors and crosses party lines in that regard. To different degrees, people in this category share the recognition that an acknowledgment of past guilt is indispensable to move forward and redressing the wrongs is the only viable way for Japan to build mutual trust in the global world. They use a range of language from human rights and transitional justice to friendships and pluralism, and they emphasize the requirements of good relations with regional neighbors. Embraced by an eclectic mix of internationally minded leaders in politics, business, scholars, and civic activists, people vary along a spectrum from aggressive to moderate in their quest for redress and justice, and from realist to idealist in pursuing rapprochement.[19] This approach is cosmopolitan, presupposing justice as a universal value, whether it comes from Christianity, feminism, socialism, transnational intellectual sensibilities, or declarations of international agencies.

The parallel horizons inhabited by people subscribing to these approaches were jolted into being by the new international realities of the 2000s and 2010s when military threats and belligerence increased with a multitude of international events: the missile launches from China and North Korea; the failure to be part of the victorious coalition in the Gulf War (1990); 9/11 and the ensuing "war against terror"; and the failure to gain permanent membership in the UN Security Council (reserved for the victors of WWII) (2005). Japan's ideal of peace diplomacy collided with the reality of shifting geopolitics, and reshuffling priorities became inevitable. Confidence in peace diplomacy was shaken by the realization that "checkbook diplomacy" was no longer sufficient in supporting Kuwait; at the same time, confidence in reconciliation diplomacy was shaken by the rising anti-Japan nationalist sentiments in the region. Thus contingency legislation was enacted in 2003 and 2004 in the wake of 9/11, and, soon after, the new defense guidelines that designated North Korea and China as potential threats were established (2004).[20] In the same year, Japan's Diet approved dispatching 1,000 SDF troops to southern Iraq on a "humanitarian recovery mission" as part of the UN Peacekeeping operations (2003–2008).[21] These developments among others challenged the effectiveness of Japan's peace strategy based on Article 9 and increasingly strained the established memory narratives.

The Nationalist Approach: From Defeat to Respect and National Belonging

From aggressive neonationalism to moderate civic and cultural nationalism, a nationalist approach subscribes to the notion that furthering the national interest will bring the best solution to the "history problem." Based on a sense of shared national belonging and attachment to a historical community, this approach partakes of a certain cultural resistance to cosmopolitanism.[22] Recent Japanese prime ministers making official visits to the Yasukuni Shrine on commemoration day can be identified in this category (often called "neonationalist"), as well as those who passively condone traditional symbols of national honor like the national flag and the national anthem. Many in this category favor revising the constitution, as Japan's Prime Minister Abe Shinzō described at a special new year's interview with the *Sankei* newspaper in 2014. Asked about his vision for Japan in the year 2020, the year that Tokyo will host the summer Olympic Games, he responded:

> [I foresee that by 2020] the constitutional revision will be done. At that stage, I want Japan to fully recover its prestige and be recognized respectfully for its momentous contributions to world peace and stability in the region. Japan's higher prestige will restore the balance of power in the Asia region.[23]

Emphasizing the recovery of prestige and respect, Abe makes clear that he wants to restore some fundamentals of nationhood that he believes were lost after defeat. His often-quoted ambition to "leave behind the postwar regime" (*sengo rejiimu karano dakkyaku*) is precisely about ending the long defeat, overcoming the cultural trauma of "a weaker Japan" that has been the subtext in postwar political culture, and gaining equal recognition in the world. In practical terms, this means strengthening Japan and ending military disempowerment and the one-sided dependence on the United States as a "client state." An example of this nationalist vision is encapsulated in the revised draft constitution (*kenpō kaisei sōan*) announced in April 2012 by Abe's political party (LDP): it is a nativized, domesticated version of the constitution, emphasizing tradition, patriotism, and duties to the state; and, significantly, it changes Article 9, replacing the renunciation of possessing a military force with the establishment of a National Defense Army (*kokubōgun*).[24]

The nationalists' impetus to inculcate national pride and patriotism in the country is readily explicable when we consider the erosion of support for traditionalist sentiments in recent decades. National pride has declined in recent decades from 57% in 1983 to 39% in 2008, and it is consistently lower in the younger generations.[25] Japanese high school students, for example, have the lowest sense of national pride compared to American and Chinese counterparts.[26] Japan's younger generations born after the baby boom also report that they have no religion (neither Buddhism nor Shintoism) and no sense of attachment to the Emperor.[27] The nationalists' drive to cultivate patriotism in schools today actually emanates from a sense that their power base is eroding among the new generations who are disengaged and disinterested. In this sense, the mutual provocations that fan the perceptions of threat in relations with China are effective tools to promote a stronger sense of national belonging and solidarity among disenfranchised groups.

This approach to "overcoming" the past is complicated. The accusation by the West that Japan is not doing enough to accept responsibility for World War II war crimes invites anger from nationalists who resent not being a member of the established Western clique. Not being firmly established in the European order, Japan's path to shedding the stigma and asserting its established position is more arduous than Germany's. Taking account of this international stratification, the hurdle for *recognition* for non-Western, nonwhite nations is doubly high and perpetually hard to clear.[28] *Nationalistic remembering* is, then, not directed to reconciliation efforts but to gaining moral and strategic superiority.[29] In this sense, the moral recovery from the long defeat is directed to revising the script of defeat, questioning the legitimacy of the Tokyo Trials, the devaluing of the Yasukuni Shrine, and China's victory in the Asia-Pacific War. From this vantage point, China is a country that exploits historical grievances to promote political gain. Relations with South and North Korea should also be "normal," that is, uncompromised by Japan's guilt and uninhibited by constitutional constraints.

In this perspective, an apology is not a compelling, ennobling act that exemplifies strength of character and courage to take responsibility for the dark past, but a self-defaming and belittling act that exposes weakness and gives license to opponents to endlessly disgrace and diminish Japan.[30] Drawing on the earlier discussion on *generational proximity* in family memory, it is not surprising that the children and grandchildren of the wartime power elite strongly resist apologizing for Japan's wartime deeds. As an inheritor of a political dynasty and family memory, Prime Minister Abe Shinzō's case is a well-known example.[31]

The Pacifist Approach: From Defeat to Healing and Human Security

The pacifist creed has long been an important counterweight to nationalism in postwar Japan, and its proponents delivered on that mission months after Japan dispatched the SDF to southern Iraq to take part in its first "humanitarian recovery mission." In June 2004, a group of nine prominent Japanese public intellectuals gathered in Tokyo to announce the founding of the "Article 9 Association" (A9A, Kyūjō no kai) to protect the constitution from the state's intensified efforts to revise it. The high-profile cast ensured that the group would draw wide public attention. All the founding members were of the wartime generation and had well-established credentials as postwar pacifists: Oda Makoto and Tsurumi Shunsuke had been leaders of the anti-Vietnam War movement; Ōe Kenzaburo, the Nobel laureate, is known for his pacifist conscience and outspoken public criticism of the state, evoking comparisons with Germany's Günter Grass. Miki Mutsuko had been active in the movement to attain redress for "comfort women" and joined the Asian Women's Fund in 1995. Others included Kato Shūichi, a leading public intellectual, and Okudaira Yasuhiro, a prominent constitutional scholar. The Article 9 Association's manifesto reads as follows:

> Let our Constitution Article 9 shine upon this [changing] world, so we may hold hands with our fellow pacifist citizens around the world. For this purpose, we must reselect Japan's constitution and Article 9 as sovereigns of this nation . . . as it is our responsibility to shape the future of this country.
> We appeal to the world to do everything possible to prevent the revision of this Constitution, and to protect it for future peace in Japan and the world.[32]

The popular response to this appeal was resounding: within a year and a half, more than 4,000 local citizens' groups of the Article 9 Association sprang into action. Ten years later, there are more than 7,500 A9A groups of all imaginable stripes: A9A for film makers, poets, women, children, the disabled, patients, doctors, musicians, scientists, the fisheries business, trading companies, the mass media, Buddhists, Greens, the Communist Party, and so on; and local community groups have sprouted by the thousands across towns, cities, and prefectures.[33] An international petition drive ensued, organized by the Global Article 9 Campaign to Abolish War, which was established by the youth movement Peace Boat (2005).

The accusation by the West that Japan is suffering from collective self-pity in its vow never to allow another war that would create more Hiroshimas and Nagasakis, misses the significance of pledging disarmament for a country with 700 years of military tradition and three victories in international wars.[34] The pride in this radical break with the past is such that a citizen's group nominated Article 9 for the Nobel Peace Prize in 2014.[35]

The popular appropriation of Article 9 as a form of civic identity was long in the making. Japan's postwar pacifism, historian Akazawa Shirō explains, was born out of a profound skepticism for state-defined "justice" that wrought massive sacrifices and immoral acts of violence.[36] As war memory fostered persistent antipathy for the military and mistrust of the government's ability to control the military, Article 9 came to function as an important constraint on the government that allayed those fears. What emerged over time was an antiwar pacifism based on a desire for human security, regret for a violent past, and a promise to be model global citizens in the future. Peace is therefore a civic identity and a strategy of moral recovery, expressing contrition as well as an aspiration for an elevated moral status in the eyes of the world. This multifaceted discursive practice of peace is therefore fundamentally different from an antiwar pacifism based on questions of war responsibility.

The A9A was a corrective to defy the resurgence of aggressive nationalism in the 2000s; it reasserted the pride in a pacifist identity that had become a standard moral framework learned in schools and historically found role models in both Christian pacifists—like Nitobe Inazo, Yanaihara Tadao, and Uchimura Kanzo—and atheist pacifists—like Bertrand Russell and Albert Einstein who led the Pugwash movement dedicated to eliminating "all weapons of mass destruction (nuclear, chemical and biological) and of war as a social institution to settle international disputes."[37] However, only six months after the A9A was launched, the Japanese government announced the new National Defense Program Outline (NDPO) that broadened and realigned the range of SDF activities to react rapidly and multifunctionally to domestic and international emergencies. In this policy, China and North Korea were identified as "potential threats."[38]

More recently, new civic organizations and networks have sprung into action to defend the integrity of Article 9 and the constitution in response to the cabinet's decision, announced on July 1, 2014, to reinterpret Article 9 to permit the SDF to participate in some level of collective self-defense. Those civic groups, consisting of scholars, public intellectuals, activists, and other public figures, who are mostly of the postwar generation, vow to safeguard constitutionalism and constitutional democracy, and hold the government accountable to them. An example of these groups is Save Constitutional Democracy. Like the movement to petition the Nobel Peace Prize Committee mentioned above, it represents an updated brand of pacifism that seeks a broader constituency to hold off further challenges to Article 9 by the nationalists in government.[39] From this perspective, constitutional pacifism embraced by popular, democratic choice symbolizes the ultimate moral recovery from the long defeat.[40]

The Reconciliationist Approach: From Defeat to
Justice and Moral Responsibility

A reconciliationist approach to overcoming the past prioritizes international dialogue to build relations with regional neighbors with
antagonistic histories, based on mutual respect and, ultimately, mutual
trust. Japan's acknowledgment of its history of aggression is indispensable in this regard, together with an acceptance of guilt and an effort
to redress the wrongs. In the West German case, the effort to promote
mutual understanding of the antagonistic histories with its neighbors
started within years of the war's end. Under UNESCO's auspices, West
Germany started an international dialogue first with France (1951),
and then, with the advent of *Ostpolitik*, with Poland (1972). The joint
textbook commissions carried out bilateral reconciliation work successfully by all accounts, and continue the efforts today with ongoing
institutional support and state funding.[41] By contrast, Japan's joint
history research projects with South Korea and China started only in
the 1990s and 2000s, and with limited institutional and supranational
resources compared to the German case. During this time Japan carried out both state and civilian projects with South Korea and China.[42]
One such effort was a trinational joint history textbook called *History
that Opens the Future* published in 2005 by a group of 54 scholars, teachers, and citizens from Japan, China, and South Korea; it was the first
textbook of its kind in East Asia published in all three languages.[43]
The preface reads as follows:

> [This textbook] is about the history of East Asia in Japan, China,
> and South Korea.
>   East Asia's history in the nineteenth and twentieth centuries is
> scarred by the wounds of invasion, war, and human oppression
> that cannot be washed away.
>   But . . . East Asia also has a long tradition of cultural exchange
> and friendship as many people work across national boundaries,
> committed to building a bright future.
>   We can build a brighter, peaceful future on this beautiful earth
> by inheriting the positive assets of the past, while thoroughly
> reflecting [*tetteitekini hansei*] on the mistakes as well.
>   How can we learn from the lessons of history to build a future
> that guarantees peace, democracy, and human rights in East
> Asia? Let's think about it together. (*History That Opens the Future*
> [*Mirai o hiraku rekishi*] 2005)[44]

A joint history textbook project presumes that a shared historical perspective is possible based on some shared universal values such as peace building, democracy, and human rights, as this preface describes. The effort calls for a search for a common language, and, as much as possible, a shared framework of understanding and interpretation. The common language behind *History That Opens the Future* is Japan's history of imperial aggression and its damage to modern East Asia. The language of perpetration ties the three national histories together in what might be considered a primer on the origins of Japan's "history problem." Here the perpetrators are delineated clearly (Japan), as are the heroes who resisted the incursions (China and Korea), and the victims who suffered (China, Korea, and Japan). It also provides a blueprint for a possible resolution, which is that Japan must offer a full "apology and restitution [*shazai* and *hoshō*]" for its imperialism, invasions, and exploitation if East Asia is to find true healing, justice, and long-term reconciliation.[45]

Finding this common language is central in reconciliation work, yet hard to attain.[46] Korean-American sociologist Gi-Wook Shin points to four key areas of reconciliation in East Asia—apology politics, joint history research, litigation, and regional exchanges—where the search for common ground is necessary for progress to be made.[47] At a pragmatic level, it means that former adversaries, former perpetrators, and victims must set aside the hate and prejudice that have stewed for decades and find a reservoir of patience and good will. This process is also complicated ideologically by the "universal" international norm that defines a common language of justice in the global arena: human rights, democracy, and international norms such as crimes against peace (wars of aggression) and crimes against humanity (genocide, torture, persecution, etc.).[48] It was precisely the failure to find common ground in the understanding of "justice" that eventually ended the government-sponsored bilateral history research committees of the 2000s.[49]

Indeed, recent polls show that only a small fraction of Chinese and South Korean people (less than 11%) actually believe that Japan embraces pacifism or reconciliationism, while much larger proportions (one-third to one-half of respondents) believe that Japan upholds militarism. At the same time, many in China and South Korea point to Japan's "history problem" and the territorial disputes as obstacles that stand in the way of building better relationships.[50] At the same time, Japanese views favoring China and South Korea have also declined significantly and are currently at an all-time low. Japanese who said they liked China peaked in 1980 (78.6%) and declined to the lowest level in 2012 (18%). The decline was sharp particularly after the Tiananmen Square massacre (1988), the anti-Japan riots (2005), and the flare up of confrontations over the Senkaku/Diaoyu Islands disputes (2010). Japan's view favoring South Korea reached a peak (62.2%) in 2011—rising steadily after President Kim Dae-Jung lifted the ban on importing Japanese popular culture (1998), through jointly hosting the FIFA World Cup (2002), and the growing popularity of the Korean "wave" of popular culture (K-Pop)—but promptly plummeted (to 39.2%) after President Lee Myung-Bak inflamed the Takeshima/Dokdo Island dispute with his visit to the island in 2012.[51]

Indeed in the second phase of the trilateral scholars' efforts to build international dialogue and mutual understanding in the 2010s, the political and social climate had grown considerably worse than in the 2000s. The follow-up publication,[52] which had set itself the ambitious task of providing an overarching regional history of East Asia, reflected this difficult climate. Finding common ground on the understanding of "justice" seemed strained, as evidenced by the failure to synthesize the section on collective memory that could have led to an understanding of the most pressing issue facing the three nations, the territorial disputes. Yet it is this type of painstaking and persistent work of cultivating civilian dialogue, however difficult it may be, that ultimately paves the way for future generations to pursue the task of East Asia's reconciliation. These efforts join the assiduous work of many activist-scholars like Utsumi Aiko, Ōnuma Yasuaki, and others who have labored to achieve transitional justice in Asia over the decades.[53]

As Germany's reconciliation history shows, rapprochement ultimately presupposes a compelling apology, an admission of wrongdoing, to achieve a common sense of justice. In this approach, an apology is an ennobling act that enhances the public perception of the apologizer for the profound courage to admit one's evildoing. Precisely contrary to the Japanese nationalists' view noted earlier, staring down one's own capacity for evil and accepting responsibility for it enhances rather than diminishes a person's moral stature. An apology here becomes a pathway to transcend stigma, serving one's interest in accruing symbolic capital, in a cultural milieu where self-reflection is highly prized. Not all cultures, however subscribe to the notion that "an unexamined life is not worth living." When cultural resources do not exist that allow for a pathway to prize apology through self-reflection, the prospect of reconciliation is diminished.

The nationalist, pacifist, and reconciliationist approaches have been at odds, vying for dominance in different disputes over the past decades. They do not coalesce into a unifying national strategy for overcoming the past, and they demand different strategies for political legitimacy and politics of social integration. The pacifist approach has been particularly strong in the areas of family memory and the school curriculum, as the previous chapters in this book showed. Mending the broken fences and healing the deep scars of history, however, will take more than the advocacy and practice of pacifism, however well-intentioned and well-practiced. Moral recovery in current geopolitics is achievable only when respect can be gained from past adversaries and victims. The new tensions between Japan, China, and the Koreas make this task even more difficult.

Is There a Global Model of Reconciliation?

In the shifting world of memory making, the German model of repenting the past is fast becoming something of a "global standard," recognized by the successive Truth and Reconciliation commissions in different parts of the world. The Holocaust has become a globalized cultural trauma that may serve also to represent universal moral sensibilities.[54] Whether a "global standard" to right past wrongs—derived from a belief system that conceives sin to be addressed by repentance, forgiveness, and redemption—can acquire profound resonance outside the Judeo-Christian civilizational orbit remains an unanswered question. Whether a model of atonement for the Holocaust based on European anti-Semitism can find effective political traction in Asia and elsewhere, and be recognized as a "universal model" to reconcile disparate national memories in the global world, is sure to become one of the major problems in the politics of memory in the future.

This "global norm" is a "Western liberal norm," which suggests today that *not* addressing past wrongs through truth-seeking, confession, apology, and forgiveness is uncivilized, backward, narrow minded, self-serving, and, by implication, unworthy of full membership in the established Western world. In this process, the ideals of human rights and freedom, born out of a Euro-American Weltanschauung and centered on a liberal democratic discourse are imposed on the non-West, which aspires to join the civilized world.[55] On the one hand, this global discourse has made inroads into Japan's memory culture, enabling the burgeoning redress movements, often in the form of litigation that continue to this day. On the other hand, it has radicalized racial antagonism from those who resent the implication of moral inferiority in the "insufficient" reckoning with the past. In the emergent "politics of regret" that has come to dominate the global discourse on wars and atrocities since the 1990s,[56] an explicit *hierarchy* of "civilized" behavior has also emerged.

In discussing the culture of defeat in Turkey, Russia, and Japan, Turkish-American political scientist Ayse Zarakol emphasizes that the quest for security and equal recognition of an "outsider nation" is structurally different from that of an "insider nation." Suggesting a complex, structural explanation for Japan's predicament of defeat, she claims that the requirements of recognition and the burden of stigma are different in the East from the West. The outsider nations have always had intense anxieties about not being an integral part of the international system. In the desire to gain international stature under the gaze of the West, the defeated, like Japan and Turkey, made special efforts to emulate the West after defeat. The reluctance to apologize for war crimes is costly for both nations, but they are both hesitant to apologize because doing so requires a self-redefinition that is incompatible with their long-standing goal of attaining equality with the West. Admission of "barbarism" and the capacity to carry out unjustified violence not only "challenge[s] the integrity of the narrative of state identity," but it also ironically casts the nation as falling short of the normative standards of the West that they have striven to attain for years—such as progress, rationality, and scientific achievement.[57]

Japan's nationalists, pacifists, and reconciliationists today fall into the quandary of wanting to be recognized as a civilized nation espousing the "global standard," yet also wanting to be recognized as a civilized nation that would not carry out barbaric deeds so unworthy of civilized nations. Conforming to the global standard accrues symbolic capital and carries the approval of the world, yet at the same time confirms the West's stereotype of the yellow peril menacing white societies. Increasingly, China's and South Korea's demands for apology are articulated within this global framework even if they do not apply it to themselves for their own dark histories of oppression.

A Comparative Look at Germany

In *Shattered Past*, Konrad Jarausch and Michael Geyer examine the diverse memory narratives of Hitler's war, the Nazi regime, and the Holocaust since reunification (1989) in Germany, and illustrate how different individuals and social groups take diverse perpetrator, victim, and bystander perspectives, replete with contending recollections that highlight different lessons. They highlight how people do not produce a cohesive sense of the past, notwithstanding the official German contrition policy. War stories of perpetrators, victims, and bystanders coexist in everyday life, based on different perceptions, experiences, and self-interests that are not unified as an account for the whole nation.[58] These divided memories have emerged out of particular social and political conditions: the rift between the West-East political regimes in the Cold War, different generational perceptions, the diversity of battlefront and home front memories, and distinct ideological orientations. Different beliefs and memories of wartime experiences and the Third Reich have become evident, especially in the decades after reunification, that reveal how partial, selective accounts lead to irresolvable differences.[59] This diversity of memory narratives in Germany seems not altogether different from other nations with difficult pasts, such as Japan as discussed in this book, as well as others like postwar France and Austria.[60]

The *official* approach of managing the Holocaust legacy, however, emerged as a relatively consistent contrition policy since the 1970s and 1980s, which looked to the deeply flawed past, called for self-incrimination, a radical break, and a reconstruction of a new collective self.[61] Notwithstanding the diversity of popular narratives—for example, the traditionalists' long resentment of the contrition approach that was formulated by the 1968 generation, the war stories of heroes and victims produced on the silver screen, the private narratives of German suffering and innocence at home—Germany's politics of contrition has managed to control and efface many dissenting voices.[62] There were geopolitical and domestic conditions that made this not only possible but also necessary. In postwar West Germany, reconciliation was an imperative: West Germany's economic and political survival depended on establishing an official policy of reconciliation and integration, formulating a new cooperative framework with its neighbors starting most importantly with France, integrating itself in Europe, joining NATO, becoming part of the European Union, and forging a European identity that made up for a German identity that was viewed with deep suspicion. The political dynamics at home produced conditions favorable to this approach especially when the Social Democrats (SPD) governed for two decades (1969–1982 and 1998–2005) and implemented a number of critical policies in foreign relations (*Ostpolitik*) and education (the Holocaust and Third Reich curriculum). These structural conditions of reconciliation are markedly different from those of postwar Japan, which faced a different set of imperatives *not* to reconcile with its communist neighbors: China, North Korea, and the Soviet Union.[63]

This German approach was different from its approach after the defeat in World War I when it marshaled narratives of fallen heroes and betrayed victims to heal and unite the nation.[64] The self-incriminating approach that emerged from the second defeat amalgamated lessons learned from the failures of the first half of the twentieth century: the Holocaust and the Third Reich, as well as the failures of two world wars, and the failure of democracy in the interwar Weimer republic.[65] Germany's reformed parliamentary system supported this approach by allowing Germany proactively to control "extreme ideologies" like nationalism and communism whose parties were banned in the 1950s.[66] It also controlled any mushrooming "fringe" voices in parliament by setting an electoral threshold for party representation at 5% of the vote.[67] These institutional tools, and others designed to stabilize democracy, allowed Germany to prevent its official policies for overcoming the past from being held hostage to opposition from the extreme left or right. Thus, even though protecting and rehabilitating former Nazi's was salient in German society until the 1960s, they could be effaced once the Social Democrats and the youth generation were in a position in the 1970s to define the perpetrator narrative that demarcated German guilt.

This work of constructing moral social boundaries between perpetrators and victims also carried over to civil discourse.[68] The German heroes to be looked up to in postwar society as models of courage were those who opposed the Third Reich by risking their lives—Claus von Stauffenberg who attempted to assassinate Hitler, Hans and Sophie Scholl who led the White Rose student resistance movement, and Dietrich Bonhoeffer, the Christian anti-Nazi dissident who was incarcerated and executed, among others. Narratives of victimized Germans were effaced and made less significant than perpetrator narratives, even though millions of Germans were expelled from Poland and Czechoslovakia after 1945; hundreds of thousands were killed by air raids in Hamburg, Bochum, Mainz, Kassel, and a host of other cities; and the hundreds of thousands of soldiers perished from starvation and disease on the eastern front. Over time, civil discourse extended the circle of perpetrators to include more "ordinary" Germans who enabled the Holocaust. The circle of perpetrators remains open even today because the state abolished the statute of limitations on war crimes prosecutions (genocide and crimes against

humanity, 1979) and also outlawed the expression of neo-Nazi sentiments described as the "Auschwitz lie" (1993).[69]

The German identity polluted by the Holocaust and the Third Reich
could also be reconstructed effectively. A new collective self could be
built on Europeanism and the notion of constitutional patriotism,
which are the foundation of the European Union today.[70] In time, contrition and atonement for the past itself became a form of civic identity
fostered by a sense of national purpose modeled by the examples set
by Chancellor Willy Brandt who kneeled at the Warsaw ghetto memorial and President Richard von Weizsäcker who pronounced German
guilt at the Bundestag in 1985. The civic identity among the postwar
generations is also referred to as *Sühnestolz* (repentance pride), a new
source of national pride.[71] In the 2000s, the pendulum began to swing
the other way in civil discourse as more victim narratives garnered
popular attention. For example, Jörg Friedrich's bestseller *The Fire*
(*Der Brand*, 2002) is about the trauma of air raids in Germany,[72] and
the television miniseries *Generation War* (*Unsere Mütter, unsere Väter*,
2013) told stories of innocent German soldiers and civilians caught
in a bad war. The demarcation of perpetrators and victims in these
narratives is more fluid, blurred around the edges in ways similar
to the "gray" perpetrator-cum-victim narratives in Japan discussed
in chapter 3. At the same time, the difficult task of reckoning with
how ordinary men and compatriots transform into serial killers defies
definitive explanations.[73]

Rejoining the World as a "Normal" Country

Many more transnational wars have now been fought since World War
II: the Korean War, the Vietnam War, the Afghan War, the Gulf War,
the War in Kosovo, and the Iraq and Afghan Wars. These wars caused
escalating civilian casualties and used technologies that were ever
more potent and destructive. Accordingly, the narrative of war and
peace is in need of rethinking and reformulation for the post–Cold
War twenty-first century. The distinction between the good war and
the bad war is no longer clear-cut; the heroes and villains are no longer obviously apparent; the moral codes begin to blur from black
and white to shades of gray. There are many instances that call for
the understanding of the gray zone:[74] the Jewish *kapos* who cooper-
ated with the Nazis in concentration camps during the Holocaust; the
Soviet liberators who raped scores of German women in the Third

Reich's capital; American soldiers who destroyed whole villages inhabited by Vietnamese civilians; and Iraqi prisoners detained and tortured in Abu Ghraib and Guantanamo. As these gray zones proliferate, the construction of moral frameworks for war is becoming more and more tenuous. If the social construction of a moral framework is based fundamentally on our ability to code the distinction between good and bad legitimately, as Jeffrey Alexander suggests, the very legitimacy of those codes is called in question.[75]

Ultimately this social construction of moral boundaries is "an ambivalent endeavor" where the demarcation of good from bad and guilty from innocent is inherently unstable and open to dispute.[76] Japan's three options to bring closure to the long defeat and resolve the "history problem" are part of this complicated endeavor, as this chapter has shown. At the heart of this complexity is Japan's ambivalence about drawing lines and demarcating guilt, while the globalizing memory norms demand greater clarification of those very boundaries. The "normalization" discourse surrounding Article 9 illustrated in this chapter represents the tension between line-drawing and line-erasing, a tension that tears at the national social fabric. The impasse will continue to deny closure to the long defeat.

Japan's sense of postwar progress relied largely on the growth of tangible wealth and prosperity.[77] While this gauge worked for parents and grandparents, it no longer makes sense to the younger generations who will henceforth have to carry on the task of Japan's postwar memory work. Economic security, gradually declining since the 2000s, has become even more precarious for young Japanese workers who cannot count on employment in the manufacturing sector as their parents did a generation ago. Those jobs have now moved to the emerging economies. Young Japanese men and women contending with this bleak job market have become weary, cautious, and suspicious of their future prospects.[78] Some are embittered by a sense of broken promises and betrayal;[79] others try to transcend the national confines to seek gainful pursuits elsewhere.[80] Sensational accounts of gloom and doom notwithstanding, reports on these young Japanese reveal that they are not entirely unhappy with their relatively unambitious lives. Whether they are genuinely contented with the here and now or entrapped in a false consciousness of the oppressed, a surprisingly large portion of this young generation reports a high level of happiness in their lives.[81]

At the same time, these generations are left to seek their own raison d'être without much guidance or many role models in modern Japanese history. An intransigent minority among them has established itself by vocalizing frustration and xenophobic hate toward "racialized others" in popular Internet groups. Commenting on the emerging populist nationalism in the 2000s, Japanese sociologists Oguma Eiji and Ueno Yōko point to its new features: the members find appeal in patriotism but are relatively indifferent to the Emperor; many members are men in their 20s and 30s—a generation after the baby boomers—who are conspicuous in their hate for the left, the *Asahi* newspaper, China, and the teachers union, but they are not LDP supporters. Oguma believes they occupy the amorphous middle ground of the politically uncommitted, looking for a place to share values to secure their identity, and seeking respite from the harsh economic realities by identifying with strong politicians like Koizumi Junichirō and Ishiwara Shintarō.[82] Commenting on the emerging fringe groups that promote xenophobic hate in the 2010s, critics have shown that these groups offer solace and belonging to motivate members to join.[83]

Japan's younger generations are confronting a world that has become, and is likely to remain, unstable economically and geopolitically. The spectacular global economic and political transformations of recent decades have surely impacted many Japanese both old and young, just as they did for the rest of East Asia. China's explosive economic rise surpassed Japan's economy in the early 2010s, jolted Japan's self-confidence, and evoked fear over its future domination.[84] At the same time, China is now Japan's largest trading partner, surpassing the United States and accounting for as much as $345 billion of business a year.[85] Japan's economic response to this sea-change has been diverse and also stratified: opportunistic investors are always happy to capitalize on a burgeoning market, and strategic producers may be well poised to take advantage of China's rise, but there are as many workers for whom the swinging economic momentum has meant a painful loss of livelihood to an upstart rival. The growing anti-Japan sentiments have also cast a shadow on further Japanese investments in China's economy. It would be a mistake to generalize that the impact has been uniformly favorable or problematic in the same way for everyone.[86]

International relations experts Kosuge Nobuko and Fujiwara Kiichi believe that Japan–China relations will continue to be strained without any true "reconciliation" until China achieves greater national successes that can supplant the success of defeating Japan in 1945—until it has fully "caught up" with the postindustrial nations and feels it has fully joined the world leaders.[87] In the meantime, China's politics of patriotism, its uses of anti-Japanese sentiments to marshal national solidarity, its quest to overcome the "century of humiliation," and its spiraling defense budget and nuclear arsenal are likely to continue fueling strained relations with Japan.[88] For its part, Japan will be adding two more aegis ballistic missile destroyers to its fleet of six aegis destroyers,[89] and continues to update its military aircrafts and tanks, while stepping up its cooperation with the US military to train troops for contingencies. These actions are reinforced by the government's new reinterpretation of the peace constitution in July 2014 to allow the exercise of collective self-defense. The nation is treading the path of "normalization."

According to a public opinion survey published in 2014, over half of Chinese adults (55.2%) considered Japan to be a military threat, second only to the United States (57.8%). A major reason for this perception is trepidation over Japan's past and present military power: over half (58.2%) felt that Japan's military capability today is already threatening, while a similar proportion (52.4%) felt that the history problem was an indication of future threat. At the same time, two-thirds of Japanese adults (64.3%) perceived China to be a military threat, second only to North Korea (68.6%). The outlook for the future is relatively grim: almost half of Japanese adults (42.7%) were pessimistic about relations with China, feeling that the history problem between them will never be resolved. The Japanese respondents were more pessimistic than their Chinese counterparts (26.9%) in foreseeing this bleak future for the Japan–China relationship.[90]

Even with the increased tension in relations in East Asia, the portion of Japanese people who would volunteer to fight in a hypothetical invasion has been consistently low, around 5 to 6% (1978–2012). There is, however, a steady increase (39.3% to 56.6% in 1994–2012) in those who would "support the SDF in some way." The younger the age of respondents, the lower is their willingness to participate in a military response against invaders. At the same time, the young-age cohorts also have a stronger sense than others that Japan is in danger of getting involved in a war.[91]

Ultimately, Japan's moral recovery cannot be complete without constructing a new collective self, and a political identity that extends beyond the alliance with the United States. Japan has envisioned this new identity in the body of world governance, the United Nations. Japan's ultimate ambition for moral recovery has been to become a permanent member of the United Nations Security Council—a goal that the nationalists, pacifists, and reconciliationists can agree on. Such an achievement would take Japan beyond the long defeat, garnering a transnational identity acceptable to the victors and the world, comparable to Germany's integration into the EU and NATO. It would also dismantle the monopolistic power structure of the Security Council that is shaped by the veto powers of the winners of World War II (the United States, Russia, China,

France, and the United Kingdom). This bid, however, will continue to be frustrated by China's objection. This issue may not be resolved until China no longer needs to use anti-Japanism to draw attention away from its domestic problems.[92]

Wolfgang Schivelbusch's observations on the culture of defeat that explained postwar myth making by the aspiration never to be defeated again, now requires a post–World War II update.[93] Democratic societies can generate new, multifaceted options for overcoming defeat that the vanquished in the pre–World War II era did not have. These options involve education to overcome lingering hate and prejudice against inherited enemies; civil discourse to redefine the norms of disobedience against authorities; and transnational institutional frameworks to maintain rules, solidarities, and dialogue among former adversaries. At the same time, national memories of war are no longer self-contained in a globalizing culture of memory, and forgetting is no longer an option as it had been in the past. The new international world order demands imaginative concessions and innovative compromise to break the logjams of historical grievances.[94] For the Japanese this will mean giving up their comfort zone of ambiguity in the amorphous middle ground between guilt and innocence in World War II. For their part, Japan's former adversaries and victims will have to extend hope of forgiveness.

Although postwar culture is shaped by memories of violent conflicts that leave a deep imprint in national collective life long after the event, individuals living under those conditions do not necessarily choose the same strategies to overcome them. While the multiple war narratives of the twentieth century may eventually be generalized and stabilized over several more generations, this does not mean that differences of moral and political understandings will be *settled*.[95] Cultural trauma is reproduced by assorted memories and irreconcilable stories that are interconnected, sutured together, by common reference to the national rupture.[96] It is at once integrative and fractured, kept alive and effaced, in ways that renew collective identity. The divisiveness of cultural trauma makes it all the more difficult for the nation's past to be fully comprehended by later generations, but it ensures that those memories are kept alive in a continuous struggle to imagine the nation's future.

Notes

Chapter 1

1. Burke, "History as Social Memory"; Olick, *In the House of the Hangman*.
2. Dower, *Embracing Defeat*; Gluck, "The Past in the Present"; Seraphim, *War Memory and Social Politics in Japan*; Igarashi, *Bodies of Memory*.
3. The disputes refer to the Senkaku/Diaoyu Islands, Takeshima/Dokdo Island, and Hoppō ryōdo/the Kuril Islands, respectively.
4. The Yasukuni Shrine memorializes the war dead including the Class A war criminals indicted and executed for crimes against peace in World War II.
5. "Comfort women" were forced into servicing Japanese soldiers during the war.
6. The Act on National Flag and Anthem 1999 (*Kokki oyobi kokka ni kansuru hōritsu*) mandated the use of the national anthem and flag in schools. The controversy continues today in litigations and dismissals of dissenting teachers.
7. Atarashii rekishi kyōkasho o tsukurukai (Committee to Write New Textbooks) ignited the controversy over "revisionist" history by publishing the bestseller *Kyōkashoga oshienai rekishi*, edited by Fujioka and Jiyūshugishikan Kenkyūkai.
8. Law to aid the victims of atomic bombings 1994 (*Genshibakudan hibakusha ni taisuru engo ni kansuru hōritsu*).
9. Wagner-Pacifici and Schwartz, "The Vietnam Veterans Memorial"; McCormack, *Collective Memory*; Macleod, *Defeat and Memory*; Neal, *National Trauma and Collective Memory*.
10. Blight, *Race and Reunion*; Schivelbusch, *Culture of Defeat*.
11. Mosse, *Fallen Soldiers*; Bessel, *Germany after the First World War*.
12. Zarakol, *After Defeat*.
13. Schivelbusch, *Culture of Defeat*.
14. Halbwachs, *On Collective Memory*. American sociologists who have pioneered the study of this phenomenon include Barry Schwartz, Jeffrey Olick, Howard Schuman, and Michael Schudson. See Olick, Levy, and Vinitzky-Seroussi, eds., *Collective Memory Reader*.
15. Alexander, "Toward a Theory of Cultural Trauma," 1.
16. Eyerman, "Cultural Trauma."
17. Smelser, "Psychological Trauma and Cultural Trauma."

18. Margalit, *Ethics of Memory.*
19. Huyssen, *Present Pasts*, 15.
20. Nora, *Realms of Memory.*
21. Takahashi, *Kokka to gisei.*
22. Moeller, "War Stories."
23. Bhabha, *Nation and Narration.*
24. Karasawa, *Kyōkasho no rekishi: Kyōkasho to nihonjin no keisei.*
25. Yoneyama, "For Transformative Knowledge and Postnationalist Public Spheres," 338.
26. Giesen, *Triumph and Trauma.*
27. Barkan, *Guilt of Nations.* Prinz, *Emotional Construction of Morals.*
28. Orend, *Morality of War.*
29. Friday, *Samurai, Warfare and the State in Early Medieval Japan* and "Might Makes Right."
30. Friday, "Might Makes Right."
31. Mosse, *Fallen Soldiers.*
32. M. Yoshida, *Requiem for Battleship Yamato*, 40. Throughout this book, I use official or professional translations in print whenever available. Otherwise all translations of Japanese titles, letters, speeches, and other popular texts are my own.
33. This statement attributed to Usubuchi has been cited often in language arts textbooks and recounted in political speeches, such as the speaker of the diet's official speech on August 15, 2006, the 61st anniversary of the end of the war.
34. Fukuma, *Junkoku to hangyaku: 'Tokkō' no katari no sengoshi*, 56.
35. Winter, *Sites of Memory, Sites of Mourning*, 119.
36. Orr, *Victim as Hero.*
37. Nakazawa, *Hadashi no gen jiden*; Morris-Suzuki, *The Past within Us*, 160; Spiegelman, "Forward: Comics After the Bomb."
38. Dower, *Embracing Defeat*, 243–44, 248–49.
39. Itō, "'Hadashi no gen' no minzokushi: Gakkō o meguru manga taiken no shosō," 152. *Gen* is also a staple of television reruns: most recently, a popular dramatization of *Gen* (from 2007) was rebroadcast on Fuji Television at the end-of-war commemoration in 2014 over two days, on August 14 and 15.
40. Yamanaka, "Yomare'enai 'taiken', ekkyō dekinai 'kioku': Kankoku ni okeru 'Hadashi no gen' no juyō o megutte."
41. *Hotaru no haka* (animation film 1988); *Satōkibibatake no uta* (television drama 2004); *Kono sekai no katasumini* (graphic novel 2007).
42. Browning, *Ordinary Men.* See also Goldhagen, *Hitler's Willing Executioners.*
43. Throughout this book, references to Japanese persons writing in Japanese or working in Japan follow the Japanese convention: family names first, followed by given names. Ienaga, Saburō, *The Pacific War*, and *Sensō sekinin*, and *Taiheiyō sensō.*
44. Nozaki, *War Memory, Nationalism, and Education*, 154.
45. Nozaki, and Inokuchi, "Japanese Education, Nationalism, and Ienaga Saburo's Textbook Lawsuits," 116.
46. Original in "Jūgonen sensō ni yoru shi o dō kangaeruka" [Reflections on the war dead of the Fifteen Year War] *Rekishi dokuhon* (expanded issue, March 1979) in *Ienaga Saburōshū*, vol. 12, 260; cited and translated by Richard Minear in *Japan's Past, Japan's Future*, 148.
47. Aramaki, "Jiyū, heiwa, minshushugi o motomete: Musubini kaete," 233.

48. Ōe Kenzaburo won the case in 2008.
49. A. Assmann, "Transformations between History and Memory"; Smelser, "Psychological Trauma and Cultural Trauma," 54; Olick, *Politics of Regret*. Vinitzky-Seroussi, "Commemorating a Difficult Past." Smith, *Why War?*
50. Jarausch and Geyer, *Shattered Past*, 340.
51. Herf, *Divided Memory*. Olick, "Genre Memories and Memory Genres." Bartov, *Germany's War and the Holocaust*. Moses, *German Intellectuals and the Nazi Past*. Bude, *Bilanz Der Nachfolge*.
52. Rousso, *The Vichy Syndrome*; Lagrou, *Legacy of Nazi Occupation*.
53. Art, *Politics of the Nazi Past in Germany and Austria*.
54. Zarakol, *After Defeat*.
55. Mark, *Unfinished Revolution*.
56. Berger, *Cultures of Antimilitarism*; Katzenstein, *Cultural Norms and National Security*; Koseki, 'Heiwa kokka' nihon no saikentō*; Oros, *Normalizing Japan*.
57. In July 2014, the Cabinet Decision on Development of Seamless Security Legislation to Ensure Japan's Survival and Protect its People (*Kunino sonritsu o mattōshi, kokumin o mamorutame no kiremenonai anzenhoshōhōsei no seibinitsuite*) "reinterpreted" the constitution to allow collective self-defense under limited conditions. This revision in the meaning of pacifism is an ongoing political development, expected to unfold through the upcoming revision of the US-Japan Defense Cooperation Guidelines and an anticipated contest in the parliament over revising the security laws to align with the reinterpretation. For further discussion of these developments, see chapter 5.
58. Weinberg, *A World at Arms*.
59. A. Fujiwara, *Uejini shita eireitachi*.
60. Yui, Daizaburo. "Sekai sensō no nakano ajia-taiheiyō sensō," 261.
61. A. Fujiwara, *Uejini shita eireitachi*.
62. Fujita, *Sensō hanzai towa nanika*.
63. Almost 5,700 men were prosecuted and over 4,400 indicted in B and C Class war crimes trials across East and Southeast Asia after the war. Seven were executed as Class A war criminals, and 920 were executed as Class B and C war criminals. See Dower, *Embracing Defeat*, and Fujita, *Sensō hanzai towa nanika*.
64. Dower, *Embracing Defeat*.
65. Berger, *Cultures of Antimilitarism*; Katzenstein, *Cultural Norms and National Security*; Igarashi, *Bodies of Memory*; Orr, *Victim as Heroes*.
66. Soh, *Comfort Women*.
67. Lind, *Sorry States*.
68. Dudden, *Troubled Apologies*; Gluck, "Operations of Memory"; Seraphim, *War Memory and Social Politics in Japan*; Hein and Selden, *Censoring History*.
69. Sakaiya, *Daisan no haisen*; Yoshimoto, *Daini no haisenki: Korekarano nihon o dōyomuka*. Bungei Shunjū, "Daini no haisen: Dankaikoso senpanda."
70. Makita, "Nihonjin no sensō to heiwakan: Sono jizoku to fūka"; Saaler, *Politics, Memory and Public Opinion*; Seaton, *Japan's Contested War Memories*.
71. Yomiuri Shinbun Sensō Sekinin Kenshō Iinkai, *Kenshō: Sensō sekinin 1*, 209
72. Asahi Shinbun Shuzaihan, *Sensō sekinin to tsuitō: Rekishi to mukiau 1*, 230.
73. Saaler, *Politics, Memory, and Public Opinion*; Seaton, *Japan's Contested War Memories*.
74. United Nations Development Programme (UNDP), *Human Development Report 2013*, Table 9: Social Integration, pp. 174–77. For a discussion of this

long-standing trend in Japan, see Pharr, "Public Trust and Democracy in Japan"; Inoguchi, "Social Capital in Ten Asian Countries"; Putnam, *Democracies in Flux.*

75. Schmitt, and Allik, "Simultaneous Administration of the Rosenberg Self-Esteem Scale in 53 Nations." The survey asked people to rate how strongly they agreed or disagreed with statements such as "I am able to do things as well as most other people," "I take a positive attitude toward myself," and "All in all, I am inclined to feel that I am a failure."

76. Eviatar Zerubavel calls this type of work social pattern analysis, and drawing on the work of Erving Goffman and Georg Simmel, he suggests that "the wider the range of our evidence, the more generalizable our findings." Following this approach, I present cases from a wide range of cultural settings so that their cumulative weight increases the plausibility of the findings and generalizations. See Zerubavel's "Generally Speaking: The Logic and Mechanics of Social Pattern Analysis," 134.

77. I am grateful to Alberta Sbragia for suggesting this term.

78. Smelser, *Comparative Methods in the Social Sciences.*

79. J. Assmann, "Communicative and Cultural Memory."

80. White, *The Content of the Form.*

81. Hirsch, *Family Frames*; Welzer, "The Collateral Damage of Enlightenment"; Welzer, Moller, and Tschuggnall. *"Opa war kein Nazi": Nationalsozialismus und Holocaust im Familiengedächtnis.*

82. Lind, *Sorry States.*

83. Olick, *Politics of Regret.*

84. Alexander, *Trauma: A Social Theory*, 95.

Chapter 2

1. Orr, *Victim as Hero.*

2. Hirsch, *Family Frames*; and Hirsch, *Generation of Postmemory.*

3. Makita, "Nihonjin no sensō to heiwakan: Sono jizoku to fūka," 10.

4. Ōtsuka, *Sengo minshu shugi no rihabiritēshon: Rondan de boku wa nani o katatta ka*, 380–81.

5. Kawaguchi and Eya, *Sakebe! "Chinmoku no kokka" nippon.*

6. Rosenthal, "National Socialism and Antisemitism in Intergenerational Dialog." Caruth, *Unclaimed Experience.*

7. Rosenthal, "Veiling and Denying."

8. Rosenthal, "National Socialism and Antisemitism in Intergenerational Dialog," 244.

9. Hess and Torney, *Development of Political Attitudes in Children.*

10. Eliasoph, " 'Close to Home,' " 621; Eliasoph, *Avoiding Politics*; Eliasoph, " 'Everyday Racism.' "

11. Asahi Shinbunsha. Tēma Danwashitsu. *Sensō: Chi to namida de tsuzutta shōgen.* 2 volumes, 1987; Asahi Shinbunsha, *Nihonjin no sensō*, 1988 ; Asahi Shinbunsha, *Senjō taiken: "Koe" ga kataritsugu rekishi*, 2003; Asahi Shinbunsha, *Sensō taiken: Asahi shinbun e no tegami*, 2010. The three volumes published in 1987–1988 together contain 1,238 cases; the 2003 volume contains 132 cases; and the 2010 volume collects 171 cases. My sample consists of 135 cases from these five volumes, and 295 cases from Asahi's Kikuzō archive of 2006–2013. All these testimonies were published in the daily paper between July 1986 and August 2013.

12. Bungei Shunjū, "Shōgen: Chichi to haha no sensō ." Bungei Shunjū, "Kagayakeru shōwajin : Ketsuzoku no shōgen 55."

13. Buchholz, "Tales of War: Autobiographies and Private Memories in Japan and Germany." I am grateful to Franziska Seraphim for pointing out Buchholz's work. See also Figal, "How to Jibunshi."

14. Ueno, Kawamura, and Narita, "Sensōwa donoyōni katararete kitaka," 24.

15. S. Takahashi, '*Senkimono' o yomu: Sensō taiken to sengo nihon shakai*, 60; Y. Yoshida, *Nihonjin no sensōkan*.

16. Lifton, *Death in Life*.

17. Sōka Gakkai Seinenbu Hansen Shuppan Iinkai's project alone generated 80 volumes of oral history from 1974 to 1985. The series are published under the title *Sensō o shiranai sedai e*. Two volumes are available in English. Another pioneering work of oral history available in English is by Haruko Cook and Theodore Cook, *Japan at War: An Oral History*.

18. Y. Yoshida, *Heishitachi no sengoshi*.

19. Bruner, *Acts of Meaning*, 138.

20. Fujii, *Heitachino sensō*, 297

21. The Japanese term is *kataranai sedai* (the untalkative generation).

22. Bar-On, *The Indescribable and the Undiscussable*; Ambrose, *Band of Brothers*.

23. Y. Yoshida, *Nihonjin no sensōkan*, 120; S. Takahashi, '*Senkimono' o yomu*, 60.

24. Hosaka, "Heishitachi no seishinteki kizuato kara yasukuni mondai o kangaeru," 105.

25. Y. Yoshida, *Gendai rekishigaku to sensō sekinin*, 37–39.

26. Yoshimura, "Tōsho, hitosamazama." The first letter was published after the Russo-Japanese War.

27. The featured series have been titled differently over the decades: the feature in the 2000s was titled *Dokushaga tsukuru kioku no rekishi shiriizu* [The Readers' Historical Memory Series].

28. Gibney, *Sensō*.

29. For the reader's ease of reference I cite whenever available the collected volumes as sources of the testimonies excerpted in this chapter. The translations are mine, unless the excerpts appeared in Gibney's volume.

30. Kokubo Yumio, Gibney, *Sensō*, 153.

31. Yamaguchi Hideo, Tēma Danwashitsu, *Sensō 2:* 77–78.

32. Matsuo Shigemitsu, ibid., 248.

33. Y. Yoshida, *Gendai rekishigaku to sensō sekinin*.

34. Ikoji Munetsugu, Asahi Shinbunsha, *Sensō taiken*, 69.

35. Isozaki Yūjirō, ibid., 72.

36. Anonymous, *Asahi Shinbun*, Tokyo edition, June 16, 2008.

37. Chamoto, et al., "Zadankai: Sensō sedai no kataru sensō," 144. This classification is A. Fujioka's.

38. Buchholz, "Tales of War."

39. Y. Yoshida, *Nihonjin no sensōkan*, 193

40. Kumagai, "Zadankai: Wakamonotachini kataritsugu sensō sekinin," 24.

41. Oyasato Chizuko, Asahi Shinbunsha, *Sensō taiken*, 78–79.

42. Motoki Kisako, *Asahi Shinbun*, Tokyo edition, August 23, 2007.

43. Kikuchi Tsuyako, Asahi Shinbunsha, *Sensō taiken*, 89–90.

44. Bungei Shunjū, "Shōgen: Chichi to haha no sensō"; "Kagayakeru shōwajin."

45. "Tsugi no tēma: Senjō taiken," *Asahi Shinbun*, August 4, 2002, 14.

46. Bungei Shunjū, "Genkō boshū: Wagaya no sengo 50 nen," 505.

47. "Jitchan o mamore!" For a discussion, see T. Takahashi, *Sengo sekininron*, 106, 172.

48. Hashimoto and Traphagan, "The Changing Japanese Family."
49. Hashimoto, *Gift of Generations*.
50. Hashimoto, "Culture, Power and the Discourse of Filial Piety in Japan"; Hashimoto and Ikels, "Filial Piety in Changing Asian Societies."
51. Oguma, *1968*, 94–95. Patricia Steinhoff discusses the students' closeness with their parents in "Mass Arrests, Sensational Crimes, and Stranded Children."
52. A. Assmann, "On the (In)Compatibility of Guilt and Suffering in German Memory."
53. Kōno, *"Gendai nihon no sedai: Sono sekishutsu to tokushitsu"*; Nakase, "Nichijō seikatsu to seiji tono aratana setten."
54. Japan Naikakufu, "Dai 8 kai sekai seinen ishiki chōsa: Kekka gaiyō sokuhō." http://www8.cao.go.jp/youth/kenkyu/worldyouth8/html/2-1-1.html.
55. Welzer, Moller, and Tschuggnall, *"Opa war kein Nazi."* Welzer and colleagues use the term "lexicon" to describe the official narrative, in contrast to "family album" to describe the unofficial narrative.
56. For interesting discussions of intergenerational memory in families of German wartime elites, see Lebert and Lebert, *My Father's Keeper: Children of Nazi Leaders: An Intimate History of Damage and Denial*; and Posner, *Hitler's Children: Sons and Daughters of Leaders of the Third Reich Talk About Their Fathers and Themselves*.
57. Kuroki Hiroko, Tēma Danwashitsu, *Sensō 2*: 205.
58. Iwasaki Mariko, Tēma Danwashitsu, *Sensō 1*: 305.
59. Sakuma Yōichi, Asahi Shinbunsha, *Senjō taiken*, 187–88.
60. Sakurazawa Takao, *Asahi Shinbun*, Tokyo edition, August 20, 2007.
61. Oikawa Kiyoshi, *Asahi Shinbun*, Tokyo edition, October 20, 2008.
62. Bar-On, *Fear and Hope: Three Generations of the Holocaust*, especially chapter 1. See also Sichrovsky, *Born Guilty: Children of Nazi Families*.
63. Rosenthal, "National Socialism and Anti-semitism in Intergenerational Dialog."
64. Ambrose, *Band of Brothers*.
65. Bar-On, "Holocaust Perpetrators and Their Children."
66. Rosenthal, "Veiling and Denying."
67. Hecker, "Family Reconstruction in Germany," 75–88.
68. Burchardt, "Transgenerational Transmission."
69. Ōtake Kyōko, Asahi Shinbunsha, *Senjō taiken*, 164.
70. Kishida Mayumi, Tēma Danwashitsu, *Sensō 1*: 301.
71. Kumakawa Ken, Asahi Shinbunsha, *Senjō taiken*, 46.
72. Eyerman, "The Past in the Present."
73. Buckley-Zistel, "Between Pragmatism, Coercion and Fear," 73.
74. Amino Sachie, *Asahi Shinbun*, Tokyo edition, August 20, 2007.
75. Matsubara Hiroko, *Asahi* digital edition, August 15, 2013. http://digital.asahi.com/articles/OSK201308140191.html?ref=comkiji_redirect. For a discussion of the returnees from Manchuria, see Tamanoi, *Memory Maps: The State and Manchuria in Postwar Japan*.
76. S. Takahashi, *Kyōdō kenkyū senyūkai*.
77. Y. Yoshida, *Nihonjin no sensōkan*, 192–93; Y. Yoshida, *Heishitachi no sengoshi*, 124, 160.
78. Watanabe Hiroko, Tēma Danwashitsu, *Sensō 1*: 28.
79. Suda Atsuko, Tēma Danwashitsu, *Sensō 1*: 127–28.

80. Anonymous, Tēma Danwashitsu, *Sensō 1*: 369.
81. Fukuma, *Sensō taiken no sengoshi*, 249.
82. Narita, *'Sensō keiken' no sengoshi*, 175
83. Bungei Shunjū, "Shōgen: Chichi to haha no sensō," 262–63. Yamamoto Yoshihisa is Yamamoto Isoroku's son. Ibid., 269–71. Imamura Kazuo is Imamura Hitoshi's son. Army General Imamura Hitoshi was indicted as a war criminal and imprisoned for eight years. Ibid., 274–75. Nishi Yasunori is Nishi Take'ichi's son. Baron Nishi was a gold medalist at the Los Angeles Olympics and died in the battle of Iwo Jima.
84. Buckley-Zistel, "Between Pragmatism, Coercion and Fear," 73.
85. Polletta, *It Was Like a Fever*; White, *The Content of the Form*.
86. Fukuma, *Sensō taiken no sengoshi*, 147 and 259; Y. Yoshida, *Gendai rekishigaku to sensō sekinin*, 34.
87. Eliasoph, " 'Close to Home.' "
88. Cohen, *States of Denial*, 79.
89. BBC's "WW2 People's War" website collected and archived 47,000 stories and 15,000 images between June 2003 and January 2006. http://www.bbc.co.uk/history/ww2peopleswar/; Noakes, "The BBC's 'People's War' Website."
90. Nihon Seishōnen Kenkyūjo, *Kōkōsei no seikatsu ishiki to ryūgaku ni kansuru chōsa 2012*, http://www1.odn.ne.jp/~aaa25710/ research pp. 5–6.
91. Japan Naikakufu, *Shakai ishiki ni kansuru chōsa*.
92. Hashimoto, "Culture, Power and the Discourse of Filial Piety in Japan"; Hashimoto, "Power to the Imagination."
93. Noda, *Saserareru kyōiku, tozetsusuru kyōshitachi*.
94. Hess and Torney, *Development of Political Attitudes in Children*, 101.
95. Kodomo no Taiken Katsudō Kenkyūkai, *Kodomo no taiken katsudō tō ni kansuru kokusai hikaku chōsa*. A large proportion of Japanese youth also reported that their parents did not teach them to be truthful (never taught by father 71%; by mother 60%).
96. Yomiuri Shinbun Sensō Sekinin Kenshō Iinkai. *Kenshō: Sensō sekinin I*. In this survey, 47% felt that the Japanese should continue to feel responsible for the damage they brought to the people of China. Of these, the largest group thought that the responsibility should continue indefinitely; also, 57.9% thought that postwar Japan has not had sufficient debate on the war responsibility problem of wartime political and military leadership.
97. Nohira, Kaneko, and Sugano, "Sengo sekinin undō no korekara, " 269.
98. Kurahashi, *Kenpei datta chichi no nokoshitamono*. This volume is available in English, translated by Philip Seaton. Ushijima Sadamitsu is the grandson of Army Commander Ushijima Mitsuru responsible for the Battle of Okinawa in 1945. Mitsuru's last order 'to fight to the very end' ensured the deaths of countless soldiers. Mitsuru took his own life a few days later. Sadamitsu found out about his grandfather's last order only when he went to the peace museum in Okinawa, *Yomiuri Shinbun*, June 23, 2005. Komai Osamu is a son of Komai Mitsuo who was indicted as a B-C Class war criminal and executed after the war. Osamu was shielded from his father's deeds until 1994 when he saw official documents about his father's indictment charges. After 55 years, he was in the process of contacting the surviving prisoners in London to offer a personal apology. *Yomiuri Shinbun*, April 12–13, 2005.

Chapter 3

1. From editorials of August 15, 2002. "Heiwa na seiki o tsukuru kufū o: Shūsen kinenbi ni kangaeru [Creating a peaceful century: Reflections on commemorating the end of war]" *Asahi Shinbun*; "Rekishi o sunao ni minaoshitai [Revisiting history honestly]" *Yomiuri Shinbun*; "Genten wa kiyoku mazushiku yume ga atta [At the beginning, we were poor and pure, and we had a dream]" *Mainichi Shinbun*; "'Haisen' kara nanimo manabitoranai kunino higeki [The tragedy of a nation that learns nothing from defeat]" *Nikkei Shinbun*; "'Chi' o ikashita saishuppatsu—Tsuginaru kokumuniteki gōi o kangaeru [Making a prudent fresh start: Reflections on the next national consensus]" *Sankei Shinbun*; "Shūsen kinenbi heiwaga nanika kangaeru hi ni [Commemorating the end of war as a day to reflect on peace]" *Okinawa Times*.

2. "Nihon yaburetari [Japan was defeated]" *Bungei Shunjū*, November 2005; Matsumoto, Ken'ichi. *Nihon no shippai: Daini no kaikoku to daitōa sensō [Japan's Failure: The Second Opening and the Greater East Asia War]*; Komuro, *Nihon no haiin: Rekishiwa katsutameni manabu [Causes of Japan's Defeat: Learning from History to Win]*; Handō et al., *Ano sensō ni naze maketanoka [Why Did We Lose That War?]*.

3. For a thoughtful discussion on the meaning of 1945 in postwar history, see Gluck, "The Past in the Present." For a discussion at the transnational level, see Buruma, *Year Zero: A History of 1945*.

4. Sato, *Hachigatsu jūgonichi no shinwa*, 32.

5. Sato, *Hachigatsu jūgonichi no shinwa*; Sato, "Kōfuku kinenbi kara shūsen kinenbi e."

6. Hammond, "Commemoration Controversies," 102; Sato, *Hachigatsu jūgonichi no shinwa*, 61–63.

7. Gillis, *Commemorations*, 18; Olick, "Genre Memories and Memory Genres"; Spillman, *Nation and Commemoration*; Schwartz, "The Social Context of Commemoration."

8. Neal, *National Trauma and Collective Memory*, 24; Giesen, *Triumph and Trauma*, 112.

9. Cohen, *States of Denial*, 79.

10. Anderson, *Imagined Communities*.

11. Rahimi, "Sacrifice, Transcendence and the Soldier."

12. Schivelbusch, *Culture of Defeat*.

13. Wakatsuki, *Nihon no sensō sekinin: Saigo no sensō sedai kara*.

14. Oguma, *'Minshu' to 'Aikoku'*.

15. Koizumi visited the Yasukuni Shrine also in the previous year, but on August 13, not August 15.

16. "Resolution of Remorse (*Fusen ketsugi*)," 1995. The official title is "Resolution to Renew the Determination for Peace on the Basis of Lessons Learned from History (Rekishi o kyōkun ni heiwaeno ketsui o aratanisuru ketsugi)." The English translation of this text is available at http://www.mofa.go.jp/announce/press/pm/murayama/address9506.html.

17. Statement by Prime Minister Tomi'ichi Murayama: "On the Occasion of the 50th Anniversary of the War's End," 1995. The English translation of this text is available at http://www.mofa.go.jp/announce/press/pm/murayama/9508.html.

18. Fukuma, *'Hansen' no media-shi*.

19. Prime Minister Hosokawa Morihiro foreshadowed this trend as the head of a non-LDP coalition in 1993 when he made explicit but *unofficial* statements about Japan's "invasion."

20. Mukae, "Japan's Diet Resolution on World War Two"; Rose, *Sino-Japanese Relations*; Dudden, *Troubled Apologies*.

21. Prime Minister Junichiro Koizumi's statement on August 15, 2005, is available at http://www.kantei.go.jp/foreign/koizumispeech/2005/08/15danwa_e.html.

22. Koizumi's tenure spanned 2001–2006.

23. Confino, *Germany as a Culture of Remembrance*.

24. Orr, *Victim as Hero*.

25. Kōno Yōhei convened a meeting of four former prime ministers to pressure Koizumi not to visit the Yasukuni Shrine for the 60th anniversary; he also addressed Japan's war responsibility in his speech at the Budōkan ceremony on August 15, 2006.

26. Abe reiterated this stance also a year later at the commemoration in 2014.

27. Alexander, *The Performance of Politics*; Shils and Young, "The Meaning of Coronation"; Olick, "Genre Memories and Memory Genres."

28. Kōno and Katō " 'Nihonjin no ishiki' chōsa nimiru 30nen."

29. T. Takahashi, *Yasukuni mondai*, 44.

30. Akazawa, "Senbotsusha tsuitō to yasukuni jinja mondai o dō kangaeruka."

31. Field, "War and Apology," 20.

32. My analysis in this section covers five national newspapers, *Asahi*, *Mainichi*, *Yomiuri*, *Sankei*, and *Nikkei*; the findings are generally consistent with prior studies that assessed fewer newspapers. See Tsutsui, "The Trajectory of Perpetrators' Trauma"; Nakano, "Tennosei to media 2"; Nezu, "Sengo 8-gatsu 15-nichizuke shasetsu ni okeru kagai sekinin no ronsetsu bunseki (jō)"; Nezu, "Sengo 8-gatsu 15-nichizuke shasetsu ni okeru kagai sekinin no ronsetsu bunseki (ge)."

33. "Statement by the Chief Cabinet Secretary Yohei Kōno on the Result of the Study on the Issue of 'Comfort Women'," August 4, 1993, http://www.mofa.go.jp/policy/women/fund/state9308.html

34. Yoshimi, *Jūgun ianfu*; Yoshimi, *Comfort Women*.

35. Michiba, *Teikō no dōjidaishi*, 188.

36. Lind, *Sorry States*.

37. Fujioka, and Jiyūshugishikan Kenkyūkai, *Kyōkashoga oshienai rekishi*.

38. Revision of the Fundamental Law of Education (Kyōiku kihonhō), 2006.

39. The Act on National Flag and Anthem (Kokki oyobi kokka ni kansuru hōritsu), 1999.

40. Oguma and Ueno, *'Iyashi' no nashonarizumu*.

41. For example, " 'Sengo' o itooshimu riyū," *Asahi Shinbun*, 1996; "8 gatsu 15 nichi: 'BC kyū senpan' omo wasuremai," *Yomiuri Shinbun*, 2004; "Keizoku to danzetsu to," *Nikkei Shinbun*, 1997; "Kokka ishiki to senryaku o motsu kunini," *Sankei Shinbun* 1997; and "Shūsen kinenbi: Yaburareta chinkon no shijima," *Mainichi Shinbun* 1999.

42. "8 gatsu 15 nichi: 'BC kyū senpan' omo wasuremai," *Yomiuri Shinbun*, August 15, 2004.

43. "Shishatachino kioku o tadoru," *Asahi Shinbun*, August 15, 2000.

44. "Shūsen kinenbi: Tongarazu yasukuni o katarō," *Mainichi Shinbun*, August 14, 2005.

45. Izawa and Yomiuri Shinbun Ronsetsu Iinkai. *Yomiuri vs Asahi*, 154.

46. Figures as of February 1, 2014, www.kuchiran.jp/business/newspaper.html.

47. For example, "Naze ayamachi wa kurikaesarerunoka," *Asahi Shinbun*, August 15, 1994; "Sensō o yondemiyō," *Asahi Shinbun*, August 15, 1998; and "Rekishi ni taisuru sekinin towa," *Asahi Shinbun*, August 15, 2001.

48. Asahi Shinbun 'Shinbun to Sensō' Shuzaihan, *Shinbun to sensō*.

49. "Sengo 60nen o koete' kenkyoni shitatakani kokusaishakai o ikinuku," *Nikkei Shinbun*, August 15, 2005.

50. The *Mainichi* newspaper was founded in 1872.

51. "Shūsen kinenbi tongarazu yasukuni o katarō," *Mainichi Shinbun*, August 14, 2005.

52. "Fukaku shizukana chinkon no hi ni," *Sankei Shinbun*, August 15, 2006.

53. Fukuma, *'Hansen' no media-shi*; Orr, *Victim as Hero*.

54. Eliasoph, " 'Everyday Racism' in a Culture of Avoidance," 497; Eliasoph, " 'Close to Home.' "

55. Sturken, *Tangled Memories*.

56. Dittmar and Michaud, *From Hanoi to Hollywood*. Even as the focus shifted from military heroism to the soldiers' personal victimhood, only limited attention is directed to the injured Vietnamese civilians.

57. Bodnar, *The "Good War" in American Memory*, 3.

58. Fukuma, *Sensō taiken no sengoshi*; Yoshida, *Nihonjin no sensōkan*; Seraphim, *War Memory and Social Politics in Japan*.

59. Yomiuri Shinbun Sensō Sekinin Kenshō Iinkai [War Responsibility Reexamination Committee]. *Kenshō sensō sekinin 1~2*. The English translation is *From Marco Polo Bridge to Pearl Harbor: Who Was Responsible?* Tokyo: Yomiuri Shinbun, 2006. For in-depth reviews of this reexamination by historians, see Y. Kato, *Sensō o yomu*, and also Morris-Suzuki, "Who Is Responsible? The Yomiuri Project and the Enduring Legacy of the Asia-Pacific War,"

60. Watanabe and Hosaka, " 'Sensō' towa nanika," 133–34.

61. Asahi Shinbun Shuzaihan, *Sensō sekinin to tsuitō: Rekishi to mukiau 1*.

62. NHK 'Sensō Shōgen' Purojekuto, *Shōgen kiroku: Heishitachi no sensō 1~7*. [The Soldiers' War, an Oral History Project for the 70th Anniversary of the Pacific War]. The project recorded oral histories from over 800 veterans which are available on the project's website. Fifty episodes were broadcast between August 2007 and March 2012.

63. Yoshida, *Gendai rekishigaku to sensō sekinin*.

64. *Shōgen kiroku: 2*, 52, 166–67; *Shōgen kiroku: 3*, 247.

65. *Shōgen kiroku: 1*, 296; *Shōgen kiroku: 3*, 248.

66. *Shōgen kiroku: 2*, 40, 53, 122–23.

67. Ibid., 61.

68. *Shōgen kiroku: 1*, 209; *Shōgen kiroku: 2*, 265–66.

69. *Shōgen kiroku: 4*, 53, 127.

70. *Shōgen kiroku: 1*, 58, 252; *Shōgen kiroku: 3*, 150.

71. *Shōgen kiroku: 2*, 43, 213.

72. Ibid., 164.

73. Ibid., 42; *Shōgen kiroku: 3*, 149.

74. Ibid., 253–55.

75. *Shōgen kiroku: 1*, 194–95.

76. *Shōgen kiroku: 5*, 53, 65.

77. Noda, *Sensō to zaiseki*. Noda's work was serialized in the monthly *Sekai* over 17 months in 1997–1998.

78. Lifton, *Home from the War*.

79. For the history of Chūkiren (Chūgoku kikansha renrakukai) and its survivor mission, see Okabe, Ogino, and Yoshida, eds., *Chūgoku shinryaku no shōgenshatachi: 'Ninzai' no kiroku o yomu*.

80. Interview with Yuasa Ken, *Shūkan Kinyōbi* no. 303, 2000 February 18, reprinted in Hoshi, *Watashitachiga chūgokude shitakoto,* 172–77. His testimony is also available in *Shōgen kiroku: 6,* 258–61. Noda's analysis of Yuasa's case is available in Noda, *Sensō to zaiseki,* chapter 1.

81. Sakurai, *Terebi wa sensō o dōegaite kitaka: Eizō to kioku no ākaibusu,* 6.

82. NHK Supesharu Shuzaihan, *Nihon kaigun 400 jikan no shōgen: Gunreibu sanbōtachi ga katatta haisen* (Tokyo: Shinchōsha, 2011).

83. NHK Shuzaihan, *Nihonjinwa naze sensō e to mukattanoka (jō) and (ge)* (Tokyo: NHK Shuppan, 2011).

84. NHK Supesharu, *Chōsa hōkoku: Nihongun to ahen,* August 17, 2008.

85. NHK Supesharu Shuzaihan, *Nihon kaigun 400 jikan no shōgen.*

86. For an informative discussion of the project's findings by historical experts, see Sawachi, Handō, and Todaka, *Nihon kaigun wa naze ayamattaka.*

87. NHK Shuzaihan, *Nihonjinwa naze sensō e to mukattanoka.*

88. Ibid. The closing narration of the fourth broadcast, March 6, 2011.

89. Ozawa and NHK Shuzaihan, *Akagami.*

90. Akazawa, "Senbotsusha tsuitō," 101.

91. Michiba, *Teikōno dōjidaishi;* Gluck, "Operations of Memory"; Kawasaki and Shibata, *Kenshō: Nihon no soshiki jānarizumu: NHK to Asahi shinbun;* Kawasaki and Shibata, *Kenshō: Nihon no soshiki jānarizumu: Zoku NHK to Asahi shinbun.*

92. Fukuma, *'Hansen' no media-shi.*

93. For example, claims over NHK's "bias" in characterizing Japan's colonization of Taiwan resulted in high-profile lawsuits in 2009 regarding *NHK Special's* four-part program called "JAPAN Debut."

94. Goffman, *Stigma,* 12–13; Link and Phelan, "Conceptualizing Stigma," 364.

95. Charles Inoue notes this trend in recent samurai films such as Yōji Yamada's *Twilight Samurai* (2002).

96. Hashimoto and Traphagan, "The Changing Japanese Family."

97. "Kābē *(Mother)*" 2008; "Watashi wa kai ni naritai *(I Want to be a Seashell)*" 1994, 2007; "Manatsu no oraion *(Last Operations under the Orion)*" 2009; "Kyatapirā *(The Caterpillar)*" 2010; "Shōnen H *(A Boy Called H)*" 2013; "Kaze tachinu *(The Wind Rises)*" 2013.

98. Hyakuta, *Eien no zero;* Feature film "*Eien no zero (Eternal Zero)*" 2013.

99. NHK Special: "Anatanitotte nippon towa? Sensō o shiranai kimitachi e: Sedai o koete tettei tōron" [What Does Japan Mean to You? For Those Who Didn't Know the War: A Debate across Generations]. August 15, 2001.

100. Fukuma, *'Hansen' no media-shi,* 330–31.

101. Arai, *Sensō sekininron.*

102. Takasaki Ryūji cited in *Bokura wa ajia de sensō o shita: Kyōkasho ni kakarenakatta sensō Pt. 3* edited by Utsumi, Aiko, 47.

103. Sakurai, *Terebi wa sensō o dōegaite kitaka,* 97 and 326.

104. N. Kato, *Haisengoron;* Oguma, *'Minshu' to 'Aikoku';* Oda, *Nanshi no shisō;* Yoshida, *Nihonjin no sensōkan;* Tsurumi, Ueno, and Oguma, *Sensō ga nokoshita mono.*

105. Hyōdō, "Kagaisha de ari, higaisha de arukoto."

106. NHK survey of 1995 cited in Y. Yoshida, *Gendai rekishigaku to sensō sekinin,* 27; Makita, "Nihonjin no sensō to heiwakan."

107. Yomiuri Shinbun Sensō Sekinin Kenshō Iinkai, *Kenshō: Sensō sekinin I.*

108. Asahi Shinbun Shuzaihan, *Sensō sekinin to tsuitō.* "Rekishi ninshiki ni kansuru yoron chōsa kekka," 229–43.

109. Levi, *The Drowned and the Saved*, 43.
110. Oda, *Nanshi no shisō*.
111. Eliasoph, " 'Close to Home.' "
112. Ienaga, *Sensō sekinin*, 310.
113. Nakamasa, *Nihon to doitsu*, 44–51 and 60; Orr, *Victim as Hero*.
114. For discussions of the traumatic memory of Hiroshima see Yoneyama, *Hiroshima Traces*; Treat, *Writing Ground Zero*; Hein and Selden, *Living With the Bomb*; Hogan, *Hiroshima in History and Memory*; Saito, "Reiterated Commemoration"; Shipilova, "From Local to National Experience."

Chapter 4

1. Margalit, *Ethics of Memory*.
2. Alexander, "Toward a Theory of Cultural Trauma"; Yamabe, "Nihon no heiwa hakubutsukan wa ajia-taiheiyō sensō o ikani tenji shiteiruka."
3. Murakami, *Sengo nihon no heiwa kyōiku no shakaigakuteki kenkyū*, 351.
4. This does not include the museums within Self-Defense Force bases that are not regularly open to the public. See Sabine Früstück's *Uneasy Warriors: Gender, Memory and Popular Culture in the Japanese Army*. For an in-depth account of the development of war and peace museums and the controversies surround them, see Hein and Takenaka, "Exhibiting World War II in Japan and the United States since 1995."
5. Yamane, "List of Museums for Peace in Japan" and "List of Museums for Peace in the World except Japan" (2008).
6. Yasukuni Jinja, *Yūshūkan zuroku*. Kindai Shuppansha, 2009.
7. A. Assmann, *Der lange Schatten der Vergangenheit*.
8. A. Assmann, "On the (In)Compatibility of Guilt and Suffering in German Memory."
9. Hashimoto, "Divided Memories, Contested Histories."
10. Sutton, "Between Individual and Collective Memory."
11. Hein and Selden, "The Lessons of War," 4; Vinitzky-Seroussi, "Commemorating A Difficult Past: Yitzhak Rabin's Memorials."
12. Antoniou and Soysal, "Nation and the Other in Greek and Turkish History Textbooks."
13. FitzGerald, *America Revised: History Schoolbooks in the Twentieth Century*.
14. Hein and Selden, "The Lessons of War."
15. Dower, *Embracing Defeat*; Karasawa, *Kyōshi no rekishi: Kyōshi no seikatsu to rinri*; Okano and Tsuchiya, *Education in Contemporary Japan*; Yoneyama, *The Japanese High School*.
16. Nakauchi, et al., *Nihon kyōiku no sengoshi*; Rekishi Kyōikusha Kyōgikai, *Rekishi kyōiku 50-nen no ayumi to kadai*.
17. Personal interviews with the author in Kanagawa Prefecture, February 1997.
18. Sakamoto, *Rekishi kyōiku o kangaeru*.
19. Ishiyama, "Sengo no kokumin no sensō ninshiki to kyōkashosaiban."
20. Nagahara, *Rekishi kyōkasho o dō tsukuruka*.
21. Nozaki, "Japanese Politics and the History Textbook Controversy, 1982–2001," 607; Chung, "Kan'nichi ni tsukimatou rekishi no kage to sono kokufuku no tame no kokoromi," 253.
22. Rohlen, *Japan's High Schools*. See also Duus, "War Stories." An examination of middle school history textbooks can be found in Dierkes, *Postwar History Education in Japan and the Germanys*.

23. Those different meanings of war and peace can also be remolded by the school teachers who use those textbooks. Author's focus group interviews, May–July 2003. See also Fukuoka, "School History Textbooks and Historical Memories in Japan."

24. World History A and World History B are excluded from this analysis.

25. Watanabe, "2010 nendo kōkō kyōkasho saitaku jyōkyō—Monkashō matome (jō)," *Naigai Kyōiku*; Watanabe, "2010 nendo kōkō kyōkasho saitaku jyōkyō—Monkashō matome (chū)." The five publishers in the sample are Jikkyō Shuppan, Tokyo Shoseki (also referred to by the shorthand Tōsho), Daiichi Gakushūsha, Yamakawa Shuppan, and Shimizu Shoin. The first three are the largest players in the entire high school textbook market, each accounting for the sales of about four to five million copies of various subjects in 2010. Yamakawa is the largest publisher of Japanese history textbooks in the social studies market; their books are heavily favored for university entrance exam studies. Yamakawa, Jikkyō, and Daiichi specialize in texts only at the high school level, while Tōsho operates in school markets at all levels, and Shimizu at the middle school and high school levels.

26. My secondary comparative sample of 31 textbooks consisted of texts for Japanese History A (4), Japanese History B (8), Contemporary Society (7), Politics/ Economy (7), and Ethics (5). A detailed comparative analysis of 18 high school texts for Japanese history before 1987 is available in Nakamura Fumio's *Kōkō nihonshi kyōkasho: Kentei kyōkasho 18 satsu o hikaku kentō suru.*

27. Japanese History was split into two courses—History A and History B—in the 1989 high school curricular revision. History A mainly covers modern and contemporary history. The variation among these textbooks has also grown overtime. I am grateful to Robert A. Fish for sharing his insights on textbook diversity.

28. White, *Content of the Form.*

29. Yamakawa Shuppan, *Shōsetsu nihonshi B*, 2014, 361 and 353.

30. Tokyo Shoseki, *Nihonshi A: Gendai karano rekishi*, 2014, 128

31. Jikkyō Shuppan, *Kōkō nihonshi B*, Shinteiban edition, 2010, 197. "Spread the war" was changed to "take military action" in the 2014 edition, 207.

32. These categories are used by Richard Haass and John Dower. See Haass, *War of Necessity*; and Dower, *Cultures of War.*

33. Jikkyō Shuppan, *Kōkō nihonshi B*, 2014; Tokyo Shoseki, *Nihonshi A*, 2014; Tokyo Shoseki, *Shinsen nihonshi B*, 2014; and Daiichi Gakushūsha, *Kōtōgakkō nihonshi A*, 2014.

34. Jikkyō Shuppan, *Kōkō nihonshi B*, 2014, 207.

35. Tokyo Shoseki, *Nihonshi A*, 2014, 136.

36. Yamakawa Shuppan, *Nihonshi A*, 2014, 162; Yamakawa Shuppan, *Shōsetsu nihonshi B*, 2014, 361.

37. Yamanaka's texts are dominant in the market (16% in Japanese History A, and 59% in Japanese History B). However, the combined non-Yamakawa contingent that describes the "war of choice" (e.g., Jikkyō, Tōsho, Daiichi, Shimizu, Sanseidō, and Kirihara) comprises a legitimate counterweight in the market. See Watanabe, "2010 nendo kōkō kyōkasho saitaku jyōkyō—(jō)," and "2010 nendo kōkō kyōkasho saitaku jyōkyō—(chū)."

38. The text *Saishin nihonshi* favored by neonationalists and published by Meiseisha in 2009 (and revised in 2013) is excluded from this analysis because of its very

low circulation figure (0.9% in the Japanese History B market). The text offers a heroic narrative of the Greater East Asia War that was ostensibly waged in self-defense and to "liberate" Asia from Western colonialism. It was originally was published by Hara Shobō in 1987.

39. Seaton, *Japan's Contested War Memories.*
40. Jikkyō Shuppan, *Kōkō nihonshi B*, 2014, 206–17. This text is ranked third in circulation figures (6.4%).
41. Daiichi Gakushūsha, *Kōtōgakkō nihonshi A*, 2014, 114–21, 166.
42. Tokyo Shoseki, *Nihonshi A: Gendai karano rekishi*, 2014, 124–45.
43. Ibid., 132, 136.
44. Ibid., 172–73.
45. Yamakawa Shuppan, *Shōsetsu nihonshi B*, 2014, 345–68.
46. Daiichi Gakushūsha, *Kōtōgakkō nihonshi A*, 2014, 114–19.
47. Jikkyō Shuppan, *Kōkō nihonshi B*, 2014, 217, 255; Tokyo Shoseki, *Shinsen nihonshi B*, 2014, 226, and 247.
48. Tokyo Shoseki, *Nihonshi A*, 2005, 139, 153. These photographs are not available in the 2014 edition.
49. Tokyo Shoseki, *Shinsen nihonshi B*, 2014, 217, 221.
50. Jikkyō Shuppan, *Kōkō nihonshi B*, 2014, 209.
51. Tokyo Shoseki, *Nihonshi A*, 2014, 144, 152.
52. Ibid., 132.
53. Tokyo Shoseki, *Shinsen nihonshi B*, 2014, 225; Jikkyō Shuppan, *Kōkō nihonshi B*, 2014, 217.
54. Jikkyō Shuppan, *Kōkō nihonshi B*, 2014, 217; Daiichi Gakushūsha, *Kōtōgakkō nihonshi A*, 2014, 131.
55. Tokyo Shoseki, *Nihonshi A*, 2014, 145.
56. Yamakawa Shuppan, *Nihonshi A*, 2014, 153, 166.
57. Yamakawa Shuppan, *Shōsetsu nihonshi B*, 2014, 356–57.
58. Tokyo Shoseki, *Gendai shakai*, 2014, 61; Jikkyō Shuppan, *Gendai shakai*, 2014, 94.
59. Ishida, *Nihon no seiji to kotoba 2: 'Heiwa' to 'kokka.'*
60. Jikkyō Shuppan, *Gendai shakai*, 2014, 94.
61. Daiichi Gakushūsha, *Kōtōgakkō kaiteiban gendai shakai*, 2010, 161. This phrase was, however, eliminated in the 2014 edition.
62. Tokyo Shoseki, *Gendai shakai*, 2014, 176.
63. Eyerman, "The Past in the Present."
64. Jikkyō Shuppan, *Kōkō seiji keizai*, 2014, 27; Daiichi Gakushūsha, *Kōtōgakkō seiji keizai*, 2014, 29.
65. Yamamuro, *Kenpō 9-jō no shisō suimyaku.*
66. K. Fujiwara, *Heiwa no riarizumu*, 15; Ishida, *Nihon no seiji to kotoba 2: 'Heiwa' to 'kokka,'* 94; Izumikawa, "Explaining Japanese Antimilitarism Normative and Realist Constraints on Japan's Security Policy"; Koseki, *'Heiwa kokka' nihon no saikentō*, 96.
67. Samuels, *Securing Japan.* See chapter 1 and chapter 5 for further discussions of the current political debate about collective self-defense.
68. The top three textbooks in Contemporary Society and the top three textbooks in Politics/Economy analyzed together in this section are Daiichi Gakushūsha, *Kōtōgakkō gendai shakai* 2014; Tōkyo Shoseki, *Gendai shakai* 2014; Jikkyō, Shuppan *Gendai shakai* 2014; Daiichi Gakushūsha, *Kōtōgakkō seiji keizai* 2014; Tokyo Shoseki, *Seiji keizai* 2014; and Jikkyō Shuppan: *Kōkō seiji keizai* 2014. Students typically elect one, but not both courses.

69. Jikkyō Shuppan, *Kōkō seiji keizai*, 2014, 31.
70. Tokyo Shoseki, *Seiji keizai*, 2014, 46.
71. Hein and Selden, "The Lessons of War."
72. Daiichi Gaakushūsha, *Kōtōgakkō seiji keizai*, 2014, 105.
73. Tokyo Shoseki, *Seiji keizai*, 2014, 102.
74. Ethics is the high school counterpart of Moral Education taught in middle and elementary schools.
75. The national curricular guidelines suggest that Ethics is instrumental in forging the civic identity and moral ideals of peace and democracy. Ministry of Education and Science, *Kōto gakkō gakushū shidōyōryō*, 2009. The three top-selling Ethics texts sampled here are Tokyo Shoseki's *Rinri* 2014, Shimizu Shoin's *Kōtōgakkō gendai rinri* 2014, and Daiichi Gakkushūsha's *Kōtōgakkō rinri* 2014.
76. Shimizu Shoin, *Kōtōgakkō gendai rinri*, 2014, 104, 108–109, 111–12. 117.
77. Some public figures are singled out for their principled opposition to war, dissent against the authoritarian state, and paying the ultimate personal price for it. Such public intellectuals of prewar Japan who appear consistently across texts include the Christian pacifist Uchimura Kanzō who was prosecuted for lèse-majesté when he refused to bow to the Imperial Rescript, and the socialist-anarchist pacifist Kōtoku Shūsui who was executed for treason by the government. Ibid., 111–12; Daiichi Gakushūsha, *Kōtōgakkō rinri*, 101.
78. Tokyo Shoseki, *Rinri*, 2014, 99, 197.
79. Study manga often target school children in the latter years of elementary school and in middle school, typically ages 10–15.
80. Morris-Suzuki, *The Past Within Us*, 170; Penney, "Far from Oblivion."
81. Gakken Manga, *Nihon no rekishi*, vols. 1–17, 1982; Shōgakkan Shōnen Shōjo Gakushū Manga, *Nihon no rekishi*, vols. 1–21, 1983; Shūeisha Gakushūmanga, *Nihon no rekishi*, vols. 1–20, 1998
82. "Sensō o nikumu." Shōgakkan Shōnen Shōjo Gakushū Manga, *Nihon no rekishi*, vol. 20, 1983, 110.
83. "Sensō—iyadane, sensō." Shūeisha Gakushūmanga, *Nihon no rekishi*, vol. 18, 1998, 58.
84. Gakken Manga, *Nihon no rekishi: 15*, 121
85. Shōgakkan, *Nihon no rekishi: 20*, 102.
86. Ibid., 157.
87. Shūeisha, *Nihon no rekishi: 18*, 72,75, 98–104.
88. Shōgakkan, *Nihon no rekishi: 20*, 53, 58.
89. Ibid., 81.
90. Shūeisha, *Nihon no rekishi: 18*, 103. Shōgakkan, *Nihon no rekishi: 20*, 106.
91. Ibid., 115.
92. Shūeisha, *Nihon no rekishi: 18*, 111.
93. Ibid., 114.
94. Gakken Manga, *Nihon no rekishi: 15*, 121.
95. Nichinōken and Fujiko, *Doraemon no shakaika omoshiro kōryaku*. Quotes on pages 192, 195, 195, 199, 201.
96. Ibid., 200–201.
97. As of this writing, a new edition of this series edited by Hamagakuen has changed the format of the book, and it is now geared toward presenting facts didactically to help students study for the middle school entrance exams. Nobita's humorous asides are no longer available in the 36 pages of text about the war in the

new edition, and the depiction of Japan as shadow perpetrator has also been reduced considerably. Hamagakuen and Fujiko. *Doraemon no shakaika omoshiro kōryaku: nihon no rekishi 3 (Edo jidai kōhan—gendai), Doraemon no gakushū shiriizu.*

98. Mizuki, *Sōin gyokusai seyo! (Onward Toward Our Noble Deaths!)*, 357.
99. Penney, "'War Fantasy' and Reality."
100. Mizuki, *Komikku Shōwashi.* 8 vols. To date, one half of this series is available in English translation.
101. For example, Mizuki describes graphically how only one-tenth of the soldiers survived the disastrous Imphal Campaign in 1944, in *Komikku Shōwashi,* 5: 26.
102. Ibid., vol. 8: 248.
103. Ibid., 261–63.
104. Ishinomori, *Manga History of Japan,* 53: 22–23.
105. Ashplant, Dawson, Roper. "The Politics of War Memory," 44.
106. Schivelbusch, *Culture of Defeat.*
107. Sōka Gakkai Seinenbu, *Cries for Peace.*
108. Murakami, *Sengo nihon no heiwa kyōiku no shakaigakuteki kenkyū.*
109. Hochschild, *The Managed Heart*; and Hochschild, "Emotion Work, Feeling Rules, and Social Structure."
110. Asahi Shinbun Shuzaihan, *'Kako no kokufuku' to aikokushin: Rekishi to mukiau 2*; Takahashi, *Nihonjin no kachikan: Sekai rankingu.* These data are also consistent with successive Chūgakusei Shinbun surveys of middle school children in the 1990s.
111. Rekishi Kyōikusha Kyōgikai, *Rekishi kyōiku shakaika kyōiku nenpō 2005.*
112. Japan Naikakufu, "Shakai ishiki ni kansuru yoron chōsa." From 21.1% in 1997 to 45.0% in 2006.
113. T. Takahashi, *Nihonjin no kachikan.*
114. Japan Naikakufu, "Shakai ishiki ni kansuru yoron chōsa."
115. Nihon Seishōnen Kenkyūjo, *Kōkōsei no gakushū ishiki to nichijō seikatsu: Nihon, amerika, chūgoku no 3 kakoku hikaku,* 8.
116. Buruma, *Wages of Guilt.*
117. Sakamoto, *Rekishi kyōiku o kangaeru.*
118. Hein and Takenaka, "Exhibiting World War II"; Yamabe, "Nihon no heiwa hakubutsukan."
119. Kobayashi, *Sensōron,* 1998; *Sensōron 2,* 2001; and *Sensōron 3,* 2003.
120. Tsukurukai abbreviates Atarashii rekishi kyōkasho o tsukurukai (Committee to Write New Textbooks).
121. Sato Takayuki, *Asahi Shinbun,* Nagoya edition, May 21, 2006.
122. Itō Megumi, *Asahi Shinbun,* Nagoya edition, December 8, 2003.
123. Tamura Hiroki, *Asahi Shinbun,* Nagoya edition, May 13, 2002.

Chapter 5
1. The original Japanese phrases are "shigoto wa heiwa" and "mamoritai hito ga iru."
2. It was first named Keisatsu yobitai (Police Reserve Force), then re-named Hoantai (Security Force), before it was finally named Jieitai (Self-Defense Force) in 1954.
3. Berger, *War, Guilt, and World Politics after World War II.*
4. Magosaki, "Senkaku mondai: Nihon no gokai."
5. The full text of Article 9 is *Aspiring sincerely to an international peace based on justice and order, the Japanese people forever renounce war as a sovereign right of the nation and*

the threat or use of force as means of settling international disputes. (2) To accomplish the aim of the preceding paragraph, land, sea, and air forces, as well as other war potential, will never be maintained. The right of belligerency of the state will not be recognized.

6. Kosuge, *Sengo wakai.*

7. Ibid., 38–39.

8. General Douglas MacArthur's statement on September 12, 1945, cited in Dower, *Embracing Defeat,* 44. For further discussion of this perception and its consequences, see Buruma, *Year Zero,* and also Wagner-Pacifici, *The Art of Surrender.*

9. Dower, *Embracing Defeat.*

10. Ōtake, *Saigunbi to nashonarizumu.*

11. Japan's military expenditure was $60 billion in 2012; 10% of this sum goes to maintaining the US forces.

12. Those in favor of constitutional revision were 43% in 2014. Yomiuri Shinbun, "Kenpō yoron chōsa," 2014. http://www.yomiuri.co.jp/feature/opinion/koumoku/20140317-OYT8T50000.html. Yomiuri Shinbunsha Yoron Chōsabu, *Nihon no yoron,* 477; Yomiuri Shinbun, "Kenpō yoron chōsa," 2008, http://www.yomiuri.co.jp/editorial/news/20080407-OYT1T00791.htm.

13. Arms Control Association, "Fact Sheet: North Korea's Nuclear and Ballistic Missile Programs," July 2013, http://armscontrolcenter.org/publications/factsheets/fact_sheet_north_korea_nuclear_and_missile_programs/; "North Korea Fires 2 More Ballistic Missiles," *New York Times,* July 8, 2014.

14. Cabinet Decision on Development of Seamless Security Legislation to Ensure Japan's Survival and Protect Its People, July 1, 2014.

15. "Shūdanteki jieiken kōshi yōnin kettei, hantai ga 54%," *Nikkei Shinbun,* July 2, 2014.

16. For the viewpoints of proponents and opponents of this issue, see Pempel, "Why Japan's Collective Self-Defence Is So Politicised"; Green and Hornung, "Ten Myths About Japan's Collective Self-Defense Change"; Wakefield and Martin, "Reexamining "Myths" About Japan's Collective Self-Defense Change." In Japanese, see Toyoshita and Koseki, *Shūdanteki jieiken to anzen hoshō.*

17. Hashimoto, "Japanese and German Projects of Moral Recovery."

18. Samuels, *Securing Japan*; Izumikawa, "Explaining Japanese Antimilitarism"; Katzenstein, *Cultural Norms and National Security*; Berger, *War, Guilt, and World Politics.* For a cogent discussion of how this point on multivalence applies also to the politics of the monarchy in postwar society, see Ruoff, *The People's Emperor.*

19. Reconciliationists often cross party lines and include both LDP politicians (such as Gotōda Masaharu, Katō Kōichi, Kōno Yōhei, and Miyazawa Kiichi) and socialist politicians (such as Murayama Tomi'ichi).

20. National Defense Program Outline (NDPO) [*Bōei yōkō*] 2004.

21. The SDF was stationed in a "noncombat zone" from December 2003 to December 2008. The mission consisted mainly of generating water supply, restoring schools and roads, and medical support.

22. A. Smith, *National Identity,* 11–13, 66.

23. Sankei Shinbun, "Gorin no toshi, nihon wa? Shushō: 'Kaikenzumi desu ne'" January 1, 2014, http://sankei.jp.msn.com/life/news/140101/trd14010122450004-n1.htm.

24. Higuchi, *Ima, "kenpō kaisei" o dō kangaeru ka: "Sengo nippon" o "hoshu" surukoto no imi.*

25. Kōno, "Gendai nihon no sedai"; NHK Hōsō Bunka Kenkyūjo, *Gendai nihonjin no ishikikōzō*.
26. Japan had the highest proportion of people who are not proud of their country (48.3%) compared to the United States (37.1%) and China (20.3%), Nihon Seishonen Kenkyūjo, *Kōkōsei no gakushū ishiki to nichijō seikatsu*, 8.
27. Kōno, "Gendai nihon no sedai"; Kōno and Takahashi, "Nihonjin no ishiki henka no 35-nen no kiseki (1)"; Kōno, Takahashi, and Hara, "Nihonjin no ishiki henka no 35-nen no kiseki (2)."
28. Zarakol, *After Defeat*, 198, 243, 253.
29. Kosuge, *Sengo wakai*, 192.
30. This view of apology echoes nationalistic sentiments elsewhere; an oft-cited example is that of US Vice President George H. W. Bush who refused to apologize for the US military shooting down an Iranian Air aircraft carrying 290 civilians in 1988 ("I will never apologize for the United States of America. I don't care what the facts are"), *Time*, September 12, 1988, 86.
31. By all accounts, Abe has inherited much of his conservative agenda from his grandfather Kishi Nobusuke, a wartime cabinet minister who was jailed but never tried as a war-crimes suspect. Kishi became prime minister in 1957 but resigned three years later after ramming through parliament the ratification of the US-Japan Security Treaty. Wakamiya, *Wakai to nashonarizumu*. For illustrations of *generational proximity* in the families of wartime elites, see Hayashi, *Senpan no mago*. Forty percent of LDP lawmakers are children and grandchildren of lawmakers. "Japan's Political Dynasties Come under Fire but Prove Resilient," *New York Times*, March 15, 2009.
32. Founding statement of the Article 9 Association, June 10, 2004, http://www.9-jo.jp/news/news_index.html#2013poster.
33. Article 9 Association: http://www.9-jo.jp/news/undou/20060206zenkokukou ryuu-yobikake.htm. "Ōe Kenzaburōshi mo tōjō," *Sankei Shinbun*, June 21, 2014.
34. Ikegami, *The Taming of the Samurai*; Yamamuro, *Kenpō 9-jō no shisō suimyaku*, 236; K. Fujiwara, *Heiwa no riarizumu*.
35. Dudden, "The Nomination of Article 9 of Japan's Constitution for a Nobel Peace Prize."
36. Akazawa, *Yasukuni jinja*, 7, 257–60.
37. For example, see Daiichi Gakushūsha's Ethics textbook *Kōtōgakkō rinri*, kaiteiban edition, 2010, 192. Pugwash Conferences on Science and World Affairs. "Principles, Structure and Activities of Pugwash for the Eleventh Quinquennium (2007–2012)." The Pugwash movement won the Nobel Peace Prize in 1995.
38. K. Fujiwara, *Heiwa no riarizumu*.
39. "Scholars form 'Save Constitutional Democracy' to Challenge Abe's 'Omnipotence'," *Asahi Shinbun Asia & Japan Watch*, April 18, 2014. http://constitutionaldemocracyjapan.tumblr.com/media.
40. Okuhira and Yamaguchi, *Shūdanteki jieiken no naniga mondaika*.
41. Sakaki, *Japan and Germany as Regional Actors*; Kondo, *Kokusai rekishi kyōkasho taiwa*; Schissler and Soysal, *The Nation, Europe, and the World*.
42. Sakaki, *Japan and Germany as Regional Actors*; Yang and Sin, "Striving for Common History Textbooks in Northeast Asia."
43. This text has been described variously as a textbook, supplementary guide, or a teachers' guide.
44. Nitchūkan 3-koku Kyōtsū Rekishi Kyōzai Iinkai, *Mirai o hiraku rekishi: Higashiajia 3-koku no kingendaishi* [*History That Opens the Future*].

45. *History That Opens the Future*, 199, 217.

46. Kasahara, "Shimin karano higashiajia rekishi kyōkasho taiwa no jissen"; Kim, "Higashiajia no rekishi ninshiki kyōyū e no dai ippo."

47. Shin, "Historical Reconciliation in Northeast Asia."

48. Ibid. Park, "A History That Opens the Future"; Sneider, "The War over Words."

49. The reports of the official Japan-ROK (South Korea) Joint History Research Committee (2002–2005 and 2007–2010) are available at http://www.mofa.go.jp/region/asia-paci/korea/report0506.html; http://www.mofa.go.jp/announce/announce/2010/3/0323_02.html. The reports of the Japan-China Joint History Research Committee (2006–2009) are available at http://www.mofa.go.jp/mofaj/area/china/rekishi_kk.html. For an assessment of how textbooks' contents differ on controversial events, see Yoshida, *The Making of the "Rape of Nanking."*

50. Genron NPO, "Dai 2 kai nikkan kyōdō yoron chōsa," 2014, http://www.genron-npo.net/pdf/forum_1407.pdf; Genron NPO, "Dai 10 kai nitchū kyōdō yoron chōsa kekka," 2014, http://www.genron-npo.net/pdf/2014forum.pdf. Those who thought of Japan as a pacifist society were 10.5% in China and 5.3% in South Korea; those who thought of Japan as a reconciliationist society were 6.7% in China and 3.9% in South Korea. Those who believed that Japan espoused militarism today were 36.5% in China and 53.1% in South Korea. In China, respondents believed that the "history problem" (31.9%) and the Senkaku/Diaoyu Islands (64.8%) were major obstacles for developing a good relationship; in South Korea, the respondents ranked Takeshima/Dokdo Island (92.2%) and the "history problem" (52.2%) highly as major obstacles for building friendships.

51. Japan Naikakufu, "Gaikō ni kansuru yoron chōsa."

52. Nitchūkan 3-koku Kyōtsū Rekishi Hensan Iinkai, *Atarashii higashiajia no kingendaishi (jō)*, vol. 1; Nitchūkan 3-koku Kyōtsū Rekishi Hensan Iinkai, *Atarashii higashiajia no kingendaishi (ge)*, vol. 2.

53. Utsumi et al., *Sengo sekinin.*

54. Alexander, "Toward a Theory of Cultural Trauma."

55. Zarakol, *After Defeat*; Mark, *Unfinished Revolution.* See also Lisa Yoneyama's assessment of the West-centric discourse of Enlightenment applied to remembering Hiroshima in *Hiroshima Traces: Time, Space, and the Dialectics of Memory.*

56. Olick, *Politics of Regret.* See also Kim and Schwartz, *Northeast Asia's Difficult Past.*

57. Zarakol, "Ontological (in)Security and State Denial of Historical Crimes," 7.

58. Jarausch and Geyer, *Shattered Past*, 106.

59. Fulbrook, *Dissonant Lives*; Herf, *Divided Memory*; Moses, *German Intellectuals and the Nazi Past*; Morina, *Legacies of Stalingrad.*

60. Art, *The Politics of the Nazi Past in Germany and Austria*; Rousso, *The Vichy Syndrome*; Lagrou, *The Legacy of Nazi Occupation.*

61. Jarausch and Geyer, *Shattered Past*, 10.

62. Cohen-Pfister and Wienröder-Skinner, *Victims and Perpetrators, 1933–1945*; Niven, *Germans as Victims*; Moeller, *War Stories.*

63. Hashimoto, "Japanese and German Projects of Moral Recovery."

64. Mosse, *Fallen Soldiers*; Bessel, *Germany after the First World War.*

65. Referring to the analogous Dutch case, Ron Eyerman calls this phenomenon "accumulated traumas." Eyerman, *The Assassination of Theo Van Gogh.*

66. The Federal Republic of Germany banned both the neo-Nazi Nationalist Party (1952) and the Communist Party (1956) from parliament. See Berger, *War, Guilt, and World Politics*, 56–57.

67. Currie, *The Constitution of the Federal Republic of Germany.*
68. Giesen, *Triumph and Trauma.*
69. "Chasing Death Camp Guards with New Tools," *New York Times*, May 6, 2014.
70. Müller, *Constitutional Patriotism.*
71. Berger, *War, Guilt and World Politics*, 35.
72. Friedrich. *Der Brand, Deutschland im Bombenkrieg 1940–1945.*
73. Bartov, *Germany's War and the Holocaust.*
74. Levi, *The Drowned and the Saved.*
75. Alexander, *The Meanings of Social Life.*
76. Giesen, *Triumph and Trauma*, 155.
77. Gordon, *Postwar Japan as History.*
78. Yoda, "A Roadmap to Millennial Japan."
79. Akagi, " 'Maruyama Masao' o hippatakitai: 31sai friitā."
80. Schoppa, *Race for the Exits.*
81. Furuichi, *Zetsubō no kuni no kōfuku na wakamonotachi.* In a 2013 survey, young people in their 20s reported the highest level (78.4%) of life satisfaction compared to other age cohorts. See Japan Naikakufu, *Kokumin seikatsu ni kansuru yoron chōsa.*
82. Oguma and Ueno,*'Iyashi' no nashonarizumu*, 215.
83. Yasuda, *Netto to aikoku*; Kitahara and Paku. *Okusama wa aikoku.* These dynamics are similar to those that produce solidarity within the ranks of racist hate groups in the United States. See Blee, *Inside Organized Racism.*
84. Magosaki, "Senkaku mondai: Nihon no gokai," 85.
85. "China Passes U.S. in Trade with Japan," washingtonpost.com, January 27, 2005; "What's at Stake in China-Japan Spat," *Wall Street Journal: China Real Time Report*, September 17, 2013, http://blogs.wsj.com/chinarealtime/2012/09/17/whats-at-stake-in-china-japan-spat-345-billion-to-start/.
86. These ambiguities and tensions have to be kept in mind in assessing the likelihood that mutual economic interests or some form of economic integration may, as has been the case in Europe, be a pathway to stabilizing regional relations in East Asia.
87. Kosuge, *Sengo wakai;* K. Fujiwara, "Ajia keizai gaikō no saiken o."
88. He, *The Research for Reconciliation*; Zheng, *Discovering Chinese Nationalism in China.*
89. "Japan to Build Two More Aegis Destroyers to Boost Missile Defense," *Japan Times*, November 5, 2013.
90. Genron NPO, "Dai 10 kai nitchū kyōdō yoron chōsa kekka."
91. Japan Naikakufu, "Jieitai. Bōei ni kansuru yoron chōsa."
92. He, *The Research for Reconciliation.* Japan's next bid to reform the UN Security Council is planned for 2015. Mainichi Shinbun, "Anpori kaikaku: Teian e," July 21, 2014. For the modern history of Japan and China's rivalry caught in the global West-dominated world, see Iriye, *China and Japan in the Global Setting.*
93. Schivelbusch, *Culture of Defeat.*
94. Kosuge, *Sengo wakai*, 210.
95. Assmann, "Four Formats of Memory," 30.
96. Eyerman, Alexander, and Breese, *Narrating Trauma*; Giesen, *Triumph and Trauma*, 117.

Bibliography

Akagi, Tomohiro. 2007. "'Maruyama Masao' o hippatakitai: 31sai friitā. Kibōwa
    sensō." *Ronza* 1:53–59.
Akazawa, Shiro. 2005. *Yasukuni jinja: Semegiau 'senbotsusa tsuitō' no yukue.*
    Tokyo: Iwanami Shoten.
———. 2004. "Senbotsusa tsuitō to yasukuni jinja mondai o dō kangaeruka." *Sekai*
    9:97–103.
Alexander, Jeffrey C. 2012. *Trauma: A Social Theory.* Malden, MA: Polity Press.
———. 2010. *The Performance of Politics: Obama's Victory and the Democratic Struggle for
    Power.* New York: Oxford University Press.
———. 2004. "Toward a Theory of Cultural Trauma." In *Cultural Trauma and
    Collective Identity*, edited by Jeffrey C. Alexander, Ron Eyerman, Bernhard Giesen,
    Neil Smelser, and Piotr Sztompka, 1–30. Berkeley: University of California Press.
———. 2003. *The Meanings of Social Life: A Cultural Sociology.* New York: Oxford
    University Press.
Alexander, Jeffrey C., Ron Eyerman, Bernhard Giesen, Neil Smelser, and Piotr
    Sztompka. 2004. *Cultural Trauma and Collective Identity.* Berkeley: University of
    California Press.
Ambrose, Stephen E. 1992. *Band of Brothers: E Company, 506th Regiment, 101st
    Airborne: from Normandy to Hitler's Eagle's Nest.* New York: Simon & Schuster.
Anderson, Benedict. 1991. *Imagined Communities: Reflections on the Origin and Spread of
    Nationalism.* Rev. and extended ed. London: Verso.
Antoniou, Vasilia Lilian, and Yasemin Nuhoæglu Soysal. 2005. "Nation and the
    Other in Greek and Turkish History Textbooks." In *The Nation, Europe, and the
    World: Textbooks and Curricula in Transition*, edited by Hanna Schissler and Yasemin
    Nuhoæglu Soysal, 105–21. New York: Berghahn Books.
Arai, Shin'ichi. 1995. *Sensō sekininron: Gendaishi kara no toi.* Tokyo: Iwanami Shoten.
Aramaki, Shigeto. 2003. "Jiyū, heiwa, minshushugi o motomete: Musubini kaete."
    In *Ienaga Saburō no nokoshita mono hikitsugu mono*, edited by Takashi Ōta, Hiroshi
    Oyama, and Keiji Nagahara, 233–40. Tokyo Nihon Hyōronsha.
Arms Control Association. 2013. "Fact Sheet: North Korea's Nuclear and Ballistic
    Missile Programs," July, http://armscontrolcenter.org/publications/factsheets/
    fact_sheet_north_korea_nuclear_and_missile_programs/.

Pinker

Art, David. 2006. *The Politics of the Nazi Past* in Germany and Austria. Cambridge: Cambridge University Press.

Asahi Shinbunsha. 2010. *Sensō taiken: Asahi shinbun e no tegami*. Tokyo: Asahi Shinbunsha.

———. 2003. *Senjō taiken: "Koe" ga kataritsugu rekishi*. Tokyo: Asahi Shinbunsha.

———. 1988. *Nihonjin no sensō*. Tokyo: Heibonsha.

———. 1987. Tēma Danwashitsu. *Sensō: Chi to namida de tsuzutta shōgen*. 2 vols. Tokyo: Asahi Sonorama.

Asahi Shinbun 'Shinbun to Sensō' Shuzaihan. 2008. *Shinbun to sensō*. Tokyo: Asahi Shinbun Shuppan.

Asahi Shinbun Shuzaihan. 2007. *'Kako no kokufuku' to aikokushin: Rekishi to mukiau 2*. Tokyo: Asahi Shinbunsha.

———. 2006. *Sensō sekinin to tsuitō: Rekishi to mukiau 1*. Tokyo: Asahi Shinbunsha.

Ashplant, T. G., Graham Dawson, and Michael Roper. 2000. "The Politics of War Memory and Commemoration: Contexts, Structures and Dynamics." In *Commemorating War: The Politics of Memory*, edited by T. G. Ashplant, Graham Dawson, and Michael Roper, 3–85. New Brunswick, NJ: Transaction.

Assmann, Aleida. 2008. "Transformations between History and Memory." *Social Research* 75 (1):49–72.

———. 2006. "On the (In)Compatibility of Guilt and Suffering in German Memory." *Journal: German Life & Letters* 59 (2):187–200.

———. 2006. *Der lange Schatten der Vergangenheit: Erinnerungskultur und Geschichtspolitik*. Munich: Beck.

———. 2004. "Four Formats of Memory: From Individual to Collective Constructions of the Past." In *Cultural Memory and Historical Consciousness in the German-Speaking World since 1500*, edited by Christian Emden and David Midgley, 19–37. New York: Peter Lang.

Assmann, Jan. 2010. "Communicative and Cultural Memory." In *A Companion to Cultural Memory Studies*, edited by Astrid Erll and Ansgar Nünning, 109–18. Berlin: Walter de Gruyter.

Bar-On, Dan. 1999. *The Indescribable and the Undiscussable: Reconstructing Human Discourse after Trauma*. Budapest: Central European University Press.

———. 1995. *Fear and Hope: Three Generations of the Holocaust*. Cambridge, MA: Harvard University Press.

———. 1993. "Holocaust Perpetrators and Their Children: A Paradoxical Morality." In *The Collective Silence: German Identity and the Legacy of Shame*, edited by Barbara Heimannsberg and Christoph J Schmidt, 195–208. San Francisco: Jossey-Bass.

Barkan, Elazar. 2000. *The Guilt of Nations: Restitution and Negotiating Historical Injustices*. New York: W.W. Norton.

Bartov, Omer. 2003. *Germany's War and the Holocaust: Disputed Histories*. Ithaca: Cornell University Press.

Berger, Thomas. 2012. *War, Guilt, and World Politics after World War II*. New York: Cambridge University Press.

———. 1998. *Cultures of Antimilitarism: National Security in Germany and Japan*. Baltimore, MD: Johns Hopkins University Press.

Bessel, Richard. 1993. *Germany after the First World War*. Oxford: Clarendon Press.

Bhabha, Homi. 1990. *Nation and Narration*. London: Routledge.

Blee, Kathleen. 2002. *Inside Organized Racism: Women in the Hate Movement*. Berkeley: University of California Press.

Blight, David W. 2001. *Race and Reunion: The Civil War in American Memory.* Cambridge, MA: Belknap Press of Harvard University Press.

Bodnar, John E. 2010. *The "Good War" in American Memory.* Baltimore, MD: Johns Hopkins University Press.

Browning, Christopher R. 1992. *Ordinary Men: Reserve Police Battalion 101 and the Final Solution in Poland.* New York: HarperCollins.

Bruner, Jerome S. 1990. *Acts of Meaning.* Cambridge, MA: Harvard University Press.

Buchholz, Petra. 1995. "Tales of War: Autobiographies and Private Memories in Japan and Germany." In *Memories of War: The Second World War and Japanese Historical Memory in Comparative Perspective,* edited by Takashi Inoguchi and Lyn Jackson. Tokyo: United Nations University Press. http://archive.unu.edu/unupress/m-war.html#tales.

Buckley-Zistel, Susanne. 2012. "Between Pragmatism, Coercion and Fear: Chosen Amnesia after the Rwandan Genocide." In *Memory and Political Change,* edited by Aleida Assmann and Linda Shortt, 72–88. New York: Palgrave Macmillan.

Bude, Heinz. 1992. *Bilanz Der Nachfolge: Die Bundesrepublik und Der Nationalsozialismus.* Frankfurt am Main: Suhrkamp.

Bungei Shunjū. 2014. "Daini no haisen: Dankaikoso senpanda." *Bungei Shunjū* April, 4:275–327.

———. 2007. "Shōgen: Chichi to haha no sensō." *Bungei Shunjū* September, 9:260–302.

———. 2005. "Nihon yaburetari." *Bungei Shunjū* November, 11: 261–327.

———. 1995. "Genkō boshū: Wagaya no sengo 50-nen." *Bungei Shunjū* January, 1:505.

———. 1989. "Kagayakeru shōwajin: Ketsuzokuno shōgen 55." *Bungei Shunjū* September, 9:126–223.

Burchardt, Natasha. 1993. "Transgenerational Transmission in the Families of Holocaust Survivors in England." In *Between Generations: Family Models, Myths, and Memories,* edited by Daniel Bertaux and Paul Richard Thompson, 121–37. Oxford: Oxford University Press.

Burke, Peter. 1989. "History as Social Memory." In *Memory: History, Culture and the Mind,* edited by Thomas Butler, 97–113. Malden: Blackwell.

Buruma, Ian. 2013. *Year Zero: A History of 1945.* New York: Penguin Press.

———. 1994. *The Wages of Guilt: Memories of War in Germany and Japan.* New York: Farrar Straus Giroux.

Caruth, Cathy. 1996. *Unclaimed Experience: Trauma, Narrative, and History.* Baltimore: Johns Hopkins University Press.

Chamoto, Shigemasa, Kazuhiko Ozawa, Akiyoshi Fujioka, and Kiyofumi Kojima. 1997. "Zadankai: Sensō sedai no kataru sensō." *Sekai* 9:135–51.

Chung, Jae-hyun. 2007. "Kan'nichi ni tsukimatou rekishino kage to sono kokufuku no tame no kokoromi." In *Rekishi kyōkasho mondai,* edited by Hiroshi Mitani, 248–71. Tokyo: Nihon Tosho Sentā.

Cohen, Stanley. 2001. *States of Denial: Knowing About Atrocities and Suffering.* Cambridge, MA: Polity Press.

Cohen-Pfister, Laurel, and Dagmar Wienröder-Skinner. 2006. *Victims and Perpetrators, 1933–1945: (Re)presenting the Past in Post-unification Culture.* Berlin: W. de Gruyter.

Confino, Alon. 2006. *Germany as a Culture of Remembrance: Promises and Limits of Writing History.* Chapel Hill: University of North Carolina Press.

Cook, Haruko Taya, and Theodore F. Cook. 1992. *Japan at War: An Oral History.* New York: New Press.

Currie, David P. 1994. *The Constitution of the Federal Republic of Germany.* Chicago, IL: University of Chicago Press.

erp. G. defect - why this comparison -
same time + war + she trained in Hamburg

Dierkes, Julian. 2010. *Postwar History Education in Japan and the Germanys: Guilty Lessons*. London: Routledge.

Dittmar, Linda, and Gene Michaud. 1990. *From Hanoi to Hollywood: The Vietnam War in American Film*. New Brunswick, NJ: Rutgers University Press.

Dower, John W. 2010. *Cultures of War: Pearl Harbor, Hiroshima, 9-11, Iraq*. New York: W.W. Norton.

———. 1999. *Embracing Defeat: Japan in the Wake of World War II*. New York: W.W. Norton.

Dudden, Alexis. 2014. "The Nomination of Article 9 of Japan's Constitution for a Nobel Peace Prize" *Japan Focus: The Asia-Pacific Journal*, April 20.

———. 2008. *Troubled Apologies Among Japan, Korea, and the United States*. New York: Columbia University Press.

Duus, Peter. 2011. "War Stories." In *History Textbooks and the Wars in Asia: Divided Memories*, edited by Gi-Wook Shin and Daniel Sneider, 101–14. New York: Routledge.

Eliasoph, Nina. 1999. "'Everyday Racism' in a Culture of Avoidance: Civil Society, Speech and Taboo." *Social Problems* 46 (4):479–502.

———. 1998. *Avoiding Politics: How Americans Produce Apathy in Everyday Life*. Cambridge: Cambridge University Press.

———. 1997. "'Close to Home': The Work of Avoiding Politics." *Theory and Society* 26 (4):605–47.

Eyerman, Ron. 2008. *The Assassination of Theo Van Gogh: From Social Drama to Cultural Trauma, Politics, History, and Culture*. Durham, NC: Duke University Press.

———. 2004. "The Past in the Present." *Acta Sociologica* 47 (2):159–69.

———. 2004. "Cultural Trauma: Slavery and the Formation of African American Identity." In *Cultural Trauma and Collective Identity*, edited by Jeffrey C. Alexander et al., 60–111. Berkeley: University of California Press.

Eyerman, Ron, Jeffrey C. Alexander, and Elizabeth Butler Breese. 2011. *Narrating Trauma: On the Impact of Collective Suffering*. Boulder, CO: Paradigm.

Field, Norma. 1997. "War and Apology: Japan, Asia, the Fiftieth, and After." *Positions* 5 (1):1–49.

Figal, Gerald. 1996. "How to Jibunshi: Making and Marketing Self-Histories of Showa among the Masses in Postwar Japan." *Journal of Asian Studies* 55 (4):902–33.

FitzGerald, Frances. 1979. *America Revised: History Schoolbooks in the Twentieth Century*. Boston, MA: Little Brown.

Friday, Karl. 2006. "Might Makes Right: Just War and Just Warfare in Early Medieval Japan." In *The Ethics of War in Asian Civilizations: A Comparative Perspective*, edited by Torkel Brekke, 159–84. London: Routledge.

———. 2004. *Samurai, Warfare and the State in Early Medieval Japan*. New York: Routledge.

Friedrich, Jörg. 2002. *Der Brand: Deutschland im Bombenkrieg 1940–1945*. Munich: Propyläen Verlag [English translation: *The Fire: The Bombing of Germany, 1940–1945*, translated by Allison Brown. New York: Columbia University Press, 2006].

Frühstück, Sabine. 2007. *Uneasy Warriors: Gender, Memory, and Popular Culture in the Japanese Army*. Berkeley: University of California Press.

Fujioka, Nobukatsu, and Jiyūshugishikan Kenkyūkai. 1996. *Kyōkashoga oshienai rekishi*. Tokyo: Fusōsha.

Fujii, Tadatoshi. 2000. *Heishitachino sensō: Tegami, nikki, taikenki o yomitoku*. Tokyo: Asahi Shinbunsha.

Fujita, Hisakazu. 1995. *Sensō hanzai towa nanika*. Tokyo: Iwanami Shoten.

Fujiwara, Akira. 2001. *Uejini shita eireitachi*. Tokyo: Aoki Shoten.

Fujiwara, Kiichi. 2010. *Heiwa no riarizumu*. Rev. ed. Tokyo: Iwanami Shoten.

Fukuma, Yoshiaki. 2009. *Sensō taiken no sengoshi: Sedai, kyōyō, ideorogii*. Tokyo: Chūōkōron Shinsha.

———. 2007. *Junkoku to hangyaku: 'Tokkō' no katari no sengoshi*. Tokyo: Seikyūsha.

———. 2006. *'Hansen' no media-shi: Sengo nihon ni okeru seron to yoron no kikkō*. Kyoto: Sekai Shisōsha.

Fukuoka, Kazuya. 2011. "School History Textbooks and Historical Memories in Japan: A Study of Reception." *International Journal of Politics, Culture, and Society* 24 (3–4):83–103.

Fulbrook, Mary. 2011. *Dissonant Lives: Generations and Violence through the German Dictatorships*. Oxford: Oxford University Press.

Furuichi, Noritoshi. 2011. *Zetsubō no kuni no kōfuku na wakamonotachi*. Tokyo: Kodansha.

Genron NPO. 2014. *Dai 2 kai nikkan kyōdō yoron chōsa*.

———. 2014. *Dai 10 kai nitchū kyōdō yoron chōsa kekka*.

Gibney, Frank. 1995. *Sensō: The Japanese Remember the Pacific War. Letters to the Editor of Asahi Shimbun*. Armonk, NY: M.E. Sharpe.

Giesen, Bernhard. 2004. *Triumph and Trauma*. Boulder, CO: Paradigm.

Gillis, John, ed. 1994. *Commemorations: The Politics of National Identity*. Princeton, NJ: Princeton University Press.

Gluck, Carol. 2007. "Operations of Memory: 'Comfort Women' and the World." In *Ruptured Histories: War, Memory, and the Post-Cold War in Asia*, edited by Sheila Miyoshi Jager and Rana Mitter, 47–77. Cambridge, MA: Harvard University Press.

———. 1993. "The Past in the Present." In *Postwar Japan as History*, edited by Andrew Gordon, 64–95. Berkeley: University of California Press.

Goffman, Erving. 1963. *Stigma: Notes on the Management of Spoilt Identity*. Harmondsworth, UK: Penguin.

Goldhagen, Daniel J. 1996. *Hitler's Willing Executioners: Ordinary Germans and the Holocaust*. New York: Alfred Knopf.

Gordon, Andrew, ed. 1993. *Postwar Japan as History*. Berkeley: University of California Press.

Green, Michael, and Jeffrey W. Hornung. 2014. "Ten Myths about Japan's Collective Self-Defense Change: What the Critics Don't Understand about Japan's Constitutional Reinterpretation." *The Diplomat*, July 10.

Haass, Richard. 2009. *War of Necessity, War of Choice: A Memoir of Two Iraq Wars*. New York: Simon & Schuster.

Halbwachs, Maurice. 1992. *On Collective Memory*, edited by Lewis A. Coser. Chicago, IL: University of Chicago Press.

Hamagakuen and Fujio F. Fujiko. 2014. *Doraemon no shakaika omoshiro kōryaku: Nihon no rekishi 3 (Edo jidai kōhan—gendai), Doraemon no gakushū shiriizu*. Tokyo: Shōgakkan.

Hammond, Ellen. 1997. "Commemoration Controversies: The War, the Peace, and Democracy in Japan." In *Living with the Bomb: American and Japanese Cultural Conflicts in the Nuclear Age*, edited by Laura Hein and Mark Selden, 100–21. Armonk, NY: M.E. Sharpe.

Handō, Kazutoshi, Masayasu Hosaka, Terumasa Nakanishi, Kazushige Todaka, Kazuya Fukuda, and Yōko Kato. 2006. *Ano sensō ni naze maketanoka*. Tokyo: Bungei Shunjū.

Hashimoto, Akiko. 2011. "Divided Memories, Contested Histories: The Shifting Landscape in Japan." In *Cultures and Globalization: Heritage, Memory, Identity* edited by Helmut Anheier and Yudhishthir Raj Isar, 239–44. London: Sage.

———. 2004. "Culture, Power and the Discourse of Filial Piety in Japan: The Disempowerment of Youth and Its Social Consequences." In *Filial Piety: Practice and Discourse in Contemporary East Asia*, edited by Charlotte Ikels, 182–97. Stanford, CA: Stanford University Press.

———. 2004. "Power to the Imagination." *Woodrow Wilson International Center for Scholars Asia Program Special Report* 121:9–12.

———. 1999. "Japanese and German Projects of Moral Recovery: Toward a New Understanding of War Memories in Defeated Nations." *Occasional Papers in Japanese Studies 1999–2001*. Cambridge, MA: Reischauer Institute of Japanese Studies.

———. 1996. *The Gift of Generations: Japanese and American Perspectives on Aging and the Social Contract*. New York: Cambridge University Press.

Hashimoto, Akiko, and Charlotte Ikels. 2005. "Filial Piety in Changing Asian Societies." In *Cambridge Handbook on Age and Ageing*, edited by Malcolm Johnson, 437–42. Cambridge: Cambridge University Press.

Hashimoto, Akiko, and John W. Traphagan. 2008. "The Changing Japanese Family." In *Imagined Families, Lived Families: Culture and Kinship in Contemporary Japan*, edited by Akiko Hashimoto and John W. Traphagan, 1–12. Albany: SUNY Press.

Hayashi, Eiichi. 2014. *Senpan no mago: Nihonjin wa ikani sabakarete kitaka*. Tokyo: Shinchōsha.

He, Yinan. 2009. *The Search for Reconciliation: Sino-Japanese and German-Polish Relations since World War II*. New York: Cambridge University Press.

Hecker, Margarete. 1993. "Family Reconstruction in Germany: An Attempt to Confront the Past." In *The Collective Silence: German Identity and the Legacy of Shame*, edited by Barbara Heimannsberg and Christoph J Schmidt, 73–93. San Francisco: Jossey-Bass.

Hein, Laura, and Mark Selden. 2000. "The Lessons of War, Global Power, and Social Change." In *Censoring History: Citizenship and Memory in Japan, Germany, and the United States*, edited by Laura Hein and Mark Selden, 3–50. Armonk, NY: M.E. Sharpe.

———, eds. 2000. *Censoring History: Citizenship and Memory in Japan, Germany, and the United States*. Armonk, NY: M.E. Sharpe.

———, eds. 1997. *Living with the Bomb: American and Japanese Cultural Conflicts in the Nuclear Age*. Armonk, NY: M.E. Sharpe.

Hein, Laura, and Akiko Takenaka. 2007. "Exhibiting World War II in Japan and the United States since 1995." *Pacific Historical Review* 76 (1):61–94.

Herf, Jeffrey. 1997. *Divided Memory: The Nazi Past in the Two Germanys*. Cambridge, MA: Harvard University Press.

Hess, Robert D, and Judith Torney. 2005. *The Development of Political Attitudes in Children*. New Brunswick, NJ: Aldine Transaction.

Higuchi, Yōichi. 2013. *Ima, 'kenpō kaisei' o dōkangaeruka: 'Sengo nihon' o 'hoshu' surukoto no imi*. Tokyo: Iwanami Shoten.

Hirsch, Marianne. 2012. *The Generation of Postmemory: Writing and Visual Culture after the Holocaust*. New York: Columbia University Press.

———. 1997. *Family Frames: Photography, Narrative, and Postmemory.* Cambridge, MA: Harvard University Press.

Hochschild, Arlie Russell. 1983. *The Managed Heart: Commercialization of Human Feeling.* Berkeley: University of California Press.

———. 1979. "Emotion Work, Feeling Rules, and Social Structure." *American Journal of Sociology* 85:551–75.

Hogan, Michael J., ed. 1996. *Hiroshima in History and Memory.* Cambridge: Cambridge University Press.

Hosaka, Masayasu. 2004. "Heishitachi no seishinteki kizuato kara yasukuni mondai o kangaeru." *Sekai* 9:104–107.

Huyssen, Andreas. 2003. *Present Pasts: Urban Palimpsests and the Politics of Memory.* Stanford, CA: Stanford University Press.

Hyakuta, Naoki. 2009. *Eien no zero.* Tokyo: Kodansha.

Hyōdō, Akiko. 2007. "Kagaisha de ari, higaisha de arukoto: 'Eirei' tachi no sei to shi." *Kikan Nihon Shisōshi* 71:87–103.

Ienaga, Saburō. 1986. *Taiheiyō sensō.* 2d ed. Tokyo: Iwanami Shoten.

———. 1985. *Sensō sekinin.* Tokyo: Iwanami Shoten. *the Phantom of Japan*

———. 1978. *The Pacific War, 1931–1945: A Critical Perspective on Japan's Role in World War II.* Translated by Frank Baldwin. New York: Pantheon Books.

Ienaga, Saburō, and Richard H. Minear. 2001. *Japan's Past, Japan's Future: One Historian's Odyssey.* Lanham, MD: Rowman & Littlefield.

Igarashi, Yoshikuni. 2000. *Bodies of Memory: Narratives of War in Postwar Japanese Culture, 1945–1970.* Princeton, NJ: Princeton University Press.

Ikegami, Eiko. 1995. *The Taming of the Samurai: Honorific Individualism and the Making of Modern Japan.* Cambridge, MA: Harvard University Press.

Inoguchi, Takashi. 2004. "Social Capital in Ten Asian Countries." *Japanese Journal of Political Science* 5:197–211.

Ishida, Takeshi. 1989. *Nihon no seiji to kotoba 2: 'Heiwa' to 'kokka.'* Tokyo: Tokyo Daigaku Shuppankai.

Ishinomori, Shōtarō. 1999. *Manga History of Japan.* 55 vol. Tokyo: Chūōkōronsha.

Ishiyama, Hisao. 1993. "Sengo no kokumin no sensō ninshiki to kyōkashosaiban." In *Atarashii rekishi kyōiku.* Vol. 3: *Rekishi ninshikiwa dō tsukuraretekitaka,* edited by Rekishi Kyōikusha Kyōgikai, 297–308. Tokyo: Ōtsuki Shoten.

Itō, Yū. 2006. "'Hadashi no gen' no minzokushi: Gakkō o meguru manga taiken no shosō." In *'Hadashi no gen' ga ita fūkei: Manga, sensō, kioku,* edited by Kazuma Yoshimura and Yoshiaki Fukuma, 147–81. Matsudo-shi: Azusa Shuppansha.

Izawa, Motohiko, and Yomiuri Shinbun Ronsetsu Iinkai. 2001. *Yomiuri vs Asahi: Shasetsu taiketsu 50-nen.* Tokyo: Chūōkōron Shinsha.

Izumikawa, Yasuhiro. 2010. "Explaining Japanese Antimilitarism Normative and Realist Constraints on Japan's Security Policy." *International Security* 35 (2):123–60.

Japan Naikakufu. 2014. *Shakai ishiki ni kansuru chōsa.* Tokyo: Naikakufu. http://survey.gov-online.go.jp/h25/h25-shakai/index.html.

———. 2013. *Kokumin seikatsu ni kansuru yoron chōsa.* Tokyo: Naikakufu.

———. 2012. *Gaikō ni kansuru yoron chōsa.* Tokyo: Naikakufu.

———. 2012. *Jieitai. Bōei ni kansuru yoron chōsa.* Tokyo: Naikakufu.

———. 2009. *Dai 8 kai sekai seinen ishiki chōsa: Kekka gaiyō sokuhō.* Tokyo: Naikakufu. http://www8.cao.go.jp/youth/kenkyu/worldyouth8/html/2-1-1.html

———. 2007. *Shakai ishiki ni kansuru yoron chōsa.* Tokyo: Naikakufu.

Jarausch, Konrad Hugo, and Michael Geyer. 2003. *Shattered Past: Reconstructing German Histories*. Princeton, NJ: Princeton University Press.

Katzenstein, Peter J. 1996. *Cultural Norms and National Security: Police and Military in Postwar Japan*. Ithaca: Cornell University Press.

Karasawa, Tomitarō. 1956. *Kyōkasho no rekishi: Kyōkasho to nihonjin no keisei*. Tokyo: Sōbunsha.

———. 1955. *Kyōshi no rekishi: Kyōshi no seikatsu to rinri*. Tokyo: Sōbunsha.

Kasahara, Tokushi. 2013. "Shimin karano higashiajia rekishi kyōkasho taiwa no jissen: Nitchūkan sankoku ni okeru 'Mirai o hiraku rekishi' to 'Atarashii higashiajia kingendaishi' no hakkō." *Sekai* 840:45–55.

Kato, Norihiro. 1997. *Haisengoron*. Tokyo: Kodansha.

Kato, Yōko. 2007. *Sensō o yomu*. Tokyo: Keisō Shobō.

Kawaguchi, Kaiji, and Osamu Eya. 2002. *Sakebe! "Chinmokuno kokka" nippon*. Tokyo: Bijinesusha.

Kawasaki, Yasushi, and Tetsuji Shibata. 2008. *Kenshō: Nihon no soshiki jānarizumu: Zoku NHK to Asahi shinbun*. Tokyo: Iwanami Shoten.

———. 2004. *Kenshō: Nihon no soshiki jānarizumu: NHK to Asahi shinbun*. Tokyo: Iwanami Shoten.

Kim, Mikyoung, and Barry Schwartz, eds. 2010. *Northeast Asia's Difficult Past: Essays in Collective Memory*. New York: Palgrave Macmillan.

Kim, Seongbo. 2006. "Higashiajia no rekishi ninshiki kyōyū e no daiippo: 'Mirai o hiraku rekishi' no shippitsu katei to kankokunai no hannō." *Sekai* 840 (March):225–34.

Kitahara, Minori, and Suni Paku. 2014. *Okusama wa aikoku*. Tokyo: Kawade Shobō Shinsha.

Kobayashi, Yoshinori. 2003. *Sensōron 3, Shingōmanizumu sengen supesharu*. Tokyo: Gentōsha.

———. 2001. *Sensōron 2, Shingōmanizumu sengen supesharu*. Tokyo: Gentōsha.

———. 1998. *Sensōron, Shingōmanizumu sengen supesharu*. Tokyo: Gentōsha.

Kodomo no Taiken Katsudō Kenkyūkai. 2000. *Kodomo no taiken katsudō tō ni kansuru kokusai hikaku chōsa*. Nagano: Kodomo no Taiken Katsudō Kenkyūkai.

Komuro, Naoki. 2001. *Nihon no haiin: Rekishiwa katsutameni manabu*. Tokyo: Kodansha.

Kondo, Takahiro. 1998. *Kokusai rekishi kyōkasho taiwa: Yōroppa ni okeru "kako" no saihen*. Tokyo: Chūōkōronsha.

Kōno, Kei. 2008. "Gendai nihon no sedai: Sono sekishutsu to tokushitsu." In *Gendai shakai to media, kazoku, sedai*, edited by NHK Hōsō Bunka Kenkyūjo, 14–38. Tokyo: Shinyōsha.

Kōno, Kei, and Motoyoshi Katō. 2004. "'Nihonjin no ishiki' chōsa nimiru 30-nen: Teikasuru jikokueno jishin." *Hōsō Kenkyū to Chōsa* 2:22–65.

Kōno, Kei, and Kōichi Takahashi. 2009. "Nihonjin no ishiki henka no 35-nen no kiseki (1): Dai 8 kai 'nihonjin no ishiki 2008' chōsa kara." *Hōsō Kenkyū to Chōsa* (April):2–39.

Kōno, Kei, Kōichi Takahashi, and Miwako Hara. 2009. "Nihonjin no ishiki henka no 35-nen no kiseki (2): Dai 8 kai 'nihonjin no ishiki 2008' chōsa kara." *Hōsō Kenkyū to Chōsa* (May):2–23.

Koseki, Shōichi. 2002. *'Heiwa kokka' nihon no saikentō*. Tokyo: Iwanami Shoten.

Kosuge, Nobuko. 2005. *Sengo wakai: Nihon wa 'kako' kara tokihanatarerunoka*. Tokyo: Chūōkōron Shinsha.

Kumagai Shin'ichirō. 2002 "Zadankai: Wakamonotachini kataritsugu sensō sekinin." *Shūkan Kinyōbi* 423 (2002):24.

Kurahashi, Ayako. 2002. *Kenpei datta chichi no nokoshita mono: Oyako nidai, kokorono kizuo mitsumeru tabi*. Tokyo: Kōbunken.

Lagrou, Pieter. 2000. *The Legacy of Nazi Occupation Patriotic Memory and National Recovery in Western Europe, 1945–1965*. Cambridge: Cambridge University Press.

Lebert, Norbert, and Stephan Lebert. 2001. *My Father's Keeper: Children of Nazi Leaders: An Intimate History of Damage and Denial*. Translated by Julian Evans. Boston, MA: Little Brown.

Levi, Primo. 1989. *The Drowned and the Saved*. Translated by Raymond Rosenthal. New York: Vintage.

Lifton, Robert Jay. 1973. *Home from the War: Vietnam Veterans: Neither Victims nor Executioners*. New York: Simon and Schuster.

———. 1967. *Death in Life: Survivors of Hiroshima*. Harmondsworth, UK: Penguin Books.

Lind, Jennifer M. 2008. *Sorry States: Apologies in International Politics*. Ithaca: Cornell University Press.

Link, Bruce G., and Jo C. Phelan. 2001. "Conceptualizing Stigma." *Annual Review of Sociology* 27:363–85.

Macleod, Jenny. 2008. *Defeat and Memory: Cultural Histories of Military Defeat in the Modern Era*. New York: Palgrave Macmillan.

Magosaki, Ukeru. 2012. "Senkaku mondai: Nihon no gokai" *Sekai* 836 (11):86–92

Makita, Tetsuo. 2000. "Nihonjin no sensō to heiwakan: Sono jizoku to fūka." *Hōsō Kenkyū to Chōsa* 50 (9):2–19.

Margalit, Avishai. 2002. *The Ethics of Memory*. Cambridge, MA: Harvard University Press.

Mark, James. 2010. *The Unfinished Revolution: Making Sense of the Communist Past in Central-Eastern Europe*. New Haven: Yale University Press.

Matsumoto, Ken'ichi. 2006. *Nihon no shippai: Daini no kaikoku to daitōa sensō*. Tokyo: Iwanami Shoten.

McCormack, Jo. 2007. *Collective Memory: France and the Algerian War (1954–1962)*. Lanham, MD: Lexington Books.

Michiba, Chikanobu. 2008. *Teikōno dōjidaishi: Gunjika to neoriberarizumu ni kōshite*. Kyoto: Jinbun Shoin.

Mizuki, Shigeru. 1994. *Komikku shōwashi*. 8 vols. Tokyo: Kodansha.

Moeller, Robert G. 2001. *War Stories: The Search for a Usable Past in the Federal Republic of Germany*. Berkeley: University of California Press.

———. 1996. "War Stories: The Search for a Usable Past in the Federal Republic of Germany." *American Historical Review* 101 (4):1008–48.

Morina, Christina. 2011. *Legacies of Stalingrad: Remembering the Eastern Front in Germany since 1945*. New York: Cambridge University Press.

Morris-Suzuki, Tessa. 2005. *The Past within Us: Media, Memory, History*. London: Verso.

Moses, A. Dirk. 2007. *German Intellectuals and the Nazi Past*. Cambridge: Cambridge University Press.

Mosse, George L. 1990. *Fallen Soldiers: Reshaping the Memory of the World Wars*. New York: Oxford University Press.

Mukae, Ryūji. 1996. "Japan's Diet Resolution on World War Two: Keeping History at Bay." *Asian Survey* 36 (10): 1011–31.

Müller, Jan-Werner. 2007. *Constitutional Patriotism*. Princeton, NJ: Princeton University Press.

Murakami, Toshifumi. 2009. *Sengo nihon no heiwa kyōiku no shakaigakuteki kenkyū*. Tokyo: Gakujutsu Shuppankai.

Nagahara, Keiji. 2001. *Rekishi kyōkasho o dō tsukuruka*. Tokyo: Iwanami Shoten.

Nakamasa, Masaki. 2005. *Nihon to doitsu: Futatsu no sengo shisō.* Tokyo: Kōbunsha.

Nakamura, Fumio. 1987. *Kōkō nihonshi kyōkasho: Kentei kyōkasho 18- satsu o hikaku kentō suru.* Tokyo: San'ichi Shobō.

Nakano, Masashi. 2005. "Tennosei to media 2: Sengo 60-nen Asahi Mainichi Yomiuri sanshi ni miru hachigatsu jūgonichi shasetsu no kenshō." *Asahi Sōken Report* 183:19–48.

Nakase, Takemaru. "Nichijō seikatsu to seiji tono aratana setten: Wakamono no ishiki ni miru seiji sanka no henyō." In *Gendai shakai to media, kazoku, sedai,* edited by NHK Hōsō Bunka Kenkyūjo, 59–80. Tokyo: Shinyōsha.

Nakauchi, Toshio, Tsuneichi Takeuchi, Hikari Nakano, and Sadahiko Fujioka. 1987. *Nihon kyōiku no sengoshi.* Tokyo: Sanseidō.

Nakazawa, Keiji. 1994. *Hadashi no gen jiden.* Tokyo: Kyōikushiryō Shuppankai.

Narita, Ryūichi. 2010. *'Sensō keiken' no sengoshi: Katarareta taiken/shōgen/kioku.* Tokyo: Iwanami Shoten.

Neal, Arthur G. 1998. *National Trauma and Collective Memory: Major Events in the American Century.* Armonk, NY: M.E. Sharpe.

Nezu, Asahiko. 2008. "Sengo 8-gatsu 15-nichizuke shasetsu ni okeru kagaisekinin no ronsetsu bunseki (jō)." *Kikan Sensō Sekinin Kenkyū* 59 (Spring):69–77.

———. 2008. "Sengo 8-gatsu 15-nichizuke shasetsu ni okeru kagaisekinin no ronsetsu bunseki (ge)." *Kikan Sensō Sekinin Kenkyū* 60 (Summer):67–75.

NHK 'Sensō Shōgen' Purojekuto. 2009–2012. *Shōgen kiroku: Heishitachino sensō 1~7.* Tokyo: Nippon Hōsō Kyōkai.

NHK Hōsō Bunka Kenkyūjo. 2010. *Gendai nihonjin no ishiki kōzō.* 7th ed. Tokyo: NHK Books.

Nichinōken and Fujio F. Fujiko. 1994. *Doraemon no shakaika omoshiro kōryaku: Nihon no rekishi ga wakaru 2 (Sengoku jidai—Heisei jidai), Doraemon no gakushū shiriizu.* Tokyo: Shōgakkan.

Nihon Seishōnen Kenkyūjo. 2004. *Kōkōsei no gakushū ishiki to nichijō seikatsu: Nihon, amerika, chūgoku no 3 kakoku hikaku.* Tokyo: Nihon Seishōnen Kenkyūjo.

Nitchūkan 3-koku Kyōtsū Rekishi Hensan Iinkai. 2012. *Atarashii higashiajia no kingendaishi (jō): Kokusaikankei no hendō de yomu: Mirai o hiraku rekishi.* Vol. 1. Tokyo: Nihon Hyōronsha.

———. 2012. *Atarashii higashiajia no kingendaishi (ge): Tēmadeyomu hito to kōryū: Mirai o hiraku rekishi* Vol. 2. Tokyo: Nihon Hyōronsha.

———. 2005. *Mirai o hiraku rekishi: Higashiajia 3-koku no kingendaishi.* Tokyo: Kōbunken.

Niven, William John. 2006. *Germans as Victims: Remembering the Past in Contemporary Germany.* New York: Palgrave Macmillan.

Noakes, Lucy. 2009. "The BBC's 'People's War' Website." In *War Memory and Popular Culture: Essays on Modes of Remembrance and Commemoration,* edited by Michael Keren and Holger H. Herwig, 135–49. Jefferson, NC: McFarland.

Noda, Masaaki. 2002. *Saserareru kyōiku, tozetsusuru kyōshitachi.* Tokyo: Iwanami Shoten.

———. 1998. *Sensō to zaiseki.* Tokyo: Iwanami Shoten.

Nohira, Shinsaku, Miharu Kaneko, and Sonoko Sugano. 2007. "Sengo sekinin undō no korekara." *Sekai* 8:264–73.

Nora, Pierre. 1996. *Realms of Memory: Rethinking the French Past.* Translated by Arthur Goldhammer. New York: Columbia University Press.

Nozaki, Yoshiko. 2008. *War Memory, Nationalism and Education in Postwar Japan, 1945-2007: The Japanese History Textbook Controversy and Ienaga Saburo's Court Challenges.* London: Routledge.

———. 2002. "Japanese Politics and the History Textbook Controversy, 1982–2001." *International Journal of Educational Research* 37 (6–7):603–22.

Nozaki, Yoshiko, and Hiromitsu Inokuchi. 2000. "Japanese Education, Nationalism, and Ienaga Saburo's Textbook Lawsuits." In *Censoring History: Citizenship and Memory in Japan, Germany, and the United States*, edited by Laura Hein and Mark Selden, 96–126. Armonk, NY: M.E. Sharpe.

Oda, Makoto. 1969. *Nanshi no shisō*. Tokyo: Bungei Shunjū.

Oguma, Eiji. 2009. *1968 (jō)*. Vol 1. Tokyo: Shinyōsha.

———. 2002. '*Minshu*' to '*Aikoku*': *Sengo nihon no nashonarizumu to kōkyōsei*. Tokyo: Shinyōsha.

Oguma, Eiji, and Yōko Ueno. 2003. '*Iyashi*' *no nashonarizumu: Kusanone hoshu undō no jisshō kenkyū*. Tokyo: Keio Gijuku Daigaku Shuppankai.

Okabe, Makio, Fujio Ogino, and Yutaka Yoshida. 2010. *Chūgoku shinryaku no shōgenshatachi: 'Ninzai' no kiroku o yomu*. Tokyo: Iwanami Shoten.

Okano, Kaori, and Motonori Tsuchiya. 1999. *Education in Contemporary Japan: Inequality and Diversity*. Cambridge: Cambridge University Press.

Okuhira, Yasuhiro, and Jiro Yamaguchi. 2014. Eds. *Shūdanteki jieiken no naniga mondaika: Kaishaku kaiken hihan*. Tokyo: Iwanami Shoten.

Olick, Jeffrey K. 2007. *The Politics of Regret: On Collective Memory and Historical Responsibility*. New York: Routledge.

———. 2005. *In the House of the Hangman: The Agonies of German Defeat, 1943–1949*. Chicago, IL: University of Chicago Press.

———. 1999. "Genre Memories and Memory Genres: A Dialogical Analysis of May 8th, 1945 Commemorations in the Federal Republic of Germany." *American Sociological Review* 64 (June):381–402.

Olick, Jeffrey K., Daniel Levy, and Vered Vinitzky-Seroussi, eds. 2011. *The Collective Memory Reader*. Oxford: Oxford University Press.

Ōnuma, Yasuaki. 2007. *Tokyo saiban, sensō sekinin, sengo sekinin*. Tokyo: Tōshindō.

Ōtake, Hideo. 1988. *Saigunbi to nashonarizumu: Sengo nihon no bōeikan*. Tokyo: Kodansha.

Ōtsuka, Eiji. 2001. *Sengo minshu shugi no rihabiritēshon: Rondan de boku wa nani o katatta ka*. Tokyo: Kadokawa Shoten.

Orend, Brian. 2006. *The Morality of War*. Peterborough, Ont.: Broadview Press.

Oros, Andrew. 2008. *Normalizing Japan: Politics, Identity, and the Evolution of Security Practice*, Stanford, CA: Stanford University Press.

Orr, James Joseph. 2001. *Victim as Hero: Ideologies of Peace and National Identity in Postwar Japan*. Honolulu: University of Hawai'i Press.

Ozawa, Makoto, and NHK Shuzaihan. 1997. *Akagami: Otokotachi wa kōshite senjō e okurareta*. Osaka: Sōgensha.

Park, Soon-Won. 2011. "A History that Opens the Future: The First Common China-Japan-Korean History Teaching Guide." In *History Textbooks and the Wars in Asia: Divided Memories*, edited by Gi-Wook Shin and Daniel C. Sneider, 230–45. New York: Routledge.

Pempel, T.J. 2014. "Why Japan's Collective Self-defence is so Politicised." *East Asia Forum*, September 2, http://www.eastasiaforum.org/2014/09/02/why-japans-collective-self-defence-is-so-politicised/.

Penney, Matthew. 2008. "Far from Oblivion: The Nanking Massacre in Japanese Historical Writing for Children and Young Adults." *Holocaust and Genocide Studies* 22 (1):25–48.

———. 2007. "'War Fantasy' and Reality—'War as Entertainment' and Counter-narratives in Japanese Popular Culture." *Japanese Studies* 27 (1):35–52.

Pharr, Susan J. 1997. "Public Trust and Democracy in Japan." In *Why People Don't Trust Government*, edited by Joseph S. Nye, Philip Zelikow, and David C. King, 237–52. Cambridge, MA: Harvard University Press.

Posner, Gerald L. 1991. *Hitler's Children: Sons and Daughters of Leaders of the Third Reich Talk about Their Fathers and Themselves*. New York: Random House.

Prinz, Jesse J. 2007. *The Emotional Construction of Morals*. New York: Oxford University Press.

Putnam, Robert, ed. 2002. *Democracies in Flux: The Evolution of Social Capital in Contemporary Society*. New York: Oxford University Press.

Rahimi, Babak. 2005. "Sacrifice, Transcendence and the Soldier." *Peace Review* 17 (1):1–8.

Rekishi Kyōikusha Kyōgikai. 2005. *Rekishi kyōiku shakaika kyoiku nenpo: Sengo 60-nen to shakaika kyōiku*. Tokyo: Sanseidō.

Rekishi Kyōikusha Kyōgikai. 1997. *Rekishi kyōiku 50-nen no ayumi to kadai*. Tokyo: Miraisha.

Rohlen, Thomas P. 1983. *Japan's High Schools*. Berkeley: University of California Press.

Rose, Caroline. 2005. *Sino-Japanese Relations: Facing the Past, Looking to the Future?* London: RoutledgeCurzon.

Rosenthal, Gabriele. 1998. "Veiling and Denying." In *The Holocaust in Three Generations: Families of Victims and Perpetrators of the Nazi Regime*, edited by Gabriele Rosenthal, 286–94. London: Cassell.

———. 1998. "National Socialism and Anti-semitism in Intergenerational Dialog." In *The Holocaust in Three Generations: Families of Victims and Perpetrators of the Nazi Regime*, edited by Gabriele Rosenthal, 240–48. London: Cassell.

Rousso, Henry. 1994. *The Vichy Syndrome: History and Memory in France since 1944*. Translated by Arthur Goldhammer. Cambridge, MA: Harvard University Press.

Ruoff, Kenneth James. 2001. *The People's Emperor: Democracy and the Japanese Monarchy, 1945–1995*. Cambridge, MA: Harvard University Asia Center.

Saaler, Sven. 2005. *Politics, Memory and Public Opinion: The History Textbook Controversy and Japanese Society*. Munich: Iudicium Verlag.

Saito, Hiro. 2006. "Reiterated Commemoration: Hiroshima as National Trauma." *Sociological Theory* 24 (4):353–76.

Sakaiya, Taichi. 2011. *Daisan no haisen*. Tokyo: Kodansha.

Sakaki, Alexandra, 2012. *Japan and Germany as Regional Actors Evaluating Change and Continuity after the Cold War*. Florence, KY: Routledge

Sakamoto, Takao. 1998. *Rekishi kyōiku o kangaeru: Nihonjin wa rekishi o torimodoseruka*. Tokyo: PHP Kenkyūjo.

Sakurai, Hitoshi. 2005. *Terebi wa sensō o dōegaite kitaka: Eizō to kioku no ākaibusu*. Tokyo: Iwanami Shoten.

Samuels, Richard J. 2007. *Securing Japan: Tokyo's Grand Strategy and the Future of East Asia*. Ithaca: Cornell University Press.

Sato, Takumi. 2005. *Hachigatsu jūgonichi no shinwa: Shūsen kinenbi no media gaku*. Tokyo: Chikuma Shobō.

———. 2002. "Kōfuku kinenbi kara shūsen kinenbi e: Kioku no media ibento." In *Sengo nihon no media ibento 1945–1960*, edited by Toshihiro Tsuganesawa, 71–94. Kyoto: Sekai Shisōsha.

Sawachi, Hisae, Kazutoshi Handō, and Kazushige Todaka. 2011. *Nihon kaigun wa naze ayamattaka: Kaigun hanseikai 400 jikan no shōgen yori*. Tokyo: Iwanami Shoten.

Schissler, Hanna, and Yasemin Soysal. 2005. *The Nation, Europe, and the World: Textbooks and Curricula in Transition.* New York: Berghahn Books.

✓Schivelbusch, Wolfgang. 2003. *The Culture of Defeat: On National Trauma, Mourning, and Recovery.* Translated by Jefferson Chase. New York: Metropolitan Books.

Schmitt, David P., and Jüri Allik. 2005. "Simultaneous Administration of the Rosenberg Self-Esteem Scale in 53 Nations: Exploring the Universal and Culture-Specific Features of Global Self-Esteem." *Journal of Personality and Social Psychology* 89 (4):623–42.

Schoppa, Leonard J. 2006. *Race for the Exits: The Unraveling of Japan's System of Social Protection.* Ithaca, NY: Cornell University Press.

Schwartz, Barry. 1982. "The Social Context of Commemoration: A Study in Collective Memory." *Social Forces* 61 (2):374–402.

Seaton, Philip A. 2007. *Japan's Contested War Memories: The "Memory Rifts" in Historical Consciousness of World War II.* London: Routledge.

Seraphim, Franziska. 2006. *War Memory and Social Politics in Japan, 1945–2005.* Cambridge, MA: Harvard University Asia Center.

Shils, Edward, and Michael Young. 1953. "The Meaning of Coronation." *Sociological Review* 1 (2):63–81.

Shin, Gi-Wook. 2014. "Historical Reconciliation in Northeast Asia: Past Efforts, Future Steps, and the U.S. Role." In *Confronting Memories of World War II: European and Asian Legacies,* edited by Daniel Chirot, Gi-Wook Shin, and Daniel C. Sneider, 157–85. Seattle: University of Washington Press.

✓Shipilova, Anna. 2014. "From Local to National Experience: Has Hiroshima Become a 'Trauma for Everybody'?" *Japanese Studies* 34 (2):193–211. ͻ ʃ βϲ βϲαṳṣϯ

Sichrovsky, Peter. 1988. *Born Guilty: Children of Nazi Families.* New York: Basic Books.

Smelser, Neil J. 2004. "Psychological Trauma and Cultural Trauma." In *Cultural Trauma and Collective Identity,* edited by Jeffrey C. Alexander et al., 31–59. Berkeley: University of California Press.

———. 1976. *Comparative Methods in the Social Sciences.* Englewood Cliffs, NJ: Prentice-Hall.

Smith, Anthony D. 1991. *National Identity,* Reno: University of Nevada Press.

Smith, Philip. 2005. *Why War?: The Cultural Logic of Iraq, the Gulf War, and Suez.* Chicago, IL: University of Chicago Press.

Sneider, Daniel C. 2011. "The War over Words: History Textbooks and International Relations in Northeast Asia." In *History Textbooks and the Wars in Asia: Divided Memories,* edited by Gi-Wook Shin and Daniel C. Sneider, 246–68. New York: Routledge.

✓Soh, Chunghee Sarah. 2008. *The Comfort Women: Sexual Violence and Postcolonial Memory in Korea and Japan.* Chicago: University of Chicago Press.

Sōka Gakkai Seinenbu. 1978. *Cries for Peace: Experiences of Japanese Victims of World War II.* Tokyo: Japan Times.

Spiegelman, Art. 1994. "Forward: Comics after the Bomb." In *Barefoot Gen 4: Out of the Ashes 'A Cartoon Story of Hiroshima',* by Keiji Nakazawa, v–viii. Philadelphia: New Society.

Spillman, Lyn. 1997. *Nation and Commemoration: Creating National Identities in the United States and Australia.* Cambridge: Cambridge University Press.

Steinhoff, Patricia G. 2008. "Mass Arrests, Sensational Crimes, and Stranded Children." In *Imagined Families, Lived Families: Culture and Kinship in Contemporary Japan,* edited by Akiko Hashimoto and John W. Traphagan, 77–110. Albany: SUNY Press.

Sturken, Marita. 1997. *Tangled Memories: The Vietnam War, the AIDS Epidemic, and the Politics of Remembering.* Berkeley: University of California Press.

Sutton, John. 2008. "Between Individual and Collective Memory: Coordination, Interaction, Distribution." *Social Research* 75 (1):23–47.

Takahashi, Tetsuya. 2005. *Kokka to gisei.* Tokyo: NHK Books.

———. 2005. *Yasukuni mondai.* Tokyo: Chikuma Shobō.

———. 2005. *Sengo sekininron.* Tokyo: Kodansha.

Takahashi, Saburō. 2005. *Kyōdō kenkyō senyūkai.* Tokyo: Inpakuto Shuppankai.

———. 1988. *'Senkimono' o yomu: Sensō taiken to sengo nihon shakai.* Kyoto: Akademia Shuppankai.

Takahashi, Tōru. 2003. *Nihonjin no kachikan: Sekai rankingu.* Tokyo: Chūōkōron Shinsha.

Tamanoi, Mariko. 2009. *Memory Maps: The State and Manchuria in Postwar Japan.* Honolulu: University of Hawai'i Press.

Toyoshita, Narahiko, and Shōichi Koseki. 2014. *Shūdanteki jieiken to anzen hoshō,* Tokyo: Iwanami Shoten.

Treat, John Whittier. 1995. *Writing Ground Zero: Japanese Literature and the Atomic Bomb.* Chicago, IL: University of Chicago Press.

Tsurumi, Shunsuke, Chizuko Ueno, and Eiji Oguma. 2004. *Sensō ga nokoshita mono: Tsurumi Shunsuke ni sengo sedai ga kiku.* Tokyo: Shinyōsha.

Tsutsui, Kiyoteru. 2009. "The Trajectory of Perpetrators' Trauma: Mnemonic Politics around the Asia-Pacific War in Japan." *Social Forces* 87 (3):1389–1422.

Ueno, Chizuko, Minato Kawamura, and Ryūichi Narita. 1999. "Sensō wa donoyōni katararete kitaka." In *Sensō wa donoyōni katararete kitaka,* edited by Minato Kawamura, et al., 17–54. Tokyo: Asahi Shinbunsha.

United Nations Development Programme (UNDP). 2013. *Human Development Report 2013.*

Utsumi, Aiko. 1986. *Bokura wa ajia de sensō o shita: Kyōkasho ni kakarenakatta sensō pt. 3.* Tokyo: Nashinokisha.

Utsumi, Aiko, Yasuaki Ōnuma, Hiroshi Tanaka, and Yōko Kato. 2014. *Sengo sekinin: Ajia no manazashi ni kotaete.* Tokyo: Iwanami Shoten.

Vinitzky-Seroussi, Vered. 2002. "Commemorating a Difficult Past: Yitzhak Rabin's Memorials." *American Sociological Review* 67 (1):30–51.

Wagner-Pacifici, Robin. 2005. *The Art of Surrender: Decomposing Sovereignty at Conflict's End.* Chicago, IL: University of Chicago Press.

Wagner-Pacifici, Robin, and Barry Schwartz. 1991. "The Vietnam Veterans Memorial: Commemorating a Difficult Past." *American Journal of Sociology* 97 (2):376–420.

Wakamiya, Yoshibumi. 2006. *Wakai to nashonarizumu,* Tokyo: Asahi Shinbunsha.

Wakatsuki, Yasuo. 2000. *Nihon no sensō sekinin: Saigo no sensō sedai kara.* Tokyo: Shōgakkan.

Wakefield, Bryce, and Craig Martin. 2014. "Reexamining 'Myths' About Japan's Collective Self-Defense Change—What Critics (and the Japanese Public) Do Understand About Japan's Constitutional Reinterpretation." *Japan Focus: The Asia-Pacific Journal,* September 8.

Watanabe, Atsushi. 2010. "2010-nendo kōkō kyōkasho saitaku jyōkyō—Monkashō matome (jō)." *Naigai Kyōiku* 5963:2–9.

———. 2010. "2010-nendo kōkō kyōkasho saitaku jyōkyō—Monkashō matome (chū)." *Naigai Kyōiku* 5965:6–13.

Watanabe, Tsuneo, and Masayasu Hosaka. 2006. "'Sensō sekinin' towa nanika." *Ronza* 11:128–42.

Weinberg, Gerhard L. 2005. *A World at Arms: A Global History of World War II.* 2nd ed. New York: Cambridge University Press.

Welzer, Harald. 2006. "The Collateral Damage of Enlightenment: How Grandchildren Understand the History of National Socialist Crimes and Their Grandfathers' Past." In *Victims and Perpetrators, 1933–1945: (Re)presenting the Past in Post-unification Culture,* edited by Laurel Cohen-Pfister and Dagmar Wienröder-Skinner, 285–95. Berlin: W. de Gruyter.

Welzer, Harald, Sabine Moller, and Karoline Tschuggnall. 2002. *"Opa war kein Nazi": Nationalsozialismus und Holocaust im Familiengedächtnis.* Frankfurt am Main: Fischer Taschenbuch Verlag.

White, Hayden. 1987. *The Content of the Form: Narrative Discourse and Historical Representation.* Baltimore, MD: Johns Hopkins University Press.

Winter, Jay. 1995. *Sites of Memory, Sites of Mourning: The Great War in European Cultural History.* Cambridge: Cambridge University Press.

Yamabe, Masahiko. 2005. "Nihon no heiwa hakubutsukan wa ajia-taiheiyō sensō o ikani tenji shiteiruka." *Ritsumeikan Heiwa Kenkyū* 6:3–11.

Yamamuro, Shin'ichi. 2007. *Kenpō 9-jō no shisō suimyaku.* Tokyo: Asahi Shinbunsha.

Yamanaka, Chie. 2006. "Yomare'enai 'taiken', ekkyō dekinai 'kioku': Kankoku ni okeru 'Hadashi no gen' no juyō o megutte." In *'Hadashi no gen' ga ita fūkei: manga, sensō, kioku,* edited by Kazuma Yoshimura and Yoshiaki Fukuma, 211–45. Matsudo-shi: Azusa Shuppansha.

Yamane, Kazuyo. 2008. "List of Museums for Peace in Japan." http://inmp.net/attachments/category/52/List_of_museums_for_peace_in_Japan.pdf.

———. 2008. "List of Museums for Peace in the World Except Japan." http://inmp.net/attachments/category/52/List%20of%20museums%20for%20peace%20in%20the%20world%20except%20Japan%20by%20Kazuyo%20Yamane.pdf.

Yang, Daqing, and Ju-Back Sin. 2013. "Striving for Common History Textbooks in Northeast Asia (China, South Korea and Japan): Between Ideal and Reality." In *History Education and Post-conflict Reconciliation: Reconsidering Joint Textbook Projects,* edited by K. V. Korostelina, Simone Lässig, and Stefan Ihrig, 209–30. New York: Routledge.

Yasuda, Kōichi. 2012. *Netto to aikoku: Zaitokukai no 'yami' o oikakete.* Tokyo: Kodansha.

Yasukuni Jinja. 2009. *Yūshūkan zuroku.* Tokyo: Kindai Shuppansha.

Yoda, Tomiko. 2006. "A Roadmap to Millennial Japan." In *Japan after Japan: Social and Cultural Life from the Recessionary 1990s to the Present,* edited by Tomiko Yoda and Harry D. Harootunian, 16–53. Durham, NC: Duke University Press.

Yomiuri Shinbun. 2014. "Kenpō yoron chōsa." http://www.yomiuri.co.jp/feature/opinion/koumoku/20140317-OYT8T50000.html.

———. 2008. "Kenpō yoron chōsa." http://www.yomiuri.co.jp/editorial/news/20080407-OYT1T00791.htm.

Yomiuri Shinbun Sensō Sekinin Kenshō Iinkai. 2006. *Kenshō: Sensō sekinin I–II.* Tokyo: Chūōkōron Shinsha.

Yomiuri Shinbunsha Yoron Chōsabu. 2002. *Nihon no yoron.* Tokyo: Kōbunsha.

Yoneyama, Lisa. 2001. "For Transformative Knowledge and Postnationalist Public Spheres: The Smithsonian *Enola Gay* Controversy." In *Perilous Memories: The Asia-Pacific War(s),* edited by T. Fujitani, Geoffrey M. White and Lisa Yoneyama, 323–46. Durham, NC: Duke University Press.

———. 1999. *Hiroshima Traces: Time, Space, and the Dialectics of Memory.* Berkeley: University of California Press.

Yoneyama, Shoko. 1999. *The Japanese High School: Silence and Resistance*. London: Routledge.

Yoshida, Mitsuru. 1985. *Requiem for Battleship Yamato*. Translated by Richard H. Minear. Seattle: University of Washington Press.

Yoshida, Takashi. 2006. *The Making of the "Rape of Nanking": History and Memory in Japan, China, and the United States*. New York: Oxford University Press.

Yoshida, Yutaka. 2011. *Heishitachi no sengoshi: Sensō no keiken o tou*. Tokyo: Iwanami Shoten.

———. 1997. *Gendai rekishigaku to sensō sekinin*. Tokyo: Aoki Shoten.

———. 1995. *Nihonjin no sensōkan: Sengoshi no naka no henyō*. Tokyo: Iwanami Shoten.

Yoshimi, Yoshiaki. 2000. *Comfort Women: Sexual Slavery in the Japanese Military During World War II*. Translated by Suzanne O'Brien. New York: Columbia University Press.

———. 1995. *Jūgun ianfu*. Tokyo: Iwanami Shoten. *CIVILian, O, sexual*

Yoshimoto, Takaaki. 2012. *Dainino haisenki: Korekarano nihon o dōyomuka*. Tokyo: Shunjūsha.

Yoshimura, Kōichi. 1968. "Tōsho, hitosamazama." *Shinbun Kenkyū* 10:60–65.

Yoshioka, Tatsuya. 2008. "Experience, Action, and the Floating Peace Village." In *Another Japan is Possible: New Social Movements and Global Citizenship Education*, edited by Jennifer Chan, 317–22. Stanford, CA: Stanford University Press.

Yui, Daizaburo. 2005. "Sekai sensō no nakano ajia-taiheiyō sensō." In *Ajia-taiheiyō sensō 1: Naze ima ajia-taiheiyō sensō ka*, edited by Ryūichi Narita et al., 235–74. Tokyo: Iwanami Shoten.

Zarakol, Ayse. 2011. *After Defeat: How the East Learned to Live with the West*. Cambridge: Cambridge University Press.

Zerubavel, Eviatar. 2007. "Generally Speaking: The Logic and Mechanics of Social Pattern Analysis." *Sociological Forum* 22 (2):131–45

Zheng, Yongnian. 1999. *Discovering Chinese Nationalism in China: Modernization, Identity, and International Relations*. Cambridge: Cambridge University Press.

Don't unproblematically fold female sex. trauma into the war loss.

Equates civ + mil trauma.

Index

Page numbers with an "n" indicate the note numbers of the respective entries.

Printed in the USA/Agawam, MA
March 17, 2017

649450.001